What people are saying about

Aspecting the Goddess

In *Aspecting the Goddess* Jane Meredith combines skillful and engaging storytelling with easy to follow directions on a set of tools with which you may create deep and enriching personal relationship with the feminal divine. *Aspecting the Goddess* is a joy to read. Both accessible and fresh, this creative guidebook to crafting relationship opens the door to intimate and personal communion with the Great Goddess in Her many guises.
Lasara Firefox Allen – author of *Jailbreaking the Goddess* and *Sexy Witch*

Jane Meredith's *Aspecting the Goddess* is a bold and unique look at connecting to myth and deity. While the book's main intention is to help anyone gain a stronger and deeper relationship with the feminine divine it also offers an opportunity to look at the world itself with new eyes, to see everything around us as pieces of the Goddesses (and Gods) we are reaching out to. Designed as a journey, walking the reader through the process of connection on different levels with different Goddesses, this book feels both deeply personal and deeply spiritual. A valuable addition to any pagan's library, whatever path you may follow, as it presents some wonderful food for thought and ideas for spiritual growth.
Morgan Daimler – author of Pagan Portals *The Morrigan* and *Brigid*

Aspecting the Goddess will inspire you, guide you, support you and help you connect in so many different ways with the divine in whatever shape or form you see it. This beautifully insightful book contains not only myths about goddesses from around the world, but also personal stories and experiences together with some really wonderful exercises, rituals and creative prompts to help you. Prepare yourself to be taken on a most amazing journey...

Rachel Patterson – author of *The Cailleach, Animal Magic* and *Kitchen Witchcraft*

One of the most compelling features of Paganism and Goddess spirituality is the direct experience of the Divine. *Aspecting the Goddess* provides a wealth of resources for those that are seeking a more profound connection to the Divine Feminine. Six different methodologies are described that allow you to find your way into experiencing and manifesting the Goddess in both your awareness, rituals, and in your perspectives on life. Although the focus is on Goddesses, the material presented is equally applicable to working with Gods as well as beings that are beyond gender. The book itself is like a journey that incorporates personal experiences, myths, stories, and practical magical advice. How far you go is up to you, and you may go further than you think, because you will have the benefit of experienced guides that have gone before you.

Ivo Dominguez Jr – author of *Spirit Speak* and *Casting Sacred Space*

I loved the entwining of Jane's life experience with different forms of invocation and Aspecting of Goddess, demonstrating how drawing close to Goddess affects our everyday lives.

Kathy Jones – Priestess of Avalon

This is a book about intense emotions, including grief, gradually being understood through working with the old myths. Parallels are suddenly clear from the evolving dramas that explain our own reactions and the behaviour of people. Aspects of Goddesses are shown to us through our interactions with them and how we can access them through creativity - however alien that may seem at first - and how profound the answers can be. *Aspecting the Goddess* offers reconciliation possibly, far greater comprehension of our lives probably, and, if we dare, an enthralling and rich Inner life almost certainly. There are sound chapters on the practical side of solo or group working and how one's own journey is always paramount and not deflected or confused by the presence of others.

Geraldine Beskin – The Atlantis Bookshop

Aspecting
the Goddess

Drawing Down the Divine Feminine

Aspecting
the Goddess

Drawing Down the Divine Feminine

Jane Meredith

MOON
BOOKS

Winchester, UK
Washington, USA

First published by Moon Books, 2018
Moon Books is an imprint of John Hunt Publishing Ltd., Laurel House, Station Approach,
Alresford, Hants, SO24 9JH, UK
office1@jhpbooks.net
www.johnhuntpublishing.com
www.moon-books.net

For distributor details and how to order please visit the 'Ordering' section on our website.

Text copyright: Jane Meredith 2017

ISBN: 978 1 78535 603 2
978 1 78535 604 9 (ebook)
Library of Congress Control Number: 2017939483

A CIP catalogue record for this book is available from the British Library.

Design: Stuart Davies

Printed and bound by CPI Group (UK) Ltd, Croydon, CR0 4YY, UK

We operate a distinctive and ethical publishing philosophy in
all areas of our business, from our global network of authors to
production and worldwide distribution.

Contents

Other books by Jane Meredith

Aphrodite's Magic: Celebrate and Heal Your Sexuality
Journey to the Dark Goddess: How to Return to Your Soul
Rituals of Celebration: Honoring the Seasons of Life through the Wheel of the Year
Circle of Eight: Creating Magic for Your Place on Earth
Magic of the Iron Pentacle: Reclaiming Sex, Pride, Self, Power &
Passion (with Gede Parma)

For Trinda McCarthy
~ in love and gratitude ~
1945 – 2015

she whispers in my ear, words that are just for me...

...she appears in a dream and reveals her name to me...

she takes my hand and walks beside me...

I see her, catch a glimpse of her in the cascade of a waterfall, the flight of a bird, a woman dancing, the moonlight falling in a forest...

she is in the waves curling in to shore, she is the flames of the fire, she is the deep forests and wild moors, she is the soft night breeze. I feel her holding me. I feel her raining onto my skin, her breath blowing around me, I hear her in the call of the black cockatoos. I see her in burning starlight. I raise my arms, feet on the ground and welcome her into my body. Goddess.

Aphrodite, Gaia, Inanna, Kali, Rhiannon, Lilith, Nut, Selene, Mary, Artemis, Freyja, Kwan Yin –

Goddess.

Aspecting the Goddess invites you into direct, intimate relationship with the divine.

Let yourself step inside a realm where the gods and goddesses interact with us. In this place we experience all of nature as an expression of spirit and ourselves as part of nature. The goddess is alive, we are alive and we are a part of her.

We begin with a name, a wish, a vision, a dream. We hold onto that vision or yearning, we court it, we begin a journey. We open to it. We follow this thread of goddess and begin to find books, rituals, art, nature, trance, myth and to these we bring our curiosity, desire and willingness. We seek out a world where the goddess speaks to us, dances with us, moves through our bodies and teaches us directly. This world is not a distant planet, a fantasy novel or an epic poem, it is our own world. When we enter into relationship with the goddess we meet the divine not only in ritual and sacred space but also in our daily lives, as long as we make room for her.

The concept that the gods are all around us, in the air and

earth, the stars and trees and insects, reveals the magic of nature to us. This is sometimes called pantheism, the belief that all is divine, everything is a part of divinity. When we stop separating the divine from the natural, from the world we live in, we no longer battle with that separation within ourselves. We are spirit and we are body, there is no distinction. Nature, the world and the earth are sacred, are divine. So are our bodies. We are not separate from nature, but a part of it. All of our knowledge comes through the experiences we have while inhabiting our body. Our understandings of the divine also come to us this way, from the embodied experiences we have.

Children interact easily with the natural world and we have all been children. Even adults are in love with the wild the moment our constructed lives let go a little, release us from cities, the cares of relationship, earning a living and worrying for the future. As I climb the tree I feel its body against mine and the way the wind moves through empty sky. When I taste that soil, put it on my tongue and then swallow it, I ingest the way worms do, animals, the taste of this place, this exact hillside and slope apart from all other hillsides in the world and thus belong here a little more. When I lie in the river, caught by its current until my body chills, I flow over its rocks, ripple and rush forgetting, forgotten what cold is, now I am fish and riverweed, now I am finding my true shapes. Standing under starlight or watching the sun rise I remember how small I am, yet connected to everything. This is sacred.

The more I work with deities the more I am convinced that each one is unique, while also believing they are all parts of the same thing, that we are all a part of. Nature, the universe, life force; call it spirit-in-matter or matter-in-spirit, the irreducible potential of the dust of a comet or an exploded star to seed life, to somehow *be* life...this is what we come from. Divinity, whenever we choose to be aware of it, reminds us of this enormous, simple truth. Everything we see and know – the rocks and trees, our books and computers, our food and water, the birds and animals and insects, the seas and mountains and deserts – are all this one thing, stardust on its way to becoming cosmic dust again. We are indivisible from it. For me the gods and goddesses, all of them, are this reminder, that we belong to everything.

As well as this oneness and unity each deity is like a whole species, unto itself. I believe that how we understand them currently, as some kind of glorified human-looking being, is not their original form, though it may be what we can most easily relate to. I think their secrets lie in their symbols and they are, in essence, far simpler, more powerful and elemental than anything that could exist in human form. The Norse goddess Freyja had a beautiful necklace, made by the dwarves of gold and amber. I believe Freyja is, herself, that gold and amber. She is the beauty of a seam of gold running through quartz crystal, the mystery of that fossilized golden sap; she is literally the jewels of the earth. Gold and amber are not just her symbols, they are how she appears in the world; they *are* her. I believe Zeus is lightning, not that he holds or wields it, but that it is him. Demeter is the grain, Ceridwen her cauldron, Isis is the throne of Egypt.

This belief does not lessen the powers of the gods but rather returns to them actual, real powers. The powers of the forest and the deer that are Artemis, the power of seeds growing out of the ground that is Persephone, the power of flowers we have named Blodeuwedd. When I see those things as animated, living deity I look again, filled with awe at the local waterfall, my beloved white cockatoos or the mists that rise up from the valleys aware that this, also, is an expression of deity. In effect, these *are* deities, or deity. Everything is. It does not become less special to me; but instead more special and I feel Freyja's powers lying not just within myth or when she is invoked into ritual or I am reading her stories, but each time I touch or wear or look at her precious jewels; if I wear amber I am wearing pieces of Freyja. When I go to the ocean I am gazing upon or swimming with Yemaya,

Poseidon, Aphrodite. The face of death – worn by a bird lying dead on the road, my mother in her coffin or a dead tree – is the face of Ereshkigal, Hades, or the Morrigan.

We belong to nature and also to our human world, containing stories and choices and relationships. Myths bridge these two worlds, taking us into the archetypal realm where we witness the actions of the gods and goddesses, sometimes vast and primordial, sometimes almost human. There's the sheer allure of a story, the intrigue of discovering how difficult situations and complex characters evolve. Some myths we experience as relevant to our own experience, in ways supportive, reflective or cautionary. Great myths and archetypal stories also have deeper resonances. They speak not just of a particular circumstance or challenge but about the human condition; teaching essential lessons that none of us escape. Stories of descent, death, resurrection and initiation are among these enormous, resonant stories that reverberate within us, whether we hear them for the first or thirty-first time. But what if we don't just read or listen to the myth; what if we step inside and learn to inhabit it? Not just as a passing thought but literally walking into the story.

For anyone who's ever sought the vividness of fairytale, of ritual come alive and happening all around you, I recommend this practice of entering a myth; not necessarily with props or acting but by putting one's body into it and allowing the myth's essence to speak through feeling and observation. The myth becomes three-dimensional. You may come to know the characters as if they were friends, or feel them as aspects of yourself. Your memories of the experience will be tied both into the story and your understanding of yourself. The circularity of myths means the journey takes you back to the beginning; sometimes with visions, resolution, understanding or simply the experience of mystery. This is just one way to develop deeper relationship with a deity and story.

How do you choose where to start, which myth or goddess

to explore? Perhaps you already have a connection with one or more goddesses or gods and in reading this book you may be inspired to develop those relationships. Maybe a goddess has appeared in a dream to you – or from the pages of a book, or in a ritual – and you'd like to find out more. You may be familiar with working with deity and want to read stories about how that has been for others and different ways to explore this work. The relationship we create with deity is like any other relationship, it grows through attention and interaction, communication and shared activities. We may be used to our relationship with a divine being taking place within ritual, in the realm of dreams and maybe trance, but perhaps we are not always aware of how to cultivate it, or spark it into being when we have felt it to be absent, or for clear ways to deepen that relationship.

Aspecting the Goddess explores six different techniques for developing relationship with deity. Some of these techniques are usually carried out alone whereas others often take place within ritual or with groups of people. We might call these two approaches the *inner path* and the *outer path*. Working with the inner path we focus on aspects of our personal relationship with the goddess, to some degree we travel to her realm and speak and interact with her there. Working with the outer path we focus on external expression of the goddess or her myth, seeking to bring those things into our community, group or ritual.

Three sections in this book follow the inner path. First is *Walking with the Goddess*, where we invite an awareness of a goddess into our lives and become aware of her. Next is *Researching the Goddess*, where we set out to learn more about the history and mythology of a particular goddess and finally *Dedicating to the Goddess*, when we might choose to make a dedication to a deity we feel deeply committed to. A further three sections are devoted to the outer path. Firstly *Presencing the Goddess*, when we invite or bring the goddess or a sense of her to be present, usually into a ritual or for a specified length of time.

Then *Enacting Myth*, where we embody or ritualize a specific story and lastly *Aspecting the Goddess* where we draw some of the energy of the goddess into our own bodies and in that way give her the physical expression of voice and movement.

This book is filled with stories. They are stories of my experiences with goddesses, both in and out of ritual, by myself and with others. There are stories about twelve different goddesses, from Welsh, Norse, Egyptian, Sumerian, Greek, Biblical and contemporary Feri/Reclaiming mythologies. They range from my experience of holding the mask of Nephthys and her shadowy, swooping clarity to the grit and depth of my commitment to Ereshkigal and the way my mouth feels it is filling with earth even to say her name; from the ferocity and clarity of Inanna's descent into the Underworld to the chilled magnificence of the Star Goddess. These experiences range over a period of more than twenty-five years. I have included this span and breadth of stories in order to incorporate into the book as many different pantheons, types of experiences and mythologies as possible.

Deities have different resonances from each other. When we work with one or more of them we become familiar with these and can recognize them, or the feeling that arises within us, from one time to the next. Each time I begin to work with Isis there's a distinct set of sensations or feeling-thoughts that start to come into my awareness. I could label these – they include impressions of coolness, power, breadth, intellect, deep wisdom, ferocity – but it is more than this, more than the individual components of it and more than the sum of them. Without for one moment thinking that I know, or understand Isis, still I can recognize her. Inanna feels different, Freyja different again.

When I talk with people who work with a particular goddess there is most often a very distinct presence, and we hold it in common. That is, each of us has our own individual experience of the goddess but also, within how we perceive and understand her, there is an area of overlap, often a very large one. Further, what we perceive or experience is not always what it is popularly portrayed of that goddess. Invoking Aphrodite – and this goes against much of what is written or assumed about her, although dozens of women have confirmed this – results commonly in a gentle, deep, compassionate and sparkling sensation and awareness. This is not to say that the dangerous seductress does not reside within Aphrodite – goddesses are vast beings with many, many aspects – but it does not come through, for me and many others, as predominant. When we relate to a goddess it is not one-way; we hear, feel and receive them.

Perhaps you've been curious about a particular goddess for a long while. Or you might read a story about a goddess in the pages of this book and wonder how it would be to know her more closely. Maybe your family, ancestry or heritage belongs to a particular place, religion or mythos and you will choose to begin there. Or you might want to journey with a different goddess every month for a year. Stories are invitational, they are interactive. Opening this book you might be drawn along the inner path to research, to dedication, to walking with a goddess or you might be drawn along the outer path to presencing, exploring myth and aspecting a goddess. Perhaps you will work both at once, researching a goddess you intend to aspect, or presencing a goddess you are dedicating yourself to. Set your intention, make your invocation and the journey begins.

Sometimes I have felt cool or hesitant towards a particular goddess before I have entered into relationship with her but every time, after working with her, she has come into my collection of beloveds. Each one, in her own way, has revealed herself to me – her power, her beauty, her grace and her truth – and maybe this is just the beginning of our relationship. Perhaps it is like getting to know a forest, beach, city or person; it can lead us not just into intimacy with that particular forest or person but also towards developing connections with other forests and people.

For you it might be different. Maybe your experience of deity is through your relationship with one goddess or one pantheon and that's what works for you. Or maybe you resonate more deeply with nature as goddess, or the moon, or the seasons and have no particular need to work with named deities, histories or mythologies. Perhaps you are just open to what unfolds on this journey.

Aspecting the Goddess invites you to enter the realm of relationship with deity. What happens in that relationship – and how it develops – is the dance between yourself and the goddess.

May there be many blessings in your relationships with the divine that we call goddess.

Jane Meredith
Blue Mountains, Australia 2017

How to Use this Book

Aspecting the Goddess is designed to inspire and support your connection with the goddess. You might look upon it even more broadly and use it to facilitate your relationship with the divine, both gods and goddesses, or numinous or non-gendered or other-gendered deity or deities. All of the longer stories in this book and most of the examples given concern my own relationships with different goddesses. You might choose simply to read the book or you might choose to actively work with it as you cultivate your relationship with one or more goddesses. You may have picked up this book looking for specific skills, techniques and processes to work with deity and you can find these in the exercises at the end of each section. Feel free to experiment and adapt these. I hope that in my explanations of how I do something, you might be able to find ways for you to do a similar or related thing, ways that work for you.

There are twelve stories here of my connections with twelve different goddesses, two stories placed into each of the six sections in this book. These stories are gathered from across half my lifetime. It certainly is possible to work with a different goddess each month, for example, but it might not be as meaningful as developing relationships with one or two goddesses. If you are drawn to one particular goddess, or maybe a couple, I recommend developing your relationship with those one, or two, by moving through different sections of this work with them. Thus with one goddess you might choose to cover researching, presencing and aspecting, or walking with, enacting myth and dedication. You can pick and choose sections that work for you, in the order that seems most appropriate, or you can take your work with one goddess through this whole book.

I have included so many different goddesses, rather than focusing on stories to do with the three or four goddesses I feel closest to, for a number of reasons. I wanted to bring as much variety as possible into the goddesses, pantheons and stories represented. A story about Freyja will be very different than a story about Ariadne. I also wanted the invitation to be as wide as possible. It may be that you have an affinity with Celtic, Sumerian or Greek stories or goddesses and by including many different goddesses hopefully it is conveyed that all experiences, with any goddess or god, are part of this work. There are pantheons and mythologies I have never worked with, such as Hindu and Santerian, and they are therefore not represented in this book, but I hope it is both explicit and implied that if that is where your knowledge, identity and relationship with deity resides, that is a place open for your exploration.

Many people create a private relationship with deity and do not require or wish anyone else's involvement in it. Others may do this but also be part of a group, whether a coven, women's or men's group, ritual or teaching group or some other type of group. The exercises in this book are easily adapted to group work, where each person in the group could be working with the same deity or each with a different one. A powerful alternative is to work within a myth or pantheon, so that each person is working with a different deity or aspect of deity, but they all join together. One possible model, for a group meeting every month or two months, would be to choose a chapter and individually work on it between meetings. Then one or usually two people – in turns, so it is not the same people each turn, or it could be the whole group – creates a ritual, process, discussion or other event to share and explore the group's learnings.

The book is arranged in six sections and to some extent they are sequential. The first three sections – *Walking with the Goddess*, *Researching the Goddess* and *Dedicating to the Goddess* – I think of as interior work, although of course others in both your ritual and personal life will feel the results of this. It is offered as primarily work between yourself and the deity, not essentially involving other people. The final three sections – *Presencing the Goddess, Enacting Myth* and *Aspecting the Goddess* – are more outward, they usually involve the presence and often the participation of other people. Within both those sections the intensity builds from the first, less-involved segment – *Walking with the Goddess*, in the first half and *Presencing the Goddess* in the second half – through a mid-ranking of intensity in *Researching the Goddess* and *Enacting Myth*, to two of the most intense ways I know to relate to a goddess, *Dedication* and *Aspecting*.

These are terms that are generally in use and different definitions of them abound, resulting in overlaps, uncertainty and imprecision regarding exactly what we are talking about. I have attempted to define these quite precisely in the introductions to each section, for the purposes of being able to write and read this book. These six techniques offer distinct methods of relating intimately with divine presences and allow us to train ourselves in these different ways, learning what to expect and how to hold boundaries and containers for more effective magical, ritual and even devotional work. There are inevitably overlaps, times when we are deliberately doing more than one of these things and also occasions when what is happening might slip from walking with the goddess, for example, into presencing the goddess.

The more we increase our skills, focus and experience, the more control we will have, as well as more knowledge about what is appropriate for any given ritual or time. Whether you use the same terms that are used here or not is unimportant. The focus of this book is stepping into different states of awareness and communion with the divine. I think it works better when we know what we are doing and choose how to do it. The divine – any deity, any goddess – is unimaginably far larger than we are. What will be possible for them will be far beyond what is possible for us. There may be times when it seems they desire something quite different than we desire. It may be hard to reach them, or difficult to return from relating with them. For all these reasons learning how to, and practicing, holding a strong container – clear intention, boundaries and focus while remaining grounded within ourselves – are crucial skills. There are more details on how to do these things at the end of the book under *Basic Ritual Skills*.

Throughout this book the terms *goddess*, *deity* and *divinity* are used both interchangeably and specifically. They are used interchangeably to remind us that we may be working with a named goddess, a god, an unnamed one or a larger sense of the divine. Sometimes they are used specifically, for example *the goddess Athena* or *any deity may be selected*. Where I do use the name of a goddess or god I use the common spelling and, unless it is otherwise described, I am working with that deity as they are generally to be read about within their myths and stories.

There are a number of ways you can approach this book. Each of the six sections contains a short introduction, two stories of different goddesses and two practical processes or exercises. You can read through the whole book first, later returning to sections or activities you want to work with. You can use it as an active workbook, approaching each section and trying out the activities, with the goddesses described here or others. You can read all the stories, allowing them to inspire or deepen your own relationship with the divine, whatever that might look like. You can choose to read the sections you are most interested in first, coming back to the others later. You can work solo, with a friend or partner or in a group.

How do you choose which deity or goddess to work with? For some people, this is not even a question since they already have an established relationship with one or more deities and that is what they wish to continue. Others have a name, a dream, a story and that is a valid starting point. Others may have a heritage they wish to explore – Norse or Native American or Jewish – while others may not have these things. Perhaps one of these stories will inspire you and send you reading into Egyptian, Welsh or Sumerian mythology. Perhaps you will pick a goddess almost at random, although many people will say there is no such thing as randomness when dealing with spiritual matters, and your choice will surely be deeply meaningful for you. I have limited myself, in this book, to named goddesses although certainly it is not my main or only way of working with goddess. You may choose to work with the Earth Goddess, the Moon Goddess, the Crone, the Dark Goddess, or a local deity, named or nameless, that you are familiar with.

Recently the discussion of cultural appropriation has become more prominent, as those of us in various invaded lands seek what I might call right relationship with the First Peoples whose land was stolen and whose culture is often both denigrated and reviled, then later poached and capitalized on. Thus there appears to be a returned focus to working with stories and deities who belong to our own heritage, both genetic and cultural; or at least to those cultures – such as ancient Greek, Sumerian and Egyptian – that so informed our culture and our Christian and post-Christian mythologies. Certainly in Australia, if we are not Aboriginal we would not work with an Aboriginal myth or deity without very specific circumstances, of being taught and guided in this by an Aboriginal person or group endowed with such authority. Where cultures have been invaded, degraded, and sometimes destroyed, we try not to add to the list of crimes. This is a sensitive topic and not everyone agrees on any particular approach. Some guidelines include that we should consider how our choices may act to further marginalize or oppress peoples from ethnic groups not our own; that where there are living custodians of myth and story we should, at the very least, ask permission and seek guidance from those custodians and that we should examine the privileges and assumptions that may underlie our choices of myth and deity.

I invite you to explore what seems meaningful to you in these pages, treating it as inspiration and support and venturing outwards from there

Walking with the Goddess

Walking with a goddess is a way of granting us some insight into her myth or stories. *Walking with* can be an introduction to a goddess we don't know, perhaps one who has appeared in a dream or whose name has leapt out at us. It is less intense than some other ways of working with a deity, which does not mean the experience won't be profound. Walking with a deity allows us, unlike dedicating oneself to a goddess or even presencing a goddess, to choose when we are and are not in dialogue. It is more like having a conversation with someone – at times an absorbing, surprising or challenging conversation – than inviting them to move in with you or swearing undying oaths with them. It requires our specific focus and attention for anything to really happen.

Because walking with a divinity is less intense and all-consuming than, for example, aspecting, it means it is relatively easy to stretch it out over long periods of time. A month can be an appropriate time to allow impressions and experiences to accumulate. We may also walk with a goddess for a single ritual. If this is planned for a ritual with others, often one person – preferably more than one – might spend a week or a month prior to the ritual conducting a personal walking with that deity. This is similar to how we might approach aspecting a deity in ritual – for most people, turning up to a ritual, their preparation takes place during or immediately prior to the ritual. But the person or people aspecting, and their tenders, will have spent at least hours and more probably days or weeks feeling their way into the aspecting, the story and the deity in the lead-up to the ritual.

At the Glastonbury Goddess Conference in England one year I found myself in the Circle of the Maiden for a week, aligned to the North-East (the northern hemisphere direction of Imbolc; in the southern hemisphere it would be the South-East). As well as representing maidens and the state of maidenhood, this grouping of one-eighth of the conference attendees was assigned Goewin, from the Welsh myth-cycle of the Mabinogion. Goewin is the foot holder of Math, the king. According to myth this position was always held by a maiden and among our circle were included the young girls present at the conference, pre- and early adolescents. It was a curious place to find myself and I did not feel much affinity with the Maiden; so I chose to walk with her, rather than invoke her or enact her myth.

Because I was walking with her through the week, holding her in my awareness as I moved through the activities of the conference, I began, slowly, to see things from her point of view. I saw how the young girls in our group were so immediate in their grasp of ritual and sacred space and how little explanation they needed, compared with adults. I saw their simplicity – innocence, if you like – granting them a strength and an immediacy in joy, involvement or risk where others of us were more reserved. I also witnessed the absolute, contained and complete beauty of a woman in our group, in her forties, who named herself bodily a virgin. I asked myself, *who is this foot holder of the king? Who holds the feet of the king?* – and I was thinking of the old kings, married to the land and their blood bound to its welfare and protection. The king sits on a throne. He places his feet in the lap of a young woman, a virgin. Who is she? She is seated – below him. On the floor, on a cushion. On the earth, in effect. Surely she must be a living human representation of the earth, the earth goddess. The one the king marries when he takes his oath of kingship.

This is what I learnt, walking with the maiden foot holder of Welsh myth. She is the earth. Where the king places his feet – that is the earth. The one who guards, who guides his feet – is the earth, which is the sacred feminine and any harm done to her is harm to the king. In the Mabinogion is a story describing the rape of the king's foot holder, which leaves her unfit for the role and the king's response, as well as punishing the perpetrators severely, is to marry her. Thus if she is the land, if in effect he is already married to her because he is the king, it is the perfect, circular and mythic response. Her violation makes obvious what was true all along; the king is married to the earth and her rape

– already treated as a grave, even dire act – has much wider-reaching implications; even more so in this time of exploitation of the earth's resources and widespread natural devastation than when the Mabinogion was written.

Walking with a goddess can be a way to gently introduce yourself to her. We are unlikely to feel that the deity's attention has swung sharply onto us, in critical, demanding or piercing ways, which certainly can happen when we enter into deeper relationship. Walking with a goddess is not a passive act on our part and in fact may require more deliberate ongoing attention to maintain a connection; whereas, for example, with dedication or aspecting, once we have done the invocation and made an initial commitment we may feel the whole thing is taken more or less out of our hands. Walking with a deity can also be a practical and respectful way to get to know a number of deities in a relatively short time; for example different members of one pantheon, or twelve or thirteen different goddesses during a year.

The tools of journaling, meditation, trance and ritual will assist you to stay connected, or keep connecting with the deity you are walking with. At the end of this section are two exercises to assist you in walking with a goddess.

Persephone

One dark moon night twenty years ago I sat with three other women in a shadowy room and we created a ceremony for Persephone. Perhaps the year was even heading into winter. On that night we ventured into the realms of myth and ritual, guided by the goddess and her story. I remember a palpable sense of Persephone being in the room with us. Each of us created an offering. I know that because I've kept mine, inside the box with my ritual mirror. It's black cardboard in the shape of a teardrop, there's a spiral outlined in gold and purple glitter and words, spiraling inwards. *Let me walk always towards you... Inanna Ishtar Isis Artemis Gaia Freyja Aphrodite.* Although Persephone's name isn't on it I have been walking towards her since that long ago ritual, watching her story weave in and out of mine and reflecting on our parallels and differences.

Persephone's myth is captivating, familiar and alarming to many of us. We are drawn to it, held by it, frightened by it. The innocent daughter of Greek Demeter, powerful goddess of grain, one day Persephone picks a flower. At this stage she does not even have a name, she is known as *Kore*, maiden. The earth opens up beneath her and she vanishes. In different versions of the story she went into the Underworld because she heard the dead souls calling to her; or she was abducted by Hades, Lord of the Underworld, or seduced by him. Her mother searches for her in vain and when she finally discovers where her daughter has gone, she cannot get her back. In revenge, or grief, she brings about the first winter. By the time Persephone is released from the Underworld she has eaten some pomegranate seeds and is bound to return, thus creating the round of seasons as every year the earth mourns her loss. Hecate, crone goddess of the crossroads is an almost silent player in this story. She witnesses Persephone's descent, eventually assists Demeter and offers a third way of viewing this myth.

Persephone's story takes us in and in. Her invitation – to eat of the mysteries, to become an initiate – reveals itself as soon as we begin working with her. So many times in a group of women we've taken a pomegranate and broken it open, peeled back the skin or sliced into it to reveal those red seeds, glistening, jewel-like. *Take this and eat, knowing. Knowing it binds you to the Underworld, knowing it means that, like Persephone, you'll return and return again to the dark...* We commit ourselves to the mysteries. We travel Persephone's paths without knowing where those paths will take us. We leave our mothers, surrender our daughters, we mourn and create winters and springtimes and revisit and return. We walk with Persephone.

Persephone is shrouded in mystery. Her great disappearing act, from her own story, remains fascinating to us. At the beginning of the myth she vanishes into the Underworld and then nearly all the rest of the story is about other things until, right at the end, she appears again. The story follows Demeter in the upper world as she searches and mourns for her daughter. Oh the trials of mothers, yes, we've all heard that. But what we want to know is what's happening with Persephone in the Underworld – is she dead? Alive? Does she love her husband and maybe-abductor, Hades? Hate him? Is she trying to escape? Resigned to her fate? Even when she is returned, through Demeter's efforts, to her mother's embrace and to live at least half the time in the upper world, we still don't know the answers to those questions. Her story swings around the separation from, and return to, her mother.

Mothers and daughters, the red lines of women. Within twelve months my mother dies and also one of my closest friends dies; Trinda, the woman who for twenty years mothered me in all the ways she could. Both died around the age of seventy, both as a result of long-term health conditions monitored and treated, in my mother's case over forty years, for Trinda over fifteen. Both deaths were shocking to me, though I had known about them, known they were coming, were soon – but I had never attempted to imagine what it might be like when they were dead.

When I was a small child I longed for my mother. I'm sure there were times we were close but I mainly remember the times she was an impossible distance away from me, although maybe in the same room, or just down the hall. Perhaps, really, I find this part of Persephone's story hard to imagine, that she was so close to her mother, that they moved together like one doubled being through the fields and orchards of Demeter's domain. I spent my childhood trying to win over my teachers, imagining that the affection of each of those women, in turn, could make up for my mother's lack of attention. I looked – closely, piercingly – at the mothers of other girls, wondering at their interactions with their daughters and wondering, also, how one of them could somehow become my mother. Louise's mother, Becky's mother, Eliza's mother, Michelle's mother... I watched their closeness with their daughters and envied it, longed for it.

There's that piece with the earth, when Persephone enters into the earth, which has opened up for her. My high school was alienating, difficult and frightening. I had arthritis and was in pain; that bone-deep relentless aching and the stabbing, seizing pains that arthritis combines. I could not seem to find any corners to be happy in. Sometimes, at night, I would let myself out of my bedroom and tread softly outside, barefoot. I lay on the earth, face down. I did not wish to die, exactly; I had no call towards death or suffering. But I did wish that I could turn time back and not be born. I would dig my fingers into the dirt, through the grass and leaves and sticks I lay on. *Take me back*, I whispered, into the realms of the dark, still, growing earth; *take me back*. If the earth had opened up for me then, I would have stepped through. I would have vanished.

At the beginning of Persephone's story she picks a flower she has never seen before. But this is Demeter's daughter, who spends her whole life in fields and orchards. And she had not a mortal's length of childhood, but that of a goddess. How long is that? Centuries? What type of flower is it, that she would never have seen before? Perhaps she went somewhere Demeter never went – the forest, maybe – and therefore saw flowers she'd never seen before. Some versions of the story say Hades made that flower especially for her. But the way these Greek stories work they'd tell you what flower it was, so you could find one yourself, like you could find Demeter's corn, or a narcissus, lute, a lightning bolt or pomegranate or all the other symbols those stories use. Persephone never leaves Demeter's side, or so it's said, so either the story got it wrong and they weren't so tied-together or – she'd begun wandering.

Was this was her first time away from her mother? Or perhaps she'd been stretching out the thread that bound them, further and further... Then, that flower – was it really a flower or is that just a nicety of story-telling? I've heard the story told with the flower as a symbol for her menstrual blood, or her ripening sexuality. Maybe the flower is her genitals, or even his. Hades. God of the Underworld, rising up through the earth to seize hold of her, the instant she picks that flower. A flower she's never seen before. And she's the child of a single mother; who was impregnated, if you want to go into detail, by her brother Zeus, the same one who had agreed to look the other way when their brother, Hades, wooed or maybe stole Persephone to be his wife. Okay, so her husband is her uncle; doubly so since both her parents are his siblings. But this is not a casual dalliance. He makes her his queen, is very loyal and apparently monogamous – almost unheard of for those Greek gods – and allows her to visit her mother for months on end every year. Although I notice he doesn't invite Demeter into their realm.

It is only in my mother's death that I feel myself approaching her again and then it is not as the woman she had become but as part of this mother-daughter ribbon of lives I am threaded on. I dream of a line of women, holding hands and a river flows between me and the next woman up the line, my mother. My grandmother is on the other side of her. It is the generations of us and the river, surely, is the river of death and life. On this side of the river, mine, is life and on the other side, stretching back, are the realms of the dead. The next woman to be tugged across the river, to that side, will be me. I see my mother now as one in a pattern, an archetype of French land and blood, one body in the endless line of one woman giving birth to another. The mysteries are being revealed.

My life is so different from my mother's life, my grandmother's, my great-grandmother's and great-great-grandmother's. I can imagine that for each of those women it was like watching her daughter enter into the Underworld, perhaps never to be seen again. My great-great-grandmother Aurore Ismerie was born in France. I know nothing about her life. Nothing except this: she left her mother to live in a foreign land, from which she would never return. Her daughter, my great-grandmother Josephine, bore seven children and her husband died when the youngest, my grandmother, was one year old. Five of those children were boys, the eldest of the seven her only other girl, a beauty who married when my grandmother was still a small child. Josephine was crippled with arthritis in the later part of her life and my grandmother Antonyle Yvonne, known as Neila, surrendered her dreams of becoming a nurse to stay and nurse, at home, her mother.

So the stories of mother and daughter blur together, my grandmother's story defined perhaps by being the dutiful daughter, not marrying until late and then giving birth to three children, two boys who both died shortly after being born and finally my mother, another Josephine, her only living child whom she never really forgave for being a girl. Or, perhaps, for living when her sons had died. My grandmother stayed in that narrow, home-based role; she nursed her dying husband when she was only in her fifties. Later, for many years, she nursed one of her brothers, the taciturn, abrupt, withdrawn one who was never kind or grateful to her, at least not that I ever saw or heard about. He suffered paralysis down one side of his body, half his face was frozen, making his speech even more bitten off than perhaps he would have chosen and he walked with a cane from my youngest memories.

My grandmother watched my mother go to university and have a career, although to leave home she did have to get married. She watched her daughter's children, my brother and myself, stay alive and she watched my mother have the freedoms of the sixties, seventies, eighties while she remained in a kind of time warp; even her closest friends addressed her by her married name and on principle she never did anything purely for pleasure. In a small way she had clearly gone through hard times, I remember that we were never allowed to open a packet of biscuits or a tin of soup until its exact replacement was in the cupboard.

My mother Jo, named for her own grandmother, had two profound moments with her mother in the last year of Neila's long life. My grandmother, in her nineties, finally told Jo she had been a good daughter. Which she was, loyal and endlessly visiting with my grandmother's favorite treats, things Neila would never have bought. Submitting herself to the endless story they told between them, that my mother was the wrong gender, the wrong child; that she had not pleased her mother with her choice of husband, with the life she led, with her appearance; that everything would have been different if only her brothers had lived. So to hear after fifty-something years that she was a good daughter, it was precious to her.

The other moment was just before my grandmother's death, in the day or two before; I can't check exactly when, now that they are both dead. My grandmother was not quite conscious, was already entering, perhaps, the realms of death and she called out *don't take him away from me*, which made no sense at the time but a little later my mother thought, perhaps that was her dead baby, that they were taking away, as of course they would have done in those days, with a brisk admonition that she should forget him and get on with her life and in time she would have another. Which she did. Twice. But that haunting never left her, the haunting of how it would have been if her sons had lived and now we think, I think, since I am the only one of the three of us left alive, that moment when they took him away never finished for her, those two moments since there were two dead sons. Until finally she called it out, aloud and maybe she had been calling it internally all that time. Then she could die.

Writing out this history I see the disconnection travelling from mother to daughter, down the line. Aurore lost her mother when she travelled to another land and another life. Neila lost her mother to ill-health and pain, and she did not have her around when she was a young mother and may have needed support. Jo perhaps lost her mother into this grief over dead babies and her inability to replace them; she and Neila had never been close.

I lost my mother to books. When I was young I would stand in front of her as she read. I would tell her about school, ask her questions maybe and she would half-listen and half-answer, from behind the book she was reading. Books and reading were her passion, she made a career of them. The irony of my becoming a writer, even a writer of books, has not escaped me. I always thought maybe it was my way of trying to get the first piece of her attention, that if reading those pages was so much more interesting than real life, I would be on the pages.

She did what she wanted and yet, to me, she still seemed to live a narrow life. My son tells me not to worry about it but I wonder at how little interest she took in anything outside her immediate zone of focus and how closed-off she seemed to be. She watched me walk away from her, in traditional Persephone style, but she didn't seem to try to get me back. She didn't play Demeter, perhaps because she was still playing Persephone, escaping her own mother. Perhaps we have a series of stories, in my mother-line, about loss and disconnection and the reconnection is never quite made, or made only on a death-bed, or after death.

My mother had experienced a cloying level of interference, control and opinion from her own mother, I wonder if she just went in the other direction. In return for her slight abstraction, her vagueness and absence and lack of focus on me or my activities, I thrust myself away from her. I spent my whole middle childhood saying *I will not be like that.* I will not be the one who ignores her children, who makes promises only to break them, who collapses in tears whenever she is confronted. In many ways, I am not like that. In other ways, of course, I am like her; how could I help it? That is what shaped me, what gave me form and flesh; we look alike, we have the same body type and of course that French blood, I would not want to be without that.

Actually I can believe Persephone was like this. That she longed for her mother's attention – and yet while she was by her side she never had a name, a personality, a domain of her own. Demeter has a very important job, endlessly demanding I imagine, with little time for a daughter that did anything but reflect her. Demeter was the one the songs were about, the stories, she was the one they prayed to. Perhaps they tacked *and Kore* onto the end of those prayers, but was that enough for the daughter who went on to become Persephone and Queen of the Underworld? Probably not. So she has a few hundred years of that, or a millennia, an aeon, the length of a myth, the length of agrarian time – endless – for the cycle of life to occur and occur again, unstopping before she grows up or distances herself enough at least to think, to wonder, what else is there?

What else apart from endless fertility and life, than grain sprouting and ripening and harvested, than the trunks of trees in the orchards rising to bear limbs and leaves and flowers and fruit? What else? Well. The lambs when they are born, yes some thrive and grow, many, but not all. Some die. Why do they do that? What happens to them? The grain of the fields, where does it go when it falls to the ground? What story does it tell? The tree, how is it held up? What sustains it from below, what feeds it, what mysteries lie where we cannot see? This fresh water spring that appears, where from? This endless fountaining of life begets death, many deaths. The deaths as endless as the lives; as many as the births. How does that fit into grain-and-flower-and-fruit? Where would a girl go, to discover such things?

Thus the longing, unmet and then thrust away. There are realms the mother does not have domain within, silent places, still and dark; the places that predate her powers and supersede them, what comes both before and after the grain and fruit and lamb. Death. The realms of death. Oh Persephone, no wonder you were so entirely beyond your mother's reach when you made that journey, you went the one place that was the antithesis of all your mother's knowing, all her doings and powers and attention, all her being.

Did I do that? Doesn't every daughter do that? Realms of emotion, of the mind, of sexuality; places the mother would never go, relationships she could not condone, friendships more intimate than any she has ever had, activities of which she would not approve. The man on the motorbike, the political protest, the lesbian lover, the group house, the intellectual debate, the music and books and theatre. The clothes she wouldn't wear, the dares she wouldn't take, travelling alone; the still, clear knowledge of herself she thinks her mother never had. I left my mother as my own mother had left hers, as she had been left in her turn, as she had no doubt been left, and left; as Aurore Ismerie, leaving France, left her mother in some way we will never now know.

In the Underworld, so the story goes, Persephone ate nothing for nine months – or six, or four, or however many months, but it was months – and then she was suddenly tricked into eating pomegranate seeds. Tricking someone who isn't eating, into eating... I don't know. I can't quite see it. It's hard to eat things by accident, if you're not eating anything. All I can imagine, if she ate them – and it's an essential part of the story, that she ate them – is either that she was eating all along and was tricked into the specifics of eating pomegranate seeds, or else she ate them willingly, or at least knowingly. Perhaps the whole thing was a slightly carelessly constructed story, put about afterwards to try to explain her continuing returns to the Underworld. Because one thing is certain, after her initial time in the Underworld Persephone returns there every year. She's become a part of the place, or it's become a part of her. She's the queen there, now.

Really I feel more like Persephone returning, now that my mother's dead, than I ever did while she was alive. I did the escape to a different realm and I never came back. Until now. I used to wonder if it didn't cause her pain, my distance from her; I couldn't imagine a child of mine being so removed from me as I was from her, but it looked like she didn't notice. That she had better things to do. I don't really know how she thought of me. A crucial piece of Persephone's story is that Demeter mourned for her; I wonder what happens to those of us who never felt mourned, who were never missed or were simply overlooked.

The substitute mothers I found through my adulthood, they weren't in the business of mourning for me, either. They did the support part, support and praise and unconditional love. They held me in the world, they looked at me with pride, gave encouragement and challenge, told me I was beautiful and brilliant, they didn't give advice. I felt they knew me well, better than I knew myself and that they would do anything for me. Trinda was the longest and the closest of them... I didn't ask for mourning. The mourning part –it was an undone piece. Now I have taken it up myself.

But this is Persephone's story, not just mine and in it she transforms from a young maiden goddess, with no name, even, of her own, into the powerful Persephone, Queen of the Dead. She becomes, like her mother, mistress of her own realm. That little girl, yearning to be like her mother and yet also longing to escape is deeply familiar to us. So she has escaped her and become her – both. I have escaped my mother one way and another, most finally through her death and, of course, in her death I have become her. Yes it is my own version of her but, from so many perspectives, I am just like her. Now that she is dead I am the only version of her. Persephone is a version of Demeter – she was as that maiden, clinging to her mother's side and she is as the powerful Queen of the Underworld, replicating her mother's power and majesty in the realm that mirrors her mother's realm.

We might choose to walk with Persephone as we approach times of threshold; of going within and also of emerging. Persephone takes risks, she accepts invitations. An essential part of these thresholds is that we can't know what lies on the other side of them. We have to go on instinct, or trust, or just plain daring. Here is a flower growing, that I've never seen before – what will I do? Pass it by – or – pick it? Persephone picks the flower. I prefer the versions where she goes willing into the Underworld, called by something, seeking something or simply seduced by the Dark God, but even in the most popularly told version, where she is more or less kidnapped or possibly raped by Hades, she's still the one who picked that flower.

Something about wanting to *have* that experience – not just look at the flower, admire or wonder at it, but have it for herself – that's the path that led her into the Underworld. Because she had never seen it before obviously she had no idea of its properties. It could have been poisonous, seductive, lethal, it could have summoned a god. It could have opened a doorway into the Underworld. It did. I think at that point to start crying innocent and just-passing-by or I'd-never-leave-my-mother's-side is a little disingenuous. This is not to disregard very serious, real-world events of rape, slavery, abduction and domestic violence. Women and cultures suffering from these injustices are not to be assumed responsible for what has happened to them. As more and more of us wake up to these realities, we have to hope and work for change. It is possible that Persephone's story also holds something of empowerment, for those who have experienced such extreme disempowerment.

Once Persephone is in the Underworld again there is volition, choice. She ate and drank nothing for five or six months. She is a goddess, after all. So why eat some seeds of a pomegranate, right at the last minute? Clearly not to satisfy hunger, as we think of it; a few pomegranate seeds wouldn't satisfy any ordinary hunger. But a hunger for the divine – they might satisfy that. A hunger for the mysteries of the Underworld, to integrate and own them, literally to ingest them; those seeds might meet that hunger. As a symbolic integration of what she herself would become; a seed, to be buried and then grow again – they satisfy that motif. As a metaphor for accepting the seeds of Hades into her body, well they satisfy that, too. By then there was no doubt that he was her husband. That she belonged to the Underworld and was queen of that place. When she returns to Demeter she is no longer just a daughter, Kore, maiden; she has become Persephone, Queen of the Dead.

To be Queen of the Dead is to be queen of life, as well, specifically of birth, rebirth and of spring. Demeter's realms are those of summer and autumn; grain in the fields, flowers, fruit on the trees, the wealth of the land and the abundance of crops and food. Persephone holds the other half; winter and the descent, spring and rebirth. The two goddesses between them embrace the seasons, the Wheel of the Year. Passing back and forward like a weaving dance the whole life cycle is held, the way generations pass one to the next the gifts and traits of their hereditary line.

There are dark shadows in this story of Persephone's,

of mothers and daughters. Shadows of grief and loss and powerlessness, the wrenching away of what is known and has been loved and familiar. Shadows of dealing with the masculine; the brother/ruler/father in Zeus who does not listen and cannot see, the dark lover of Hades so much older and initially more powerful than oneself. Shadows of entering the mysteries. Everyone in this story is in the realm of the unknown; Zeus finding the limits of his power, Demeter in loss and devastation, Persephone in the Underworld and Hecate standing at the crossroads, witnessing. Hades, perhaps, in love.

In Persephone's story the mother loses her daughter, then regains her. Are there meetings again, reunions, in the story of my mother line? There's my grandmother finally speaking those words to my mother. And haven't I understood, since my mother died, how I spent fifty years resisting her and therefore perhaps didn't come fully into myself? All my shyness, my social awkwardness, my avoidance of being seen; didn't that come directly from my avowal not to be like her? Like Persephone I both flung myself away from her and also returned. I have felt closer to my mother in the two years since her death than I have for a very long time, since I was a little girl. Perhaps because I feel I hold her whole life, now and she is gentler in that, across the span of it; across her childhood, teenage years, through all the phases of her adult life until her death at seventy-three, sudden and complete. I am bringing myself into a place of reunion.

Aurore, Josephine, Antonyle, Josephine, Jane.

Trinda dies a few days before I get on a plane to go to the other side of the world and so I am not there for the mourning, for her daughter, for the celebration of her life, a ritual I had promised Trinda I would conduct. Three months later when I finally return to Australia I travel north to see her daughter Mallika before she leaves, in her turn, for the other side of the world. I stay at a friend's house, a friend who is not there, away herself, but her daughter Roshana is there. This is a girl I have known since she was two; I have known her at five and eight and twelve and fifteen. Now she is twenty-two. I am jet-lagged, exhausted and in deep grief; I don't think she really knows any of that but she offers to cook me dinner. She says she is cooking anyway, she will cook some for me and if I want, I can eat it.

I watch her moving around the kitchen towards the end of the cooking process, it is my friend's kitchen and she moves like my friend. Her body, its movements in the kitchen, looks like my friend's movements. It is familiar and yet new, reborn into this body. She brings me my dinner and will barely accept thanks for it; she says it is nothing, not even very good though I try to tell her how lovely it is for me. After I have eaten I take the plate to the sink. She says, from the other room, and I knew she would say this, because it is exactly what my friend would say, exactly, the exact words and intonation, to leave it and she will deal with it. She says it kindly, generously, exactly as my friend does and I am smiling with it, not even with the words or the thought but with the replica of my friend and so I do leave it for her, though usually I would not do that.

I go to visit Trinda's daughter and when she walks towards me all I can think is, she looks so like Trinda. The lines of her face, something in the lean of her walk, the lift of her eyes. We talk for several hours and I cry, off and on, though I have already been crying for three months and I don't really want to impose my tears on her. I tell her some little, tiny pieces of what Trinda was to me and after a while she asks if I want to hold Trinda's ashes. She gets the container out of the suitcase that is already half packed and hands it to me. It is so heavy. I sit there in wonder for a while, between the worlds of life and death, imagining I am holding my friend as she died, which I didn't get to do. I am in the sadness and the awe and enormity of it and Mallika says she would like to sing to me. So she sits there with her guitar and sings the Chrissie Hynde song Trinda asked for at her funeral.

I dress as your daughter
when the moon becomes round.
I'll be your mother
when everything's gone.

She is tender with me, the same way Trinda was nearly always tender with me and I hold Trinda's ashes and sob and sob for loss and beauty and my friend's daughter in this fragile, ferocious world and there are elements of daughters and daughters becoming mothers and mothering even their own mothers, or those around them. Oh we are into the mysteries here, the Persephone mysteries. These daughters, holding the places of their mothers, in their mothers' absences. Persephone herself becoming a mother to her realm, to the dead souls, doing that in the absence of her own mother. Daughters become mothers and mothers are always daughters.

This thread is tangled in my family, perhaps it is in every family. In my life I have sought the mysteries, I have journeyed there and returned, but the women who met me on that return were not my mother and I did not have a daughter of my own. Instead the story has shifted sideways and I greet the return of my mother inside myself; ah, now I know her, hold her, because I am her, to all intents and purposes. She no longer holds shape in the world but I do, I carry that line, the DNA of it, I stand in her place, I am the literal, physical and in some ways energetic pattern of her that remains.

Trinda was Hecate for me more than Demeter; one who showed the way, watched my descents and returns, looked out for me and recognized my paths. In her death, in these double deaths, I am left holding all the pieces. Pieces of ash, of earth and bone. Red seeds of pomegranate. I leave a pomegranate offering, broken open, for Trinda under a tree she loved. I wear a silver bangle with three strands twisted together that I took from my mother's jewelry. I don't know if it was hers or my grandmother's and there is no-one to ask but I have not taken it off for two and a half years. I think it twines the three of us together. I am flesh with a heart that still beats, eyes that see, skin that feels and oh, the endless thoughts in this being of me. I am holding Trinda, I am holding my mother, I am tripled, Persephone Demeter Hecate and I am greeted by the daughters of my friends who cook a meal for me and sing me a song. Food to return to life, a song of the mysteries we hold between us, within us. Ashes of the dead.

In my mourning there is daughters greeting a mother, welcoming her home and myself as daughter mourning my mother, my mothers' absences and deaths. Daughters, we are all daughters. The pieces of Persephone's myth are here. When Roshanna cooks dinner, when Mallika sings to me, I feel some sort of return. I have eaten the pomegranate and I return again and again to this story of descent, of searching out mystery and depth and even to its framework of mothers and daughters, but all the pieces are mine and I choke, eating, when they can no longer eat, not being in the world of the living at all, but I do eat.

I live part of my time there now, in the land of the dead.

Blodeuwedd

Blodeuwedd is part of a Welsh myth, long and tangled as they mostly are.

Before she appears the story is about a golden boy, a demoted goddess cast as an abandoned and abandoning mother and a clever, bitter magician. The woman gives birth, resentful, tricked into it and cursing; the child is rescued by her brother, the magician who raises him. His mother has to name him, they trick her into it. His mother has to arm him; they trick her again. Someone has to marry him; this time they trick nature into making a woman of flowers and they are married. But this is not a happy story.No-one thought of this bride or what she might desire and she falls in love not with the bright boy but a darker god, the man of death and much death results. Death and freedom, born from curses and from magic.

Something in this story sparkles, seeks to break free of the form and it is not the mysteries of occult magic, for me; not the yearning of the unmothered child – though both of those, at other times, could draw me. As for Arianrhod, who's given birth to this Llew, named and armed him unwillingly, her whole tale seems caught up with the advent of patriarchy; when she went to claim what was surely her ancient right, to be acknowledged as goddess, the land under the throne of the king, it was denied her, on the grounds that she was not a virgin. And what is a virgin? Is it not the feminine, divine unto itself and holding loyalty to no man? The men in this story somehow prove that because she has lain with men she has no power. The son she gives birth to is evidence, no wonder she denies him. It is not even the dark turn of the story that beckons me, as they make all the wrong choices, magic and power and love turning against them as Llew's bride falls in love with someone else, undoing everything that has been done so carefully and so cleverly.

No, it is the wild one; the woman made of petals, of flowers, conjured from sunlight and summer, from softness, scent and color, the woman bees will flock to, butterflies worship; she who opens at dawn and glories all the long day and then closes, replete, at night. *Blodeuwedd.* You of the nearly unpronounceable in English, difficult-to-write name, that name that sounds like a whisper across the slope of a mountain, or an echo carried down a stream, a name that might be a breath of invitation deep in the forest. *Blod-eye-wuth*, Blodeuwedd. Made by magic into womanhood with no childhood to teach you, no mother to turn to or blaze forth from, no sisters to hold and dance with. Blodeuwedd, one of a kind, a woman from magic and flowers, desire made flesh. Perhaps Blodeuwedd is also a child of Arianrhod's, one way and another; a child of the goddess, born straight from the earth and not through a mortal woman.

How far apart is a flower from a woman; how far apart a river, a tree, a bird? Infinitely far; perhaps not very far. Within our essence all these things reside, rivers and birds and flowers and trees, memories of what our atoms once belonged to, forms of this world that predate our form. When we turn there for solace, to moonlight, the tides of the sea, to the bright flowers of summer, the golden wheat, the call of an owl at night, don't we feel as if we were a part of it and it is easier to join that beating heart of the world than it is to reach out to or understand another human being? Child of earth, of the goddess – we are all that, humans and deer, oak trees and mountain streams, flowers and mountains. All comes from her, all leads back to her.

Mountain. Ages old, the bones of the earth thrust up from seabed or birthed by volcanoes as the great plates of the earth grind against each other, or else left standing after glaciers churn their way through the landscape, relentless but, in the end, taking the easiest path and leaving the stubbornest points of landscape alone. She is there, a foretaste of her in the molten fire that burns everything in its path, only later, aeons later relaxing into rich soil rewarding those paths of flame with lush forest, fertile fields, undulant green growing life, all dedicated to her. She is there in the take-no-prisoners glaciers, the thoughtless Ice Queenness of them rolling everything in their path relentlessly into the destruction that bites out mountains and valleys and lakes. She is there in the sharp black rocks at the peaks, the rounded boulders gentled by wear, she is there in the streams carving into her hillsides, still shaping her; she is there in the mists and clouds that veil her or the icy lake where she might bathe, changed and changing.

She is in the forest that clads the slopes like her green cloak, she is there in elder, ash, in oak and thorn, in beech and rowan, hazel, willow and yew. She is in the trunk and branch and root of them, clinging to rocky hillsides or dwelling deep and lush among their kind in the valleys and softer hills. She is there, exposed to bone in winter, showing their skeletons and she is there in the spring green that kisses their limbs; she is there in the bud and flower and feathering through to seed; oh, she is there. Flower might be the part of the process that we name beautiful; flower of the field or garden or hedge, but flower is one piece only of a whole story, one moment of color, brightness and scent from a whole year long, seasons long, millennial old story, the story of flowers. A story older than that of humans, certainly, older than mammals, than birds, than lizards. A story so old that were we to consider it truly we would cower, afraid, beneath its magnitude, the severe utter beauty of it. It is a story of otherness, that some small part of it pleases the human eye is incidental. Flowers were born from the green to please wind and bee, to worship the earth. Bearers of the ancient life force they dance the dance of gods who existed long before we came to gaze upon them.

Memories of the great forest remain. We think of forests as contained places, discrete areas of green on the map. This was not contained, this was not mapable. It stretched across Europe.

For a long time the laws of that forest were the rules containing human realms. The laws of oak and beech, of ash and rowan. The laws of leaf and stem, of root and branch and trunk, of soil, of water, of sun. The cycle of bud and flower and fruit and cold interval. This was vast, unyielding and the very fabric of the land. Villages fought to keep the forest back. Those who lived at the edges of the village were distrusted, too close to the forest they were thought to be influenced by its magics. Strangers who emerged from the forest were suspect, it was hard to be certain they were properly human, let alone when they spoke or dressed oddly or talked of unfamiliar places. Later, when towns were built, they focused into the center, away from the edges; windows gave view onto civilization, not onto the wild, which was considered ugly, frightening. Those who made their living in or from the forest – herb women, woodsmen, hunters – were considered not quite civilized.

In Blodeuwedd's story two people, one with great powers and one with bare, aching need seek to control this force, to dip a handful of it up, out of the stream of creation and shape it with their wills, to human ends. To make a woman from flowers. To turn this great, green engine of our world towards domestic love and loyalty, to ask wild fertile beauty to serve another cause. We might be surprised that it worked even for a minute, that a woman of flowers was born of magic, did momentarily take that form and glimmer there, as if to promise something she could not fulfill, was not ever designed to meet or understand. Even though it is a story perhaps we can see where that imagining came from; the corresponding beauty of flowers and a woman's form, the softness of her, the secret center of her. Perhaps we can sympathize, even yearn ourselves for a glimpse of that magic.

But she had forces inside her not tied in blood to lines of women, to the getting of children and caring for humans; her offerings were sap and summer, pollen and petal and as she wielded them – and she couldn't not wield them, she was made of them, they composed her – she attracted not just her given husband, though none had asked if she wished for a husband, but anyone else who saw her, who smelled her. Like a flower. She had been forged in magic and so it swirled around her, it was in the tresses of her hair and her breath and the touch of her fingers, the gaze of her eyes and anyone caught in it drowned, a little, like bees. That magic, old, old and imperative called them into the center, no argument, compelled them and welcomed them and perhaps those ones knew her, a little; better than Llew who believed in tricks and visions; unmothered, half-formed Llew.

Take a tree, take a flower, take a bird, a breath of air with the words whispered through it, incantations, take the magic of stardust and reshape it, just as we are shaped again and again through millennia, to just this shape in this moment; take will and bind it with magic, with the processes of nature and see through it sideways, like through water, a pool or a waterfall maybe; let the twist of water become her hair, the petals her soft skin, the roots of the tree her nourishment from the earth and the bird her knowledge of the divine. Let her be birthed on the side of a mountain – a Welsh one, why not? – from the yearnings and devisings of two men, one young and hopeful and one old with knowledge but neither of them wise and let them stand for all men and the great yearning for union, now that they have lost the goddess, spurned her in Arianrhod without seeing the truth laid out before them.

Let a woman rise up from flowers, from desire and need, like summer comes from spring and let us forget, for a moment, that autumn follows, and winter and let this woman be as women are, as flowers are turning towards the sun, opening their petals and offering their pollen to who comes in the great pulsing, thrusting, generous need for the brush of wings against stamens, for the caress of wind among petals to carry golden drifts out and beyond, for the random decree of plants and the blessings they scatter to the winds.

Oh, it was bound to end badly, this story of creating a woman from flowers. Did they think, at all, about what flowers do, about what flowers are? The sex organs of primitive, unapologetic nature, before all that refinement of the animal kingdom, let alone the pack-ness, the tribe-ness, the social rules that humans broker; trading some of that primitive for other, so-called higher needs of socialization and security and social order. Gwydion, the great magician with Llew his rescued nephew; was this his attempt to bring forth life, to do what a woman could and he could not, provide a wife for his sister's son? Let us not forget the place sisters' sons occupy, pre-patriarchy; for one can always know the mother and never the father of a child, thus it is sisters' sons who are decreed to carry on the male lineage. Was this his attempt to continue his magician's line, for immortality not just of his magic as it would live in her and her children, but in his lineage through Llew?

She's called the woman of flowers but surely she's really the Goddess of Flowers – she's the power and essence of flowers, she is *flower*. So then the story makes complete sense – he tried to marry the flowers and of course they are not faithful; murdered by his rival and his wife, his was the blood-and-bone they took to nurture them through the deep winter, so come spring they could rise again in their glory. Love of the goddess, marrying the goddess has always meant death to a mortal man; death in the ways of sacred death – and his was a sacred death – and death in the ordinary way, as humans fade and die while goddesses, flowers and trees and all of nature shift and change and continue on. What he sought to do, through the magic of Gwydion, what they had always sought to do, though Llew unknowing it, was to tame and fetter the goddess, first in the form of Arianrhod, how they tricked and manipulated her again and again to get what they wanted; and then with Blodeuwedd.

Can the powers of the feminine be turned to serve the

masculine? The story shows yes, we are in a time when they can be – diverted, perverted, maybe, turned against women themselves, the goddess – but not forever. There's a payback and it results, as always, as it always did back to the oldest old, in his death. Not the death of the old, knowing one – the magician – but of the young, the beautiful, the willing sacrifice, the one who gave his love. Oh, him. We will take him. So the powers of the goddess are not what they were – not unquestioned – but they are final. Nature we can trick and change and commodify and try to tame – but she is not tame and she will, in the end, be the death of us.

Flowers turn to owls, in this story, after Blodeuwedd betrays Llew her punishment is to be turned into an owl. Birds of prey have more agency than flowers; yes flowers feed on compost, on the rotted bodies of whatever is laid in their soil and their beauty springs forth from it, but owls are hunters and killers; owls are a different face of the goddess and not a kinder one. Flower and owl, the light and dark faces, you could say, of the goddess; and if you mess with one you will meet the other – or perhaps we always meet the other, since they are intrinsically part of the same, so you cannot have flowers without owls; if you meet with owls you must also eventually return to flowers. Night and day they are; flowers opening their faces to the sun and owls awake, hunting, seeing by night. They hold the paradoxes of goddess as well; flowers that belong to the light have no caring in them, their seeds are dropped or blown, their pollen distributed by others; whereas owls build nests, lay and sit on eggs and then care for their young. It's the Dark Goddess who is nurturer, not she of the light.

There's a mountain in Wales, Cadair Idris. Twice I've been there, both times with my son Damon and both times we only got as far as the lake, halfway up. The first time it was sunny, the walk was strenuous and Damon was only six; it was a beautiful place to picnic before going back down. I had picked it off the map and we were delighted by the wildness, the starkness and strength of the landscape. Later I discovered it was written into books as a place of magic and entry into the other world. I could imagine the lake being a place of transformation, that if you entered its waters you would not emerge unchanged. When we dipped our feet in it was glacial; shockingly cold, the kind of cold it's impossible to conjure up in the mind, before encountering it. This was in summer.

The second time we went Damon was fourteen and determined to get all the way up, around the summit that loops high and rocky up behind the lake. At the start of the walk were two rowan trees with their red berries warding; we picked some to carry with us. The weather was cold, damp, part of the way up is along a narrow stream, walking up the stream, in the water. I'd forgotten how steep and tough a walk it was, even the first half, to the lake and the second half was said to be worse. There are all these sharp black rocks everywhere, shifting as you place your feet on them, tumbling downwards. Trails of mist swirled in and it took us a couple of hours to reach the lake. It was summer again but you wouldn't know it. It was cold with a kind of rain that could have just been the approaching cloud, it hovered across the scenery. I asked another walker, shepherding a flock of rugged schoolboys, how far he thought the summit was. He said four more hours, round trip and I knew I couldn't do another four hours. We got as far as the lake, foreboding and bleak, cloud lowering and I had to pull Damon away from it; too old to be tied to a mother but too young to go on his own, though had it been clear and sunny I might have let him. The school group wouldn't take him with them, no matter what we said. We left Cadair Idris its secrets for another time. It's one of those mountains where, it's said, if you spend the night on it you emerge mad, or a poet; perhaps they are the same.

I walked with Blodeuwedd for a month, once; held a connection with her in the world while others of my circle walked with Gwydion, Llew, Arianrhod. I was in love with her, for that month. Not with a wondering, gentle sense but with a raw, rough urgency. It was consuming, it consumed. My gaze narrowed, focused, into petals and bees and the drift of wind, the colors of one leaf against the next and the ripe and rotting smells of earth and garden. I could hardly draw a breath, apart from that. She was not gentle, Blodeuwedd, nor did she care about gentleness. She did not, actually, care about others, or even much about the fate of herself. She was all concentrated into the process, the moment of opening and offering and consumption, she was bold and absolute and all of herself.

With Blodeuwedd I skipped through life. I thought of petals, tight in a bud and then opening, I thought of sap pushing its way up the stems of things, pushing into leaves, pale green, unfurling, darkening. I could almost taste them. I thought of pollen at the center of the flowers, beckoning and sending its scent out on the wind; I thought of its individual grains and the sex of the brush of the legs of bees. I thought of spilling scent and richness and plenty onto the ground, into the air, of spreading myself, the desire of it. I felt the wind, the moist ground as lovers; I turned to the sun, I blushed under it. All of life was dancing through me, I had no need for human lovers or attention, they could not compete. I was all brightness. After that would be the fecund fullness of fruit and the rotting into earth; rich and strong, demanding all my senses and consuming my attention.

I didn't think about the story, I wasn't interested in it. Fascinating, instead, were the tides, the pulse of green life, the dance between sunlight and shade and the immediacy of growth. After a month of this we met and began to work with the story. I tried to explain what I had felt and seen to the others but I don't think it could be explained, not in human language. She was not human. She stayed an older strand of the goddess, so intrinsic to her story of nature she never really left it, never took on for more than a moment those human roles she was so unsuccessfully assigned, she stayed part of the unreachable, longed-for raw enchanted feminine that can't be owned but only worshipped.

They called in Blodeuwedd and in the center I looked back at them, then past them, these people who were so concerned with finding her. I felt huge indifference to this story. I stood with her and had information beating at the inside of my brain, but not information about the story, its characters or actions. Who cared what magicians did, or about the complex relationships between mothers and sons? Who cared if men needed lovers, desired women or wished for brides to hold and love in the mortal realm? Who cared for these particular humans, or humans in general? She did not. The flowers did not. Yet when Blodeuwedd was called she was forced into that story and I shared my imagining with her.

It was not my inclination, not my nature, but I was turned from my own inclinations, shaped into a nature not my own. When they called and caught and bound me I was all confusion and longing. I was flowers, yes; but in their own shapes, not this shape wished on me. The longing was to be free, to be myself again, mindless petals, not to be human-shaped, claimed or married or held to faithfulness. Flowers are not faithful. Flowers are the lovers of the world. In my confusion I was lesser, I could feel that. I still longed for the wind, the sap, the bees and sun; but they had to be translated into human forms and I was clumsy in it, lost and disconnected.

I felt the coldness settle inside; a chill, icy and serene. I was not a part of their story and whoever they named me, whatever they thought I was, I was not that. I had no interest in their questions, which did not translate into anything I understood or cared for. I sought only the wild, to be released back into it. Finally they spoke of owls, then I felt a resonance and would accept, perhaps, that they knew me a little. But not enough to hold me, not enough to fix me into the shape I had been in the story, the shape of a wife for a boy with no mother. I would wear my flowers in summer and owl wings in winter and I felt ages old, portrayed as young but in truth holding a great and ancient power, nearly untranslatable but back to the oldest goddesses.

There's a waterfall, spinning over the rocks and down through air; delicate, this one and fine, like a woman's long braid as she bends over the pool and it brushes the surface, disrupts and sends ripples through and down. This braid is spun atoms, molecules of air, really; hydrogen bonded with oxygen but become water now, this other substance, or why don't we say molecules of star, of stardust, of starheart back from the beginning, the hydrogen the beginning of it all, the simplicity from which all these complexities are born. There's a waterfall. It has a woman's name. It's a women's place, from back before the beginning of written history; maybe its names were always sacred and female, maybe rituals were born here, maybe laughter and ceremony, maybe bleeding and birthing, we don't know but we know enough to come here when there's a spell to be made, when we seek to bring something into existence, to birth it; a child or a love or a woman.

There are white flowers here, in spring, late spring, Beltaine; millions of them, tea-tree flowers, a delicate tinged-with-pink white, five petaled perfect, branch after branch of them. On the way down you pass through an avenue of them, a ceremony in itself and if you were wishing, at that time, for a union of love, well it might come true. Tea-tree is woody, brushy, these delicate flowers spring from toughness, the green of their tiny speared leaves is an Australian dark green-grey, spiky so that the rest of the year, when it's not flowering, it is completely unremarkable to the eye. It reminds me of hawthorn in that, fierce and difficult, deeply magical, ancient in its associations with spring, fertility, desire. With the essence of the goddess herself, one could say. Hawthorn is associated with May, with May Day and Beltaine; it blossoms then, in my birth month of May and so, regardless of the fact that I was born on the other side of the globe as we spun towards darkness and into death and the depths of the mysteries, hawthorn has always been a flower I felt bound to. Don't those themes of flowers, love and death go together anyway? They certainly do for Blodeuwedd.

Sometimes great spells arise of themselves. All the ingredients are there, laid out and all one has to do is notice, step sideways and give a blessing. I have a son, as Arianrhod did, born out of wedlock as it happens; one who loves Welsh mountains and mythology, one who as a child loved the name Llew so much I thought if I were to have a second child, and it were a boy, I would name him that. I have a son, raised in the ways of magic and ritual, the worship of the old gods and I don't mean the named ones, though those too; I mean the gods and goddesses of mountain and stream, of summer and winter, moon and leaf and wind, of tree and stag and bird and fish. I have a son who understands the turn of the Wheel in a way I am always envious of, not learning it as an adult and needing to constantly relearn it but from the inside, born and growing up within it, as natural as breath, close as heartbeat. I have a son who believes in magic, just enough.

The first time he came to visit me in the Blue Mountains, where white cockatoos parade through the sky as if they own it, I took him to the waterfall. It was spring. White tea-tree flowers lined the path, like a wedding. This place is not really mountains, though that's how it's named; it's a plateau pushed up from the sea a kilometer into air millions of years ago. Enough millions for the rain, the streams and rivers to eat great gorges and valleys out of the shale and sandstone, enough millions for huge vertical cliff faces to stand above the valleys, sheering off every so often to show fresh shades of soft pink and yellow that weather through to deeper earthen colors before slicing off, again. Walking, the path twists or turns and suddenly, below one almost, the landscape opens up, revealed into plunging depths and lush secrets of fern, waterfall, tumbled rock.

There were the mountains, the stream, the flowers. It was spring.

We walk down one of these fissures, there are ladders at the steeper parts and we are talking, on and off, about his life and how well so many parts of it are going and how he still doesn't have a girlfriend. He never has, really. Perhaps he's the kind of boy who girls see as a friend instead of a lover; he's genuinely kind and thoughtful, honest rather than flirtatious, humble rather than daring. He wouldn't push his luck, might not risk rejection, wouldn't ask where his heart wasn't in it. The girls he's chosen until now; really I've been grateful they haven't returned his affections. Maybe growing up with a single mother predisposes you to this, he's a bit of a rescuer; he's chosen beautiful girls with a peculiar mix of neediness and arms-length chill, there's something hard and calculating about them as they keep him dangling, hopeful, feed him enough to be their support person but never their boyfriend; they choose bold and dangerous types for that, the ones who bring passion and pain, so they'll need a good friend, to see them through.

There was the need, the yearning. We believed in magic.

I've moved out of the home we've shared together, he's on his own in the world, more than he's ever been and perhaps he's grown past that model of girl. We speak of the sacred nature of this place we're approaching, we stop on the path and I ask to bring him, as my son, if it is or was a sacred women's place and not just what it appears today, a somewhat off- the-track part of the National Park, small but with a regular stream of visitors, locals mainly. I ask the land to let me take him in, as I once carried him in my body, to let me carry him within my energy again and seek its blessing. Perhaps a door opens up, a veil where we walk between one world and the next, where our eyes open to the sacred and we breathe the air of a slightly different world, the true one. Perhaps all that explains what happens next.

When we get to the pool with the waterfall it's freezing and pristine and there's no-one else there. We take off our clothes and go in. It's not a big pool, rounded and deep in the middle, but as soon as I put my feet in I lose all sensation from the numbing cold and I only get in up to my waist. But Damon plunges in, shouting, swims over to the waterfall and lets it fall on him, climbs the rocks beside it and stands within its light spray and at this moment, from where I've retreated to the rocks I see something, an alternate scene. It slides across my eyes like a frame changing, or focusing and is gone again. But I saw it. I saw how that scene was perfect and all that had to happen, one twist of fate, one moment, one tiny change to bring his wishes was that instead of me who stood there on the bank, it was her. Beltaine, flowers, the waterfall, two naked bodies, female and male. If it were her, instead of me, if I took myself out of this scene and let my place be taken by her – then he would have what he wished.

So I did it. It was the simplest spell, a breath, an acknowledgement, a soft, willed blink of eyelashes to allow the alteration, one small ingredient that my will, my price could pay. I chose it in a breath, a stilled moment that slowed time like the shutter of a camera, *yes* and I pressed forward into that future, the way the world works anyway, the direction the water takes, past waterfall and pool into the stream that heads always in one direction, the spring that turns to summer and the flower to seedpod and the sun to night. A boy from his mother towards his lover. There are no tea-trees on the path down the cliffs, only up above and then two more, at the entrance to the pool. We stopped at them, on the way out and I told him the spell and I picked a twig of flowering tea-tree, white and pink and I put the spell into it and told him to keep it in his wallet, until he met her, so that when he did meet her that spell would be there, in his pocket, on his body.

Walking up the path I said we should define her, at least a

little, that we should name some qualities for her, so he chose three and because I was still part of the spell I chose three also. He said *intelligent, beautiful* and *affectionate* and I said *quirky* and *self-aware* and *independent*; he argued somewhat with independent. So be it; we set the spell. It was not long, just a month later as summer came that he met a girl, different from the others. One named for a flower and she didn't have that coldness, that hard edge of prettiness the others had. It took him by surprise, perhaps we are never ready for it, for magic to unfurl in the real world, for flowers and spells to step into human shape. But they met and she asked him out and she made it happen, or the spell made it happen and when they came to visit me, the first time, he took her down to the waterfall and gave her the flowers, the spell that he had carried so she, the girl with the flower name, the woman of flowers, could choose her own fate.

He gave her back the flowers and maybe that's enough to change the ending of the story. Perhaps women made of flowers are emerging out of the layers of the mythos to be our sisters, friends and lovers. Maybe the goddess is gentler when she's dealt with more gently, maybe Blodeuwedd's longings can match our human longings; so when we celebrate her rather than controlling her we can find the love we seek. After all we are part of nature, not separate from it and just possibly when we give her back her flowers, when we see her in her sacred places, when magic is conjured but does not seek to bind a will, maybe then she has a way to be with us. Flowers and women, love and magic. Blodeuwedd as the love we yearn for coming to life again and again, in every spring, every flower, every lifetime.

Ritual – Walking with the Goddess

Becoming familiar with a deity does not occur all at once. Just as when we get to know a new person, we build up cumulative layers of knowledge and familiarity over time. After the first few conversations the rapport between us can flow more easily, we begin to have an idea of how to talk to, or be with, this other being and become increasingly comfortable as we meet them again each time. This ritual is one you might want to repeat, even several times.

Choose somewhere in nature to walk: the bush, a park, the slopes of a mountain, a beach. You can suit the terrain towards the deity you are planning to walk with. If it is Aphrodite, the beach would be perfect, or anywhere near water; for Demeter you might choose fields, meadows or gardens. That is ideal, but anywhere outdoors and away from a lot of buildings and other humans will be fine. Remember to wear appropriate clothing for wherever you are walking. You might want to take your journal and pen, as well as colored pens or pencils.

Your walk with the goddess might unfold like this:

- When you arrive at the place you wish to begin the walk take some time to ground and center yourself. If you are not sure how to do this there are notes on grounding and centering at the back of this book.
- Take a few minutes to look around you, observing where you are, the terrain, season and weather. Choose which direction you will take your walk and focus your gaze in that direction. Pick out a place ahead of you, which you can clearly see but is still at least a short walk away from where you are now. Tell yourself that is the gateway where you will meet the goddess, to begin your walk together.

You might already sense the presence of the deity you are planning to walk with, internally or externally, or you might not. You might visualize a gate or doorway of some kind, or not. Send out a thought, speak aloud if that feels right, asking the goddess to join you at that place you have selected.

- This is the ideal moment to set your intention, both to yourself and the goddess. Your intention might be as simple as to take a walk together, or you may wish to know more about the connection between yourself and her, or you might be seeking answers to particular questions. As part of the intention set the parameters for your interaction, including the length of time you wish to spend together. For example: *Calliach, please join me for a walk across the moors this morning and I'd like to stay in touch with you over the coming month,* or *Tiamat, I'm asking you to spend an hour with me this evening as I walk along the beach and then I will say goodbye gratefully,* or *Artemis, I ask that you walk with me in this forest and I hope we will become close friends and allies.*

- When the grounding, centering and intention feel clear and strong within you, take a few more breaths and observe the distance between yourself and the gateway. I have run towards these gates, or walked very slowly, stopping several times, or walked steadily as the world seemed to blur around me. As you move towards the gate there is an opportunity to put yourself in a light trance, a slightly altered way of perceiving the world. If you are not sure how to do this, there are notes on entering and leaving trance states at the end of this book.

- When you arrive at the gate you have set up, acknowledge or greet the goddess you have asked to meet. You may feel a very strong sensation of her presence, or not. Either way, it is polite to acknowledge who you have called in, either internally or aloud. You may wish to pause at this gate or just continue on. Take a moment also to assess what level of trance you are in. Make sure you stay alert enough to be aware of your surrounds, where you are going, landmarks and the way to return, the ground under your feet, the time and any other people who are around. A trance state of about ten to twenty percent is ideal; that is, mostly present in the outer world, but able to receive impressions, thoughts and feelings that otherwise might be under the surface of your awareness.

- As you continue on your walk let yourself attune to the goddess you have invited to walk with you. You might ask yourself *how would this landscape seem to her? What would she notice?* Or you might pay close attention to sensations in your own body, thoughts and feelings as a way of tuning in to the environment, trusting that your impressions are being informed by your association with the deity. You may see visions, hear voices, or receive sensations that are not from your direct physical surroundings. This is not unusual but if they become particularly strong or absorbing take a moment to reorient yourself to where you are and what is happening in the outside world; moving about in the wilderness is not a time to lose yourself in trance or the other worlds.

- You may find a place where you wish to sit, stand or lie down for a while, to let yourself be more absorbed in this other world, the one you may be receiving glimpses of, information about or strong sensations from. If you choose to do this I recommend setting yourself a time limit and sticking to it, remembering you can walk with this deity again, another day. Because this process is really about moving through the physical world and letting our perceptions widen to include those related to the deity we are working with, deep inner meditations are best left to another time and a ritual specifically tailored for that.

- As you continue your walk you can ask, if you feel this is not already happening, to be able to notice what she might notice, to feel sensations she might feel or to hear the things she might hear. This will always be filtered through your own experience, even more so since you are only lightly in trance. But even these light overlays of the goddess with our own experience can be profound, deeply illuminating and quite strange to us. They can seem magical, entrancing and joyous as well as at times disturbing or challenging. For this ritual do not let these visions or sensations overwhelm you. Remain at the level you would if a friend you were walking with was describing their sensations and ways of experiencing the world around you, empathic but not allowing it to override your own reality.

- Perhaps you will choose to journal, draw or sketch while you are still on your walk, or perhaps you will save that for when you return. It is worth recording this exercise, even if you felt very little or did not have obvious impressions of the goddess. You may find, coming back to what you've written or drawn days or weeks later, that you now see or understand what you saw or felt in a different way. Some goddesses, like some people, are easier to get to know than others. It may be that our first few encounters with them are not remarkable but looking back we can see their presence or influence was there. This is, in any case, a subtle exercise and designed to spark ideas, curiosity and a sense of the goddess rather than immersive visions or experiences.

- When you return from your walk make sure to stop at your gate, thank the goddess for her presence – whatever you have felt or experienced, even if that seems to be nothing – and say goodbye to her as you would to a friend who was leaving after an activity together, unless you have clearly invited that presence to remain with you. Even if that is the case, take the remaining steps back to your beginning point as a lead-out of whatever trance state you have been in, deliberately walking yourself back fully into the outer world. If you are driving take extra time to reground and reorient yourself before getting into the car.

Exercise – Creative Expression

We may have read the story of a goddess, invoked her in rituals, talked about her with others and yet still not feel that we have an understanding of who she really is or what our connection is. Creativity opens up different ways of perceiving and can access emotions. For some of us it is the first tool we turn to, for others it comes less easily and may provoke some measure of resistance. A common guideline, in pursuing emotional and spiritual growth, is the greater the charge or resistance we have around something, the more useful or powerful the experience is likely to be.

Perhaps in undertaking this exercise we are challenging many years or decades of belief that we are not a creative person, that we're no good at writing, drawing or making things. Perhaps we see no links between those pursuits and spirituality. Perhaps we doubt the validity of our own impressions or intuition and trust only books and sources external to ourselves. But if we are treading a path of personal relationship with a goddess we must, at some point, begin to trust and learn from our own responses to that goddess; our reactions to her story, where it parallels with or questions our own story, the feeling state we enter when thinking about her or relating to her, whether in dream, ritual, trance or waking life. Working creatively is part of that. What we write, draw or make is filtered through us but because to some extent it has bypassed the intellectual and analytical parts of our brain it may feel more immediate, as if we are jointly creating with the goddess herself.

Decide how and where you will approach this exercise. Choose which medium to work with. You may have an absolute longing to work in clay, even if that is something you have never done before. Perhaps you are a mosaicist and glass mosaics seems the perfect way for you to work. Perhaps you haven't picked up colored pencils or pastels since you were a child but you keep imagining that. Perhaps you'd like to try writing and have an untouched notebook, waiting for your words. Perhaps you paint, or would like to try, or you want to sketch with charcoal. In the flow of creativity things that are not working perfectly are as valuable as the final result so allow yourself to experiment, to try the unfamiliar and to risk.

If you are painting, or creating something with craft materials, it may be most practical to be indoors. If you are writing or drawing you may choose to take yourself to an outside location that you identify with the goddess you are working with.

Steps to take in developing your creative expression:

- You may feel most comfortable undertaking this project in sacred space. In that case you may choose to cast a circle, acknowledge sacred space, the land and the elements or whatever you usually do before beginning a ritual. You may choose simply to sit in front of your altar, or to begin some other way, for example with chanting, meditation or dancing. Feel your way into it – if you usually have a very disciplined yoga and meditation practice but in relation to this project you feel more like dancing or walking in nature, try it.
- Once you are ready, take a few moments to ground and center yourself. Become aware of your breath and allow it to lead you inwards, to the place where your awareness of the divine always exists. Perhaps you can locate a specific

awareness of this particular goddess within yourself or perhaps it is more general for you. Say the name of the goddess to yourself, silently or aloud. Repeat her name a number of times, maybe in different ways, whispering it, chanting or singing, speaking it very slowly or in separate syllables. You may have your eyes closed. If they are open allow your vision to blur slightly or become unfocused. Reach within for the feelings, the thought-forms or the ideas that you associate with this goddess. You can ask the goddess to assist you as you work.

- When you connect with an image, feeling or sensation, let yourself begin to work with that. Describe it on the page if you are writing, or begin to place lines, colors or images on the paper if you are drawing or let your hands start to shape the clay if you are working with clay. Perhaps you will be starting with what you already knew, that Inanna's symbol is an eight-petaled flower, for instance. You might begin by drawing that. But let your pen, pencil, hands continue past that point and perhaps other shapes, colors and forms will emerge. Allow your writing, drawing or crafting to become an expression of feeling your way. Let your hands keep moving, continuing coloring or putting words on the page even if you are not sure entirely what you are doing.

- When you are finished you can place your work on or by your altar, in the pages of your journal or in some other way respect your creative expression. You might come back to it in a few days or weeks, to contemplate what you've learnt and maybe continue your creative expression.

Researching the Goddess

Researching a goddess through her stories, the culture she arises from and others' experiences with her can be a purpose in itself, an introduction to a deity we don't know or a search for specific information. *Researching* a goddess may be a project we undertake over a set period of time or it may be an unfolding venture, with phases over many years as our interest and knowledge develop. We may be researching a goddess because we wish to include her in a ritual, artwork or other creative project. She might be part of a pantheon we are working with, or belong to a tradition we have not much experience with or be the chosen deity of a group, event or magical working we are coming into. If we wish to get in touch with our sexuality or sovereignty or healing powers we may choose to research a goddess famous for those attributes.

Research often involves reading books and articles. There may be creative expressions – novels and plays, poetry – as well as primary or secondary sources, with material specific to that goddess or the culture she comes from in its original, often translated, form as well as commentaries on that original material. We can visit museums and art galleries that house icons, statues and other pieces from the period and culture our goddess comes from or that are related to her as well as seeking out talks, lectures and presentations live, recorded or online. We might talk with people who know more than we do; those who have already undertaken research as well as people who actively relate to that particular goddess. We may be able to visit places where that goddess was worshipped, where temples were built in her name or the locations and landscapes her mythology arises from. Research may also take us into ceremonies or rituals held for her or with her, perhaps quite different from our own rituals or worship.

Once I researched Tiamat, the great and ancient Sumerian

goddess whose body became the sky and earth. I had been assigned Tiamat for a group working and came to this research feeling only the tragedy of her; famously murdered by her own children, her story had previously seemed too sad and awful for me to examine or identify with, despite my love of other myths and goddesses from that culture. I had only a month with Tiamat so my research was limited to reading and discussing her story with others, but even this reminded me of how powerful a tool research is. Had I visited her story from a more emotional basis I might not have explored the theme of her murder by her own children and grand-children in bloody, losing battle to the new order.

Talking with people, especially mothers, offered a completely different perspective on the myth. Re-reading her story, more carefully, brought me to a new understanding of Tiamat. When trying to understand a myth, which may be a late re-telling and have been subject to all sorts of revisions, omissions and cultural overlays, I find it useful to look purely at the actions, the events in the story, taking off any prescribed motivations, emotions or conclusions.

Tiamat's dead body becomes the earth, the seas and sky. In other words, she is everything. Her body is laid down for her children. Which of us mothers does not do this, through birth and nurture and then, even more simply, by belonging to the generation before our children's, so that in the recognized order of things we are bound to age and die before them? We offer them, while living, every single thing we can, often the depth of our beings, all we know and everything we have. Even if it were to cost us our lives we would do this and mothers throughout time have done and still do this; sending a beloved child out of a warzone when they cannot make that trip themselves, educating their children although they had to leave school at a young age, wishing and striving to provide the best for their children.

Tiamat offers everything, her very life and body as the

nurturance for the next generations. Because she is a goddess – a mammoth goddess, from the times when the goddess was all – still we are receiving her bounty. Her body is the food we eat, the waters we drink, the soil we place our beloved dead into and the stars we gaze at, seeking the mysteries.

Researching a goddess can take you to obscure corners of the library and of the world. It can create a path into rituals, books and a pantheon or culture you never would have discovered otherwise. Researching is substantially different from the other activities in this book, in that it does not involve asking a deity to take an active part in relationship with us, although it may lead towards that or have evolved from that. Researching a goddess is a way to appreciate her through the work of others, who may include artisans, scholars and devotees, both ancient and contemporary. At the end of this section two approaches to research are discussed in more detail.

Isis

Isis called to me. The majesty of her cool gaze reached out of the Princess of Swords card of my Haindl Tarot deck, gazing off to the right and I wanted to know more about her. She seemed untouchable, calm about the past and negligent of the present, searching out future paths. Isis with her story of the glory of civilization, the very throne of Egypt; the kings who sat in that throne marrying the land through her, or that's how I read it. That grand passion Isis has for her twin-soul brother, beloved Osiris, her magic bringing him back to life and through that magic – sex, death, land – conceiving and bringing forth a savior, Horus. Isis who was sister and lover, mother and teacher yet remains remote, queen and high priestess, she intrigued me and I followed her story. It led me to Egypt.

The myth of Isis is woven with those of her sister and two brothers. The four of them lay together in their mother's womb, the goddess of the milky way, she who is the stars overhead, Nut. They were born on special days – days that had not existed until their births – one after the other, four in a row. Osiris and Isis marry, as was the tradition in royal Egyptian families, sisters marrying brothers, they become Queen and King of Egypt. Nephthys and Set also marry. Set, not content with his role off in the margins of things, murders Osiris. When Isis recovers the body, Set cuts it into pieces. Through her magics Isis is able to find the pieces and bring Osiris back to life long enough for her to conceive Horus. Osiris, now dead, becomes Lord of the Underworld and a guide to dead souls while Isis remains alone to rule Egypt.

As I read more about her I saw how Isis is so clearly the queen. When Osiris dies there's no question that she can't hold the throne, or she's not enough on her own. More, there is the feeling that the throne is duplicated now in the Underworld, with Osiris holding that realm and her the upper world. She is a creature of pairs, Isis, while always seeming whole unto herself. She pairs with Osiris in marriage and to rule Egypt. As combatants she pairs with their brother, Set. She pairs with her sister, Nephthys who holds the west and the setting sun, while Isis is in the east with the sun's rise. She pairs with her son to be one of the earliest mother-son couples of divinity; pictures and statues of the two of them are essentially indistinguishable from those of Mary and Jesus.

In a casual conversation with someone I barely knew I heard the words *the Temple of Isis, in Egypt* and though the conversation swirls onwards some part of my brain stopped at those words and just repeated them, echoing like bells. *The Temple of Isis, in Egypt; the Temple of Isis, in Egypt.* I want to go there. I have no idea how to get there but I want to go and I think I should go. *The Temple of Isis, in Egypt.* Some part of my internal antennae starts orienting itself.

Egypt was hard to get to, I had to insist on it and even then I'm not sure why my partner agreed; it was vastly inconvenient, at a bad time, couldn't I go by myself? But I didn't want to, Greece or France by myself was one thing but Egypt was something else altogether. Egypt was strangely frightening. Not just disorienting, with that tremendous heat and the fierce narrowness of the land; the concentrated spine of the river, road and railway track that join the country together all running parallel within a few hundred meters of each other, the language, the absent women and the insistent men wanting to practice their English in order to sell you something, never something simple like a watch but something obscure and complex provided by a relative somewhere else altogether. Possibly shares in a business deal or a three-day trip on the river in a cousin's boat. None of that mattered to me much, although it did seem sad that we never even spoke with an Egyptian woman until our final few days in Cairo, and then only an unusual Egyptian woman would talk to us, two foreigners. It's a long way for the Queen of Heaven to descend, to a place where women can't talk to strangers, or be in the street unveiled.

My trip to find Isis began on my birthday, late at night in Cairo airport. Perhaps it's different now but I remember the casualness, the ease and disarray of that airport and how I was nearly out of it before I quite realized I was in the country. I had to wait an hour or so in the open arrivals hall; I had come from Australia via Frankfurt, spending hours lying across a bank of hard chairs in a bright corridor in transit in Frankfurt airport but my partner was on a different plane, coming from England. The plane was late. At first it was late by an hour, then two and finally by four hours and I knew I could get a taxi and travel to the booked hotel room, go to bed by myself and go to sleep and I didn't want to spend the remaining hours of my birthday that way. It seemed better to wait in the hot, bustling airport, which was commercial in an off-putting, doing-a-deal kind of way, ignoring all offers of taxis, assistance, conversation.

He finally arrived and then we were in Egypt, together. The dark rush of a taxi through a foreign city at night, the utter darkness of a hotel room, cooled by air conditioning and holding him; I could have thought of how loved Osiris was by Isis, but I didn't, then. I am now. Because, of course, she lost him. The gods are only so strong. When one of them turns against another jagged rifts tear open and even divine beings fall into them. I went to Egypt seeking the mystery of Isis and she remained a mystery but everywhere I found Osiris, as if I were collecting pieces of his dismembered body. Osiris in tombs with the rites of death, Osiris painted in his green form, Osiris as we travelled through vast temples, between pillars representing reeds in the river down which souls travel in the mysteries of Osiris, Lord of the Underworld.

Nut and Hathor, Isis and Nephthys; the goddesses in Egypt are huge and larger than life, imperial, commanding palaces and temples and vast courtyards. They are as big as the sky, as bright as stars, as stark as life and death in this desert land and as fertile as the river deltas. I am following the thread of Isis into Upper Egypt, to her temple. It was moved, stone by stone in the 1970s by Unesco from the island of Philae to a nearby, higher island, when the Aswan High Dam was built. This temple is why I have come to Egypt.

We decide to go all the way to Aswan in one trip, then stop on the way back at Luxor and other, more obscure places before returning to Cairo for the final few days. We book ourselves onto a night train and we visit the Sphinx and the pyramids during the day. There's a lot of sand, heat and some wind; I already don't quite like Egypt. I am wearing long pants and a shirt with sleeves to my wrists, in order not to offend anyone. We pay to go inside one of the pyramids and are herded inside, up a corridor of sloping wood, a ramp with rungs nailed in, so you can't slip back. There are dull lights and a sense of close air, stone slabs suspended above, below and to either side of us. We are maybe fifty meters in when the lights go out. Everyone stops still and after half a minute the guide's torch turns around and something to the effect of *everyone out!* is shouted, by him and from outside.

My lover and I stand to one side, out of the way, against the wall and allow everyone else to get past, to get outside. We just wait, in darkness, holding hands. Then the pyramid is empty except for the still, cloyed black air and us, balanced on a slope not able to see a thing, even with our eyes wide open. We whisper a few words but mainly stand there in silence waiting, listening, feeling. Osiris was buried. Is dead but still alive, in some mysterious way. I feel we are within his territory. We walk cautiously a little further up the slope but don't arrive anywhere. After ten minutes or so, when the lights still don't come on we make our way slowly down to the outside world where the guards at the door semi-shout at us in surprise; they thought everyone had already left and have probably been negligent in overlooking us.

We spend the night on the train, heading north to the temple. The whole of Egypt runs up this line, river, road and railway track running north-south, three parallel lines of transport so close to each other one can easily imagine cutting Egypt in half in one stroke. This line, originally the river's, has a daily commentary by the sun and its east-west trajectory. Four directions, four corners to a pyramid. Four gods and the world divided between them. To Isis the cultivated lands, to Osiris the river and the Underworld. Nephthys holds all the in-between lands and the desert belongs to Set. We are in the safe zone, the farms-and-roads-and-water zone but out there, pressing all around, is the otherness; blasting sun and sand. Places that can bring their dangers and their gods right into the midst of civilization; into a palace, a temple, a relationship.

When we get out of the train at Aswan the heat is such that when we open our mouths they dry out, instantly. It is blasting and insistent, like standing in the mouth of a furnace. We keep our mouths closed. In the taxi there are curtains drawn across every window except the front windscreen, perhaps it alleviates the sun's striking heat, a little. We visit a street market, entranced by the colors, the bowls piled with spices, vivid yellow and deep red, bright orange and rich brown. In our hotel room we turn the ancient air conditioner to its highest setting, three snowflakes and try to sleep; we wake sweating in the sweltering room.

Towards evening we head out, onto the Nile, towards the Temple of Isis. I lean over the side of the boat and put my hand in the water – the magical Nile. I did this before anyone said not to, later I was told horrible flesh-infesting things live there and you shouldn't touch it, ever. But I did and it was cold. Not just cool, which maybe any water would have been in that context, or pleasant, but a shock of cold against my skin – cold. Impossible, how could it be? Immediately vast depths, magical powers, a completely other realm are conjured up. Cold. Of all the sensations I might have imagined it would never have been that.

We arrive at the temple. When they say that they had to move it I have always visualized temples in English garden fashion, a small structure of blue or grey stone, crumbly and weathered, carefully reconstructed to look like an ancient ruin. I don't know why; this is Egypt. The forecourt of the Temple of Isis seems about the length of a football field. It is paved in massive glaring white stone slabs. There are pillars along each side, which we cower in the shade of, the sun is still high in the sky and it's hard to look anywhere, it's so bright and enormous, completely exposed and really an assault on the eyes. Up the end – we trek there, pillar by pillar walking through narrow bands of deep shade alternating with something brighter than the brightest beach I've ever been on – there's a massively high wall, with images of gods and goddesses striding across it. There's no explanation, no commentary and I feel utterly foreign.

Where is Isis? I had imagined grottos, altars, rooms or at least, a room. Is she all this whiteness and brightness and vastness? Is she these eye-straining glittering distances, this obscurity and immensity? Certainly in severity of form there is majesty, awe and power. She is the throne of Egypt but somehow I had imagined the throne was at least – visible. Conceivable. Not that we would be beetles on the floor, not even able to tell a throne if we saw one and with no more chance of attracting the attention of the goddess than a bee flying through this vast space.

And they moved it. They picked this up from one place; piece by piece and moved it. It is all enormous and incomprehensible and really I have no idea of Isis at all, or – whatever she is, is something I have never had a sense of, before. It is stunning and I am stunned. Perhaps that is the way to approach the goddess but I feel disoriented, unsettled to a depth that even the heat, the distances, the general difficulty of Egypt have not succeeded in disturbing. Who am I, exactly, and what am I doing here, in this glare?

Shocked by Egypt we move south, in stages. The temple at Luxor is both gentler and more rich, the columns opulent with carved language, the courtyards languidly channeling one to another. It represents the reed beds that Osiris' corpse sails through on its journey to the Underworld and I can imagine that. There is a sense of him here, lurking, immanent. If the reeds are these immense columns we are reduced, again, to the size of insects, to beetles and flies, but here it is not so much an assault on the senses as a quiet reminder of our place, humans, in the scheme of things. Of course the gods are immeasurably vaster than us, but where Isis smote us with that, Osiris takes us gently in hand, like a lullaby. Ah yes, you are tiny and yet within my halls all is one; you, too, are a part of this oneness... We shelter in the reeds.

Still in Luxor we visit the Valley of the Kings and the Valley of the Queens at dawn, the agreed time for such excursions and are blasted again with sand, distance, grandeur, incomprehension and the dizzying repetition of tombs and tunnels and rocks and paintings. Though I do notice, uncomfortably, that one god shows up again and again. Painted wrapped in white as the original mummy, Osiris' death created the mysteries of embalming and that process belongs to his realm. I see him painted green, arisen in a corner with the new grain after each Nile flood. He is here again, with crook and flail, a shepherd and perhaps the original shepherd of souls, guiding the ways through death and the Underworld, into spring and rebirth.

Only one place holds us, truly holds us; our attention and compassion and engagement.

It is the tomb of Nefertari in the Valley of the Queens, delicate and nearly entire, not pillaged and blasted like many of the others. It reflects perhaps the love she was surrounded with, love that has lasted in the paintings on the walls, depicting her journey through the afterlife. The tickets are timed as well as limited in number, we have fifteen minutes to be in this place of the sacred. It is not enough. I am in love with the rich stories painted densely on the walls and the sense of Nefertari as a living woman, her life and her passions as soon as I enter, anyone would be and my partner bribes the guard for an extra fifteen minutes. Part of me is horrified, this is Egypt, these are her sacred treasures and what are we doing over-riding their rules for our own pleasure? and part of me is just in awe. The pictures. The serpents. The animals. The gods. The words that are images of the Book of the Dead crawling and parading across the walls.

But this does not feel like a place of Isis, even though she is depicted here, holding hands with Nefertari. Isis rules the lands above; the living, not the dead. This is his domain, Osiris. What an intricate dance they weave between them, life and death. Isis reaching out endlessly, for him who has been forever removed from her, so her tale becomes one of loss. She shelters in the reed beds to give birth, her sister her only companion. She holds the sovereignty of Egypt in her lap, she is the throne that kings are seated upon and she nurses Horus, the god of the next generation, hawk-eye and revenge seeker, the one who takes on the attributes of his father and surpasses him. Nefertari might have been a queen while she lived and so reflected Isis for that time but for the three thousand or so years she has been dead, she's belonged to Osiris.

We stop at a few other places on the way back to Cairo, not standard tourist places. We are discouraged by the railway staff, by police on the stations but not by the general difficulty, which certainly is high. At one place we are searching for a Temple of Hathor and we do find someone who agrees to drive us there, and to wait, which is good because otherwise we would have no way of getting back. We pay the single guard at the entrance, he wanders through ruined halls ahead of us, alternately dark and light, depending on how intact the ceiling is of that particular piece. There are piles of sand in the corners and the floor is gritty with it. I break away several times, once to stand in pitch black in a room I cannot tell the size of, surrounded by walls with the mysteries of death written on them. How obscure Egypt is – exactly like this. All you might want to know is here and it is not to be read.

I find a very small, square room with a low ceiling. Half a wall and part of the roof is missing, so I can see perfectly. There is a goddess containing the room, her fingertips touching the floor on one side and then her whole body arching up that wall, across the ceiling and her legs stretching down to the floor on the other side of the room. Nut, the night sky. The floor has sand and also small piles of building rubble, but I lie down in it and try to photograph the whole sky, to fit it into my lens. These goddesses – Nut, Hathor, Isis – they pass their attributes and their temples and concerns back and forth between each other, the full moon, the crescent, the horns of the cow. Isis blends and appears and disappears grandly, she does not seem interested enough to have me find her. Whereas Nut, in this room, has handed her mysteries to me; here I am, this is how I am. Revealed.

I went to Egypt looking for Isis and I always thought I didn't find her. I found something, the mysteries of sand and death and distance, I met Osiris inarguably, white and hovering, green and unsettling and I noticed how he seemed just for my eyes, everywhere I looked and then, when I wanted him in postcards or paintings he never showed up. They'd taken a photo of that wall, where he was and the photo stopped just short of him; they listed gods in paintings and he would be mysteriously missing, the papyrus scrolls held beauty and delicacy or power and darkness but his odd profile, the original mummy doesn't duplicate well and though the other characters of his story are here, he eludes the image makers. I found Nut in that small room that was also as big as the sky, I found the codes of Egypt engraved and painted everywhere in hieroglyphs so gorgeous I wanted to eat them. But I lost my partner, the other half of myself.

Maybe I carried Isis the whole time, travelled to Egypt with her story, for almost unbelievably my relationship begins to deteriorate and break apart in the months following this trip. Even though we were so in love, so strong and I would have said perfect together, odd combinations of fate and choice step in and tear us apart and we are never able to put our relationship back together. It's a kind of backwards research and from that trip I have a new regard for Isis, her implacable vastness and distance. I know how it feels to have your lover ripped away and what it means to go on, after that. Grief and power and the distances they impose impregnate themselves into my memories of Egypt. They are not things I could have learnt, reading, or looking at maps or pictures in a book and I am not exactly grateful but I am awed.

Mary

We say there are no goddesses left in Western theology but of course that's not true. She has churches across the Christian world. Mary has candles lit before her daily on a thousand, thousand altars in chapels dedicated in her name, old women praying and girls waiting in wonder before her, men weeping gazing at her image as they summon the mother of Christ who by default is the mother of us all, the Great Mother. Mary's crypts retain the mysteries. Her blue sky cloak symbolizes at a hundred paces her compassion, love and shelter for any who are lost. Mary is the most ordinary, the most human of goddesses; she gives birth, she nurtures a child, she loves a man, she watches her beloved die. Mary is the most exalted of women; she gives birth to a god, falls in love with a god, watches a god die, receives the god when he rises from the dead. Her stories weave the tales of the goddess – the one who changes with the seasons but never dies. Mary hovers in the sacred realms, the overlap between human and divine, as Christ did. As we all do.

There are secrets folded into this mythology. They are so much a part of our culture, we are raised so close to them we do not necessarily see what is right in front of us. But a little reading, a little research takes us through the layers. They tried to change the old story; no longer would it be a goddess, giving birth to a god, but a human woman giving birth to god. She had to be a virgin, this new-born god could not trace his lineage through human lines but must go straight to god-in-heaven. Read it a slightly different way and Mary, by giving birth to a god, is necessarily the goddess. There are records of those who take on the mantle of the god relinquishing their human origins; their names, histories subsumed in their destiny. So the birth of Christ falls in many ways into ages-old patterns of the birth of gods.

My name is Mary and they told me I would give birth to a king. That is not uncommon, of course, many women have been told such things, many kings and would-be-kings have been born. At this stage one might say it is more or less likely or unlikely, that the child will be a king, or a god. These circumstances seemed less likely than usual. Many rivals, pretenders, upstarts, potentials have been born, more than ever held thrones. They still have to be born. The women who gave birth to them might well mourn the son they hold in their arms, to her he is already lost, given to the throne, to history, the god. These acts – of giving birth, holding a child in one's arms, letting the child go – these are repeated everywhere, endlessly, all of human life is built on this pattern. They say it as if it is nothing, *you will give birth to a child* and then skip over that bit, the actual carrying, the actual birthing, as if it were not part of the story at all.

Shall I tell you what it is to give birth to a child? It is ten moons of dedication. Conception – whether holy or human – occurs and many of us know right then, that instant, that we conceived. We know, but if it is our first, we do not know what that means. Our bodies know, though, remember our own time inside our mothers and begin the relentless preparation. Some of us received messages before the conception, via Tarot cards, internal voices, angels or just gut instinct; *now, this one, tonight.* Others of us were lucky, or unlucky; we courted it or fell into it, we longed and waited for it, we planned, it was an accident or we were subjected to it. It happened within marriage, or outside it, we longed for a child, we weren't ready, we were ambivalent, it wasn't what we wanted. We were cherished, adored; we were barely seen, part of the furniture, we were raped or abused.

When it was declared we were with child the news was received variously. With joy, with condemnation, with concern, with rushed arrangements, with shame, with resignation, with awe. A child was to be born, in time, but until then we – you, I, the woman – was the carrier of it. Until it was born and separate it was bound to us, literally into our body and lifeline, our every breath, every heartbeat was shared with it and all the changes came to accommodate this to make room for it inside us and nothing we could do was separate from it. We might believe our thoughts were free of our body, but hormones flood our brains. We might think we still had our own life as we ate more, our bodies craved and rebelled, our posture changed, our walk, as already every single breath fought to preserve and develop this life.

We might will it differently but still the body presses on, stealing what it must from us if we don't give it willingly, changing everything for this passenger. When life is sacred, holy; not so much every individual life, which are lost by the thousands in the great wash and tide of life, but great life, life itself, this impulse towards life that breeds bees and mushrooms, birch and rosemary, bird and fish, zebra and snake, when Life is sacred a pregnant woman is the center of the universe. Where does the child come from, after all? Yes it comes from the woman, most obviously; from the man also, less obviously. But beyond that – and surely, when we look more deeply we have to say there's more than that – this child is the expression of life itself. Of the force of life. Life forcing itself through, into form, into becoming. And the goddess is an expression of that. Mary holds that.

There's a conversation happening, through the days and nights, an unfolding as we shape ourselves to the child, as it shapes itself inside us. Maybe we talk to this child, sing to it, tell stories of outside and inside worlds; maybe it is just the conversation of blood and heartbeat, of cells growing and duplicating, of oxygen entering and carbon dioxide leaving. It is a conversation of minerals, trace elements, of proteins and fats and carbohydrates. Perhaps it is a craving for sugar, or salt, for fish or oranges or chocolate. It might be a conversation of hope, or despair, of desperation or of love, it is a mixture of these things and not entirely within our control. Perhaps our whole identity has been rewritten, as already our body has, towards this new one, that we still shelter within us, giving everything whether we will or no.

At some stage we give birth. I have done this. Mary did it. The older goddesses did it. Many, most women do it, throughout history and across all geographies of the world. It is something we give even when it is torn out of us, bloody, even if we die in the attempt. We give birth as it was given to us and mostly it is not perfect, there is pain and distress, things go awry, too slow or fast or in the wrong place at the wrong time and mistakes are made, by us or the world or our attendants and sometimes there is a disaster but often, often enough for the human race to survive and flourish, we come through it. Alive.

This is the thing though, this is the miracle. That baby that's born, girl or boy, easily or tearingly hard, is like the first one that's been born, ever. A completely new thing, unthought of before. Unrealized. But now here. Like a message from the gods. Now ours to care for, ours to protect, well or badly and mostly a mixture of the two, while it grows. Yes, ours but also the child has some secret well within it, a source of its own being, something that existed before and will go on existing after. A self, a spirit. A soul. You could say it was the daughter or son of fate. You could say it was fulfilling its destiny, being born to this mother, this family, this time and place on earth. You could say it was a child from God. You could say it was from Spirit. You could look into this child's eyes and see, not just the ladder of inheritance back through its parents and grandparents and ancestral lines, but straight back to the unnamable, to the birth of the universe at the beginning of time, the reflection of the stars; you could say that this child, any child, every child, was the son or daughter of the gods.

Looking at this child we remember our mortality and immortality, both. We remember that because we are born, we die; all of us that are born die, some sooner and some later and age is not necessarily the determining factor, but as we come into being, so we also leave this state of being. Yet – having lived, at all – everything changes. Having become, having this spark of potential be birthed in the form of a new being we have changed matter, rewritten the lives of those around us and brought forth another dimension of the infinite. This is one of the secrets Mary holds, that she carries through from the old Pagan religions; by showing us that her child is the child of a god, in some way is a newborn aspect of god himself, she reminds us that all children are that way.

You could see her seated there on her throne holding her son as a sign that her child is the only special one or you could see that every child is a special one, each is the son or daughter of the gods, each is born to the goddess and each carries that divine spark that ties them always not just to the earth but also to the realm of the stars, the realm our Lady of Heaven and Earth inhabits, crescent moon under her feet and stars all about her, her cloak the blue of a spring sky. I've seen her in too many churches to count, I've seen her image in plaster, clay, stone, in paintings, in stained glass, carved in wood. Yesterday I walked into St Mary's Cathedral in Sydney, out of the summer rain and saw her larger than human-sized, holding Jesus in her arms, kind gentle gaze and jewels adorning her cloak, people genuflecting and meditating before her, tourists and city workers and the deeply religious, speaking silent prayers. I lit a candle and placed it in the sixty-one branched candlestick that stood in front of her.

She's all through Europe; Madonnas in tiny chapels by the roadside in the Italian countryside, Black Madonnas in the south of France. I watched in Rocamadour, in a side chapel to the main church, a fervent evening ceremony packed with men on their way home from work standing weeping and chanting, rocking back and forward before Mary. Men wearing business suits and work clothes, in their teens, their twenties, thirties and forties.

I just stood in the doorway. It felt too foreign and too crowded for me to enter. In Notre Dame in Paris she is there, Notre Dame *Our Lady,*she is dancing on the ceiling in her blue cloak, stars beneath her. Queen of Heaven you might name her, one of her names, a name older than her, one of the names of the goddess, the great goddess. That one who is mother and lover, both, to the god. She is small and high up in the ceiling but she is at the very center. The beams of the church arc towards her, she is in a round medallion and holding her baby in her arms at the highest, most central point from which everything unfolds.

She is not lit. You stumble upon her, unsuspecting, peer from far below or you chase down the image determinedly, knowing it to be somewhere above you and then gaze upwards, straining for the details. She is there in a deep blue sky, with her golden stars and standing on the moon and she looks exactly like Inanna or Ishtar, like any Queen of Heaven and Earth. Of the many guide books in the gift shop only one has that image. Perhaps it is too pagan, too old, too powerful, at the very center of the cathedral and holding up the ceiling, holding it pinned to the sky, linking the earth with the sky, the church with the heavens; Mary and her baby, the genesis of everything.

She is elsewhere in the building of course, the building named for her, as is her son. The one whom she gave birth to and whose death she watched over, she and the other Marys, the women who loved and tended him. For in every birth there is a death and sometimes it comes soon and sometimes later, sometimes the mother is the one to cradle that child in death, to contain that life in the full circle of her arms, into becoming and unbecoming, born from and returned to the greatness. Sometimes it is another but in their arms surely is remembered the mother who gave birth to them, the first one to hold them, deep inside for nine months, the whole of the universe.

Are we not all, always, striving to find again that perfect love, so encompassing and entire that there exists nothing else? Hold me in your arms that I might feel that for a moment; make love with me that we might become, again, the only two in the world; speak a blessing to me so that I remember what it is to be one with everything. Dance with me and I feel the universe swirling about us in stars, take me on a journey into mystery so that I recall how it is to stand on a crescent moon, cresting the sky. Wrap me in a cloak of love as soft as the body of my mother whom once I was a part of, sing to me that I might imagine or hear her voice in my head, that voice of stars and majesty that vibrated through my cells as I became.

Part of birthing is the dying. At each birth a promise to death is wrought; here is another one for you. A child to die – newborn, as a baby, small child, grown, middle aged or old. But yes, as birth has come so death will sweep the circle up in its arms, each one that we labor over so intently, giving our whole bodies and breath, our heart and heartbeats to, each one will die. Mary holds that, the birthing and the dying. There's a Buddhist saying that to give birth to someone is the greatest service one can give to another human being. The next greatest service is to be there as they die. To the mothers who are granted both...what words can meet that? To be there at the death of one you have borne. To hold this, the whole of your child's life, their living from first to last cradled within the circle of your arms.

Perhaps we took it more ordinarily in earlier generations, in other cultures. Not more lightly, I don't mean that, but more as part of an ordinary life whereas now it is seen as exceptional, against the natural current, almost unbelievable that such a thing could happen. Of course it happened more often, at other times and still does in places other than the privileged Western world. Death generally happened earlier and many families, maybe most, had infants die. Surely no less tragic, no less a cutting short of love and potential, no less a burial of hope. But more accepted. Now to live after your child has died seems almost a miscalculation, as if time is going in the wrong direction and I think there is a great turning away of the social eye, we no longer admit that death of a child changes everything. Everything.

When the goddess watches her beloved, her child, put to death – what happens then? All the world must mourn, as it did with Demeter when her child vanished, as it did with Ishtar when Tammuz died on the tree, or with Inanna as Dumuzi was dragged to the Underworld, as it does, yearly, with Mary at Easter at the time of the Passion. As it does each winter with the stripping away, the turning into dark and coldness. This is it – this is the light leaving the world. This is the destruction of all we held dear. This is such an ending it must be written in the stars, the explosion and end of a star is no less than this. This treasure – this gift of mine to the world and to life – has stumbled, slain, has been put out, been taken not just from me but even from their own lifetime, their own self. And so nothing is. If this – the greatness, the fullness, the forward motion of me is not, what is left? How can I be, any longer? This does not convey the ripping grief of it, where one is torn to shreds, unmade in their unmaking and left to stumble through the world, unknowing.

Torture. And torture unto death, the cruelest human imagining. Bad enough are deaths from the body's own workings or unworking, bad enough those in war, by accident, by one's own hand. But torture – the cold turns of a mind employed deliberately to break another human into pieces, with no redemption, the only surcease death. Mary's son died on the cross. An implement of torture, unto death. A perversion of the old stories, the god, the king offered up on the tree, ecstatic in madness and spirit; yes this makes him god, makes him king in death as his story, in life, was probably not enough to lift him to this greatness, but oh. The price, the indrawn breath one must survive to live that out, to watch that, to hold that as part of one's story.

Every human is born. Every human dies. By holding those as the great iconic moments of his story Christ touches us all.

At birth he was spirit encased in flesh, he was the child of god – but we all are. When he died he transcended flesh, his spirit joined with god again – but we all do that. Each single person, every one of us, is that, is the Christ or the god or spirit born to a human mother, is a piece of the divine split off and encased in story of a human life. This birth and death business is the lot of us all. Christ elevates this story not by being the only one but by being, exactly, one the same as all. Not every mother has to witness the death of those she has birthed, but each of us knows that is what we have given over to the world. This perfect being I made, at the utter stretch of my capacity with my whole self and the pinnacle of my being, where life created life, this one I give over, give away, not just to the world and to themselves, but unto death.

There are two pivotal Marys in the story of Jesus Christ. Mary, his mother and Mary Magdalene. It is an old, old pattern that the goddess gives birth to a son. Then he becomes her lover, the father of her unborn child. He dies and her son is born. It is him again, always him, the beloved, the one stretched on the tree or at the turn of the Wheel offering his life, all of it, to her and the next cycle. It is a pattern written in the seasons; she is the fertile earth shifting from burgeoning spring, lush summer, through to waning autumn and sere winter while he is the green mantle, rising and falling, sharing its fruits to last through another year. It is the pattern of grain growing in the fields, those plants that give all then to fall, mown down to lie rotting into the ground, compost, mulch while their seeds are gathered and saved, future life. It is a pattern written in the herd, of horses or deer, of the young male ascending, to be king just a short while at the peak of his strength, impregnating as many females as he can and leaving those offspring to continue in the next formation of this herd.

Researching through layers it is easy to see the Christians

overwrote their story onto the old myths, it shows through all the cracks. The young man dying on the tree. The confusion of Mary Magdalene – is she a prostitute, wife, loyal follower, mother of his future child? – in the old times she was all of those while now we are unsure. She never shifted far away from that ancient pattern, not far enough that her role is clear. Further, the Christ's mother, Mary, has the same name as that of his most devoted acolyte. Really? Even the writers of several thousand years ago surely knew you don't give two of your characters the same name, not unless you want them to be confused with each other. Or unless they are actually the same person.

The old goddess, it is true, might be pregnant without a lover, a virgin birth without impregnation, or no more than the trees are impregnated by the bees or the wind, the earth impregnated with the seeds of grain. Mary, mother of Christ, did that same thing. But then the other Mary, or the other part of that same Mary, the continuum of Mary became his lover or at least beloved, so in a circle it all links up. Even though the Christian version of the story attempts to go in a straight line – first this happened, then this then that – still we read it round in circles. Every year Christ's birth is celebrated, every year his death mourned. What is that if not a cycle? What is it if not an endlessly repeating story, wedded to the northern hemisphere seasons? His birth is at the Winter Solstice and Mithras' festival, the warriors' cult god of ancient Rome and his death is commemorated not at a fixed date but at a phase of the moon, an older calendar, its lunar time pointing back to the feminine, agrarian and cyclic time, not sunwise according to the ascending masculine religions and dates that can be pinned down, staying consistent across the years and decades.

Spring in the northern hemisphere is the time of Christ's death and spring is a very particular time, even more notable in the old world, when the seeds that were saved are planted, the earth is blessed and light returns. His birth is at the yearly turning away from darkness and towards the light and his death is at the time when light is assured, the fields coming into play again and all promises renewed. These things make sense only in myth, in stories that go in cycles, where everything unfolds within the space of a year and then repeats, every year. That the death of the adult Christ happens a few months after the birth of the baby Christ, that Mary gives birth to him and Mary is his beloved – it doesn't work in a linear tale, though if you go round in circles these distinctions fade.

Was she his lover? Mary, Mary Magdalene of whom so many different stories are told. That she was a prostitute, that she never was. That she was the bold one of two sisters, that she anointed his feet and claimed him for herself. That she was the first of his disciples, that she was his beloved, that they married, that they never did. That she was, or is in her own right a goddess, a face of the great goddess. That she was a priestess. That the love between them was platonic, or unconsummated, that it was a beautiful song, a devotion, that it was illicit, magical, the work of souls, that in her and him the old stories came to fruition. That she bore his child, that she travelled far away after his death, that she founded lineages of priestesses. That her story is linked with the sea, the stars, the moon. That she is night and the fertile dark feminine, that she knew the secret of him.

Take me then and break me golden upon the cross. I was not born of woman and will not die the death of men. We hear these words, or different words that mean the same through the years and through the layers of myth and we know, in our flesh and bones that this is true and not true. Each of us is born of woman, each of us a spark of those great dying stars that birthed our planet, each of us a piece, whatever story you speak, of the soul of all of us. Each of us dies in the flesh and yet somehow lives on, in memory, in DNA passed to our children, in deeds of greatness, acts of kindness, the energetic patterns we left in the world, our chemicals and very atoms turning to another use but some shimmer of us remains in the great, the peculiar, the mythic human story. In the song we are singing to the earth, becoming from it and unbecoming into it, in the echo we leave in our striving, our living, our loving, our failures, our griefs and tearing, our yearning.

I've always believed they were lovers, Mary Magdalene and Jesus Christ. There are so many ways to be lovers, after all. There's the flesh and sex of it, the heat and wet abandon of it, the urgency but then there are lovers whose gaze you fall into, endlessly. Lovers who might fold you in their arms, feeling each breath as their breath and merging in and out of each other's dreams like water but if they exchange a kiss it is single, brief chaste, acknowledging more than could be said in the most abandoned sex. There are lovers who sit beside you and offer you their hand when things are tough, saying nothing or speaking of inconsequential things but you know their hearts are absolute and there are lovers who gaze into your eyes across chasms of age, gender, relationship, circumstance and promise to hold the connection between you sacred, forever.

I've always believed they were lovers. Why wouldn't they be? He was a lover to the whole world; isn't that what he promised? That god is love and he is god, or we all are and we are all born from and into love of the most perilous kind, the life-kind, the death-kind and so of course he loved them all, all his disciples, his followers, his questioners, his betrayers and why or how would he not love her? She was night itself, the moon to his sun, she offered comfort and challenge and perhaps the type of stillness he longed for, the depth of shining in her eyes, her long hair, her movements. She was grace, a blessing, the feminine unfurled in front of him in the midst of his men, his supporters, his detractors; she was different, you can see that even in the filtered versions of the story we've got today.

This was and is a story. In the story she is too prominent to be nothing to the central thrust of it, the action. She does not sit neatly on the sidelines as an admirer, she does not fill the niche of supplicant, she is not servant nor incidental. She weaves her way in from different angles, was she this woman, that? Did she wash his feet with her hair, was she nearly stoned in the street, did she stand with his mother at the foot of the cross, was she the one who saw him rise from the dead? The motif of her scatters through his story often enough, noticeable enough to begin to draw the threads together; oh well there was a woman and her name seems to have been Mary, the same as his mother's name and it seems she was by his side. Maybe she came out of the tribes or maybe she held to the old ways, the temples that worshiped the great mother, after all she has the name of his mother, there's a clue if we can read it and maybe she was the flesh of his word of love, maybe she carried the goddess in her body as all women inevitably do and surely he saw that, the gentling of the harsh desert ways of the father god for he spoke of a new way, tempered with the oldest of old.

How intimate can one be with another being? One can give birth to them. One can nurture and care for them. One can be their friend, lover, comrade. One can be there for them in crisis and death. Mary holds all these roles, one or other of the Marys, the great, composite Mary, the goddess Mary. As she has all of those roles for him, the child of god, so she holds all of those roles for us, who are all children of god, of the goddess. This is the greatness of Mary, the enormity of her, the reason she cannot be held to one human body but must be mirrored in several, in many, in all of us. In all those who give birth or hold a newborn child, in all those who offer care and love, in all those who are loyal, beloved, true, in those who minister to the dying or tend the dead or listen for our voices, after we have died. Those who can witness even the worst and not lose compassion, those who can see through the veils, those who carry us.

Mary, the goddess, she who holds the life and death of us, the love of us, the great one we can never forget, who morphs into this vision or that name or is divided in such-and-such a way but then we catch a glimpse of her, a woman dancing in the stars or with her feet on the crescent moon, or cloaked in blue or holding a child and we know her, she is the one, the great mother who held us even before our birth, the one who whispers to us in the night and hears our heart's desire and she who is there at the end, receiving us into her arms. She is a reflection of the face of god, that which we cannot see but explains all things and it is into the mirror of her that we gaze and she is the one who offers ease when we can no longer bear suffering, she is the one behind and always there and she it is who mourns with us and also rejoices and she is our mother and more than our mother ever was and also our lover, the lover of the soul who draws forth the best from us and she is the one who weeps for us, when we cannot

In Sydney, while it rains outside in summer I light a candle for her among the thousand candles lit and burning, in her cathedral. One of the faces of the Great Goddess. Mary.

Research – Reading and Writing

Reading and writing are intrinsic tools of research. Our reading may happen online, in libraries, we may read journals, novels, poetry, secondary sources and commentaries, primary sources and translations. It can include academic, literary, popular and experimental works. To get a wide cross-section of understandings of the goddess you are researching, reading within each of these areas seems ideal. If, instead, you are seeking an in-depth appreciation of a goddess from within a particular tradition, you may choose to, for example, read only Buddhist writings if you are researching a Buddhist goddess.

The line between reading and writing is a fine one and perhaps it first blurs when we begin taking notes on what we are reading. You might be someone who covers your books in sticky notes, underlinings or margin notes, or fills them with bookmarks. Perhaps you photocopy or photograph sections of books that can't be removed from a library, or seek out articles published in obscure journals, collect libraries worth of books yourself or follow elaborate trails through the internet, seeking particular information. Probably at some stage you start to take notes, by hand or on a keyboard, of the most important things you are discovering and possible further sources. Doing this we are already editing our material, choosing which parts of it we will record and so making our own writing, from the reading.

At some point we may use all this reading to create a piece of writing ourselves; an essay, article, devotional poem, a play, story or novel. This is when all the research we have undertaken becomes a resource to inform, inspire and support us and our imagination is allowed to come forward and create something new. There may be pieces of the story of this deity that really sing to you, where there is a special resonance between you and that aspect of the story, myth or goddess. In this way your writing begins to take on a particular flavor, the flavor you uniquely bring to that story, because of your personality, life experience and understandings. When you write this story down, even though it may have been told and written a million times before, still it becomes fresh, in your telling of it.

You may wish to try all three of these types of writing, inspired by research. Perhaps you will only do one of them. Or you may find some combination, or another way not listed here.

Writing as a Record

Take notes of what you are reading and the source – the author, publication and date published. If you are taking extensive notes divide them into sections or files, for example, *history, different versions of the myth, cultural notes, modern retellings*. This is the type of research one might undertake for an article or essay, a work of non-fiction where you will need to be able to name your sources and it may also be useful to track the development of your thinking. It's also just how some people like to record their learning.

Writing for Inspiration

At some point in your research you may meet a block: you cannot find what you are looking for, the interpretations of myth seem simplistic, uncertain or feel not quite right to you, you have read everything you can find or you feel you are not deepening further into the myth, but instead glazing over, stuck at a surface level. At this time, or at any time, you can take up the pen yourself; turn to a blank page or open a new document and begin writing. As this writing is an exercise, to prompt further thought and exploration, try not to refer to notes you've made, but instead simply write out the story of the goddess, as best you can remember or imagine it. Try to write the whole thing in one session, without editing or looking back over what you've written.

Afterwards, read through your writing. What do you learn about your connection to this goddess, your interest in her and the ways the story is speaking to you? Does your writing suggest how your research might develop from here? Perhaps this will lead into a creative work, or more specific or in-depth research, or branch out in another direction entirely; towards a ritual, for example, an artwork, ballad or towards a dedication.

Writing as Creative Expression

There are many different forms of creative writing including poetry, song, plays, stories, novels and film scripts. Your research can form the background for your creative writing, providing some familiarity with the culture and setting of the goddess you've chosen, the pantheon she may belong to, the nuances of her story or stories and how others have related to her previously. You may choose to re-tell a myth, in a contemporary setting or in the original setting; you might place the goddess into a completely different story or if it is a brief written form, such as a song or poem, you may focus purely on the goddess' attributes and your relationship to her.

You may choose to write in the third person – *She is the bringer of harvests*; the first person – *I am the bringer of harvests*; or the second person – *You are the bringer of harvests*. Most likely you will have a sense of the goddess while you are writing or, through your writing, you might feel her presence, hear or see words to write or receive impressions about which directions to write into or the language and form to use. This type of writing may undergo many stages of rewriting, especially if it is intended for publication.

Journey – Going There

The deities we work with come from a place, a culture, a land and a period in history. It often is not our own culture or the land we live on, and perhaps not even where our ancestral lines originate. What does it mean to go to the places these goddesses arose from? To stand on that particular earth, breathe that air, watch the way the sun and moon appear over the horizon or where they hold in the sky, to visit the museums where their relics are held, to stand in the temples where they have been worshipped? To look at the same landscapes those who built the temples looked upon, to eat the same foods? This is another level of research, outside books and thinking, embodied, and it's not so much that we can't know a goddess until we've been to her places as that we learn so much when we do go there.

It is like the difference between looking at the print or image of a famous painting, one we have maybe seen a thousand times such as Van Gogh's *Starry Night* or Botticelli's *Birth of Venus* and standing before the actual painting. It's not that they are unrelated, they are totally related. But the depth, the brilliance – and I don't mean intellectual brilliance but the quality of light attendant – the life of the whole thing that clearly, once standing there, exists only in the painting and every reproduction was completely devoid of and could hardly even hint at. The difference between a phone conversation and being physically present with someone, the difference in reading a novel set in a place one has never been as opposed to reading a novel set in a place one knows – it is incomparable. I recently re-read a novel, after I visited the area of upstate New York it was set in. The book came alive for me in a way it hadn't the first time, they were actual landscapes I had seen and streets I had walked down.

To visit the home place of a goddess we might make a

pilgrimage, maybe put many years of work and saving into getting there. If we are very, very lucky we might live in or near a place our particular deity arises from; Brigid in the British Isles, for instance. In Greece I went to Crete. I realized, abruptly it seemed, that the palace of Minos was not just a story in my childhood *Greek Myths and Legends* book but an actual, physical site, open to tourists and I went there. Ariadne had not been a character I was especially following but I went and sat on the plain stony ground and let the dry air and stunted trees speak to me. I looked at the shapes and colors of the palace, what remained or had been reconstructed and it seemed I could imagine, as I watched some children playing, what it might have been like to grow up there.

There are inherent problems with travelling; carbon footprints, the issues of cultural or spiritual tourism, practicalities of time and money. These problems point to deeper conundrums; cultural imperialism, appropriation, our consumer training that leads us to believe we can shop and choose among the world's cultures, taking whatever we like from wherever we like. Those of us who live on stolen land, such as in Australia, tenuously co-habiting with indigenous peoples whose land spoke to them in myth and story, are hedged around in difficulties. Do we import styles of magic and ritual, layers of myth and deities who actually belong somewhere else, but that we inherited with our bloodlines, our own cultural or our spiritual lineage? Do we even approach those deities or presences that are sacred to the people native to this land? If so, how? As outsiders, invaders, supplicants? These questions are difficult and so complex that there can be no simple or general answers other than respect, inquiry and listening to those whose culture and land it is traditionally. Some of us will choose not to, or not be able to travel.

What if we are working with a goddess whose culture is still living, whose worship is current and where spiritual seekers are welcome? An Indian goddess, for example, whose temples are vibrant with life and whose people do not view her as one of countless goddesses from around the world and throughout time who might be chosen as some sort of personal guide, but as a potent, unquestioned living force demanding allegiance? I think we can learn, if we go there, something we could never learn staying within our strange, eclectic non-tradition of picking – or being picked by – goddesses from a variety of places, spending a month with Freyja followed by a month with Persephone, followed by a dedication to Isis or Rhiannon.

Journeying to the place of a deity has an ancient history, the history of pilgrimage. If we go humbly, attentively, as seekers and not as conquerors or repositories of truth, this type of research can be invaluable in forming an understanding of and relationship with deity. The costs and discomforts of travelling add to the liminal nature of journeying in the sacred, we are shaken out of control, our context and from our assumptions. We do not know what we will find. We may sit beside a sacred well a whole day, waiting for a vision of the goddess and only upon leaving realize what it was we came to understand, that she is in the water, or that we ourselves were bringing her through and that each woman visiting does that, or something else. Pilgrimages are sacred journeys, not just because of the places we go in the world but because of the unfolding that occurs within us when we seek the sacred.

Dedicating to the Goddess

Dedication to a deity is a significant thing. Usually *dedicating* is decided on only after many hours of thought and ritual, over months or even years. Most dedications are understood as being life-long, although it is possible to dedicate oneself for a specific period of time, usually a year, or the year-and-a-day of contemporary pagan ritual. The fundamental idea of dedication is that one makes a commitment and then it is permanent. Dedications are not necessarily exclusive – we can dedicate to more than one deity – and an example of this would be to dedicate to a pairing of deities; for example Krishna and Radha, or Inanna and Ereshkigal. One might dedicate to two different aspects of one deity, for example Artemis and Diana, or Inanna and Ishtar. Or, over time, one might dedicate to several apparently unrelated deities; for example Persephone, Kwan Yin and Oshun. Sometimes it is not a named, or specific, deity that we dedicate ourselves to but the Great Mother, the Dark Goddess or simply the Divine Feminine.

Dedication is not something that can be decided by anyone other than ourselves and similarly it is not for anyone else to say whether we are, or are not, living up to that dedication. Dedication is not usually conditional, it comes about when we feel so within the realm of that deity that we wish to hold nothing back, to – in effect – live our life as a furtherance of that goddess' existence on earth. We are offering our life force, our embodiment and actions to the goddess, saying that we will be in service to her not when it suits us but at all times, or when it suits her. Dedicating to a deity we would expect our life to change, maybe not in ways that immediately feel pleasant to us. Perhaps I was tolerating that not-quite-satisfactory job, relationship or situation – but will she? Probably not.

Devotion is linked to dedication but not the same. Devotion – in the forms of prayer, ritual, meditation – may come both before and after dedication, or on its own and does not necessarily have the same ongoing commitment as dedication. Dedication probably involves a ceremony of commitment as well as the ongoing acts that follow that ceremony. Devotion may entail keeping an altar for that deity, caring for her special places or concerns, naming her in ritual and teaching others about her and enacting some of her principles or attributes; bringing them and therefore her into the world through ourselves and the way we live.

We might view dedication very much as a two-way process, that this goddess has called to us or chosen us and we have responded, or we might perceive it more as having ourselves sought her out and chosen her. There are times, and goddesses, where it seems she does not give us a choice, that dedication is demanded of us. We do always have choices, however, to be open to, hear and respond to that demand, but it can feel very absolute. The Dark Goddess, in her many forms, is one I often hear this about. In the great imbalance we currently live in, where the light – ascendency, happiness, wealth, endless increase – is worshipped to the absolute neglect and denial of the dark it does seem that a great rebalancing is required. Possibly having many hundreds, thousands, perhaps tens of thousands of us dedicated to the Dark Goddess is one way of beginning that rebalancing. But to feel overwhelmed by a deity, taken without our consent or simply born into her realms is not the same thing as conscious dedication.

Spiritual contracts are both like and unlike legal contracts. They are similar in requiring consent. They are dissimilar in regards to their cessation or dissolution. Some believe that they can never be dissolved, perhaps not even through lifetimes. Others might think of them as relationships that can be grown out of, a kind of natural process of completion that may occur, or a development as the dedication itself leads one onto a different path. Perhaps it depends on what one believes, or experiences, as occurring between the deity and the human at the point of and as a result of that dedication. If we are asking to be remade or bound into the service and emanation of that deity, to afterwards seek to put it aside or break it seems impossible; after all, we have become that thing, or a part of it. If we think of it as more like showing up for a job, which we could choose to leave, it makes more sense. We should think and enquire deeply within ourselves, with the deity and perhaps also with others before we take this step.

Sometimes dedication may come upon us. This happened to me when I found myself in a ceremony of dedicating as a priestess to Inanna-Ereshkigal at the completion of a seven-day ritual descent. I did have a moment, a clear moment, to choose and I chose to dedicate; I knew within myself that I could have said *no* either aloud or internally and the dedication would not have taken. It felt completely within my control – until I said *yes*, whereupon I felt the shift within me, the beginning of the rewriting of me, orchestrated by her.

More often a dedication is prepared for consciously over time. We may have a dedication ceremony with others, who may also be dedicating, or already be dedicated to the deity or we may do it alone. At the end of this section a dedication ceremony is discussed, as well as the option to commit to devotion for a year.

Aphrodite

Aphrodite is the Grecian goddess of love and beauty; she is love and beauty manifest. The statues and art do our human best to describe, in a woman's body, what that might look like. But when we invoke Aphrodite we don't just want to look at her, we want to feel her, experience for ourselves what it is to live as love and beauty.

Take a breath and connect to love – whatever we love most, our children, our partners, our work, our spiritual community, nature, the animals we live with – hold that. Then – look around. Let our eyes open onto the world – the skies, the land, the birds and trees, whatever we see of wildness, of this earth we inhabit – and let its beauty infuse us. Let that love and beauty come together not as an intellectual exercise but as felt, lived – embody that. Let it speak to our bones, the placement of our limbs, the way we address each breath, to movement; the blink of eyelashes against the skin under our eyes, the minute adjustments of shoulder and neck, the awareness of the weight holding us onto the earth. This is to look with the eyes of Aphrodite.

If we turn that gaze towards a stranger on the street, towards a weed, towards a dragonfly hovering over a stream, towards the rain – how are we not filled again, filled to overflowing with that return? For love and beauty are not static but doubled under our gaze, doubled and redoubled like cells dividing, unstoppable when we do those simple things, connect to love and open our eyes. How rare it is, in the stream of moments that compose every day, for our awareness to be with that. Perhaps when we gaze into the eyes of our lover, when we contemplate a scene of great natural beauty, hug our child or work deeply on our poem, painting, song, ritual, garden. But not every moment. And yet Aphrodite is there, a whisper, a breath away, always offering. Love and beauty.

Perhaps we are all dedicated to Aphrodite. Sensuality – skin and body and flesh and sex – that's what we're born into. I've worn mine on the surface, always yearning for touch and intimacy, for skin-against-skin in a place of deep connection and reveling in meeting the gaze of a beloved, losing all else within that realm. I am dedicated to Aphrodite not because love is light and easy but because it is fierce and unrelenting, essential and driven. Aphrodite is the secret heart of me, guarded and vulnerable but deeply true. Every time I bring myself back from a place of mourning, of self-blame, of anger; confusion, betrayal, abandonment, eventually I turn to Aphrodite. When I remember myself. When I stop thinking about the past and start to remember who I am. As I yearn again for skin and joy and touch and to gaze into another's eyes with delight. As I remember kissing.

In her stories Aphrodite owns a magical girdle and whoever wears it embodies the qualities of Aphrodite herself. I think I've always known how to create that girdle, how to wear it. To wear it in the service of the divine – of Aphrodite – those moments, surely, are the most glorious. When I am able to find that place where I am wholly hers, dedicated to love, not through another human being or a relationship but just allowing that love and spilling it out into the world like nectar or moonlight or song. When I remember to do this, when I bring myself to this then all my history, pain and even longing dissolve, disappear in the delight and presence of the goddess. This is why I keep coming back to her even when I feel clumsy, awkward, not young or pretty or thin enough, not easy or open enough, not happy enough.

Aphrodite. I will make a seven-stranded girdle with intent and magic, with blood and tears if necessary. This is part of my ongoing dedication to her, to do this work not just with others but with myself. Each one of the seven strands will honor an aspect of my sexuality, each one will be dedicated to joy and healing, to Aphrodite within me and in the world. In sacred space I will journey with these strands; with my connection to the goddess, with my ways of seeing, with my truth, my heart, my body, womb and inner mysteries. I set aside a whole weekend for it, it is an act of devotion to the goddess and also to myself, my sexuality that feels so wounded, so filled with yearning and desire.

I set up an altar for her, flowers and shells and candles and the colored cords I use to weave a girdle. I place down special things, the glass goddess that fits in my hand, some photos of my son, beads and bells and feathers. My journal, my mirror. I cast a circle: to the south to anchor me, to the east for winds and breath to blow through this tangled grief and pain, to the north for heat and sunlight, the warmth of touch, of skin-to-skin; to the west for the shared whispers of lovers and for the chalice of love, of life; to the south for earth and body, my body, another's body, all our bodies.

Aphrodite, I call to you. You who are born from the sea, as all life is, emerging from that place, cells beginning to divide and the mystery we call life separating itself out from rock and salt and water and sunlight, just as each one of us was birthed from that inner sea of our mothers, just as each one of us separated out a life from the line of women who carried us. Ocean born. I call to you as the naked self, as the goddess revealed in her splendor. I call to you as the one without boundaries, without limits, as love itself – Aphrodite I call you in. I call as a woman, middle aged by now, who's had lovers, known loss, borne a child. I call to you with all my heart. I yearn for you, your presence, touch, thought. I call from my great longing for connection, joining, meeting. I call to you in sacred ritual.

Aphrodite. Remake me. Take me as a worshipper in your temple, bring my hurt and pain into the dance of life. May everything I do in your temple be a prayer for the remembrance of the sacred nature of bodies and of sexuality. May I be the offering. This longing, these tears, the hurt coldness, the distances I make between myself and all of life – and all the gift I have, may I give it. May I give it for joy and in kindness and delight, may I give it in compassion and also in passion, may I dance with it, make love with it, write with it and work with it, dream with it and act fiercely in the world inspired by this. May I find my place in your temple.

Then I begin the work for the first cord, my connection to the goddess. I let myself trance, in and back, back to the temples and I think of Greek temples, still standing and temples I've been to in Turkey and Malta and Italy and Egypt and temples I've never been to but I know are there, in Iran, Iraq and other temples, Japan and India and Scotland and temples we've constructed in ritual and between the worlds.

In my mind Aphrodite's temple is large and spacious, with many women. There are women outside tending the gardens and relaxing by the fountains and there are children playing. Inside are women sitting in a quiet corner, reading or in meditation and women dancing and women praying and maybe weeping and women gathered together and there are places for massage and healing and conversation and yet there is still space for me to feel alone and quiet within myself and seeking; to wander into alcoves with candles lit and statues, to unfurl sacred scrolls, to dip my hands in the water that runs through the temple, to sit on cushions at the feet of your statue, to dance to music playing, the flute, the many stringed santoor. To remember myself.

I seek out a tiny inner temple where I might lay my offerings on your altar. I will bring you roses pressed from a bouquet given to me in love and I will bring you seashells from the pacific ocean beaches and I will bring you lavender and rosemary from gardens I walked through and I will bring you the pieces of my broken self and I will bring you feathers of the white cockatoos I love. I place these things on the altar. In this space I will dance to you, my dance a call, a pleading cry for you to come and remind me what it is to be a woman and all of who I am. As I dance and cry, shake with it, with yearning and need, longing to reach that place to hear you and I cry harder and dance harder and offer more, yes everything I am, I give it all then I sense you like sunlight, as moonlight or stars, Aphrodite like a blessing, weaving, dancing around me and with me and you lean forward, I sense your embrace, all about me in the particles of air and you whisper into my ear one word, *beloved.*

I remember. I know. I am, I have always been, I will always be beloved. I am beloved of the goddess, beloved of Aphrodite. As this remembrance settles into me, into my thoughts and senses, into my body, it strips away whatever else I carried here; unworthiness, hiding, doubt and I feel her touch, that whisper sweeping through me, untangling, spinning gold and silver, starlight and breath and I am hers again, not that I wasn't always hers but I am remembered now, to myself. I am held again in her embrace. Beloved. I measure out a golden cord for my girdle, my connection to the goddess and whisper its name, *beloved.*

I return from trance and look about me. There is a mirror on my altar and I pick it up. This is for the second strand of my girdle, the eye of beauty. In the ordinary, daily sense it does not occur to me to look in a mirror; staying with friends I am shocked to learn they look in a mirror before they leave the house and I realize how like my mother I must be; she never did that. I never saw that and so I never have done it. How do I look? – I don't know. I think of mirrors as magical, transformational, not practical. So now I will use my round, chased with dragons, silver-backed mirror, with its jade handle to gaze within and search for what Aphrodite might see, if it were her looking at me.

I see tiredness in my eyes, grief maybe and I see the delicate skin of my face. I see my hair, that I've always loved, long and curling, generously threaded with silver. I see heredity; how similar I look to women of this same mix, Polish/French, when I have met them; how in Melbourne once a woman stopped me in the street and said *Polish Jew*, not as an accusation but in recognition and what could I do but smile at her? The pale skin, dark hair, French of a particular type; in France, as long as I don't dress like a tourist people often assume I am French so I stay as silent as I can, to pass. I smile and nod and point and only speak when I must, then proving, regrettably, that I am not one of them, watching their faces shift slightly, adjust for a foreigner.

I can imagine Aphrodite would see those lines in me, European blending and changing but brought forward into this generation. Looking closer in the mirror I see the structure of my skeleton, cheekbones, skull, the ridges above the eye sockets; that is beautiful, the foundations of a face, the strength and severity of bone. And looking at those depths I can see also the years sketched over my face, the lines still delicate, emerging and showing how I squint, smile, frown in concentration – now my face shows all that for me. There's a softness to the skin, the fine flesh over the bones of the face that gathers, gently, year by year indiscernible but, if you look at the whole sweep of time, noticeable. Then my mouth, the shape of my lower lip, which I've passed to my son, a cupid's kiss it's been called, that is particular, unusual, marks this face out.

Then I gaze and gaze into my eyes until they become all I see. My eyes that gaze upon this world, my eyes that are the goddess seeing, seeing everything I see, in this moment seeing myself. The goddess gazing upon herself, my self a bridge, a transition, a mirror. My eyes a way for her to see an aspect of herself, living. Eyes with tears, eyes with a smile – I see all that in my eyes, sadness and strength and intent. I see glimmering secrets not yet risen to the surface I see hope I see longing and there is something luminous in eyes, gazed at this intently, for this long, a shining and I see how we are all her shining ones, shining in grief and hope and drowned in mystery, each one a shining mirror of self, her self; I see myself shining. *Shining.*

Putting the mirror down I measure out a cord against the first one, a pale pink that is both delicate and flushed with promise. This is the second cord and I speak its name aloud, *shining*. I take some time to journal, to stretch and drink water and then I go back into the process, to this dedication that is owning me, remaking me.

I move to the third strand, my voice and words, the words that are the truth of my life and sexuality. As true as Aphrodite, that naked truth that doesn't hide but is just presence, revealed. In her temple I've heard truths rarely spoken, truths that might choke one with the bitterness of them, truths where the throat closes up refusing to allow them forth; or where sound deserts and only thin forced whispers remain, words like razor blades that cut and tear on their way out, words so dense with shame they cloak the hearer, miasma-like in sympathetic guilt; words of hot bile, searing tissue in their exit, fouling the mouth. There are words so broken one can barely catch the pieces of them, speaking or hearing; words which though spoken quietly have resonances that build and build about the space, echoing and declaiming so that they gain a life of their own and words that sing in pure beauty, simply, like a bell.

I speak aloud to say I've always known the power of my unbounded sexuality and rarely, only rarely have I found a lover who reflected that, could hold it or wished for it or met it. I speak of how I dream, a thousand thousand dreams, of touch and joy in skin and flesh, of being held, of merging with a lover. I keep speaking. I am damaged by mistrust, betrayal, abandonment; each time a lover leaves me I am cut in pieces by it. I make myself whole, again and again but these things I wish for – gentleness with power, integrity even when it costs, joy and delight alongside depth of spirit and surrender into union – perhaps I can never find them. Inside I am screaming so loud, simply for not being held, having no touch and no safe place, except alone, to curl up. I let the screams out.

More words spill out of my mouth. I have been raped. I have

lived feeling unsafe, bodily and within. I have learned to hold myself at a certain distance, except from those I trust. I long to give all of myself into the sex of skin-to-skin, mouth and mouth, bodies together. I have had it a few times, with a few people, long ago. Like the opening of the universe when I was the goddess herself and you, my lover, were also that. I remember. I never cease to long for that. Sex makes me and unmakes me and it is the essence of me, the depth of me. This is the truth. *Depth*.

With that word my speaking comes to a stop, I have come to truth. *Depth* is the name of my third cord and I choose a bright pink, almost fluorescent and measure it out against the others. I wind them together and loop them around my neck to fall over my heart for the next piece.

I move – it feels like I fall – into the fourth strand and the heart. My own heart. The beating heart of me. A place I feel guarded in, careful of but right now it seems like release, a home after the voice, those words that still scour my throat. This is where I belong. It is the gentlest, softest place like a nest of a bed in the afternoon sunlight with cushions piled high and a friend to talk to. It feels utterly welcoming. My heart-beat. I can't live without it, so all of my living, every piece of it has had this as an undercurrent, a backbone and a condition. I live by its graces. Shouldn't I be kind to it then and allow it openness, let it breathe – its beating unencumbered by hurt and history – let it stay in the present; one beat, this, the next, the next, ever onwards for the whole of life? The whole of its life which is the whole of my life and I find I am flooded with love, gratitude – amazement – for my heart.

So you keep on working even while I am asleep? Even when I was too young to notice? Even when I think you are breaking, you just keep on doing that, that pumping, beating, contraction and expansion that means I stay alive while I think I am dying? Everything else takes more concentration. Breathing, even, which is automatic still takes a lot of effort to slow it down, or breathe deep enough or to breathe through difficult things, sleeping takes effort sometimes, to get there or to stay awake – and yet the heart, the most essential driving part, beating before I was breathing, before I separated sleep from waking, in the womb it was beating, I was beating with it, my life unfurling and learning to glory in that sea-deep motion of a heart.

So now and into that place I unlayer my hurts to feel the tide of blood and life pumping through them. Being left by someone I have loved feels terrifying. I fear I cannot survive it, this terror, so old, back to childhood no doubt; I will not be able to live if these people leave. But listening to my heart, placing my hand on my heart I feel no variation in its pattern, it does not care. Its mechanics are not affected if this person stays or goes and this reassures me, helps me separate out the fear from the reality; I will not die from this. My heart will keep beating. In the pulse and pump of it I am able to take some breaths that are deeper, more expansive as I learn to trust – not the vagaries of human relationships but this, my own heart.

I breathe and feel the grief that stops me from reaching out, even to people who care for me. How do I keep creating my life forward when death surrounds me in every breath? My mother dead, my friend Trinda dead; this grief like a snowstorm I am out in, lost to it, I am pinned to this tiny piece of ground and I can't see anything except whirling white and my feelings are terror and loss and this huge tearing away and how can I be with that any more than I am and yet I don't move, I'm not escaping and the landscape isn't changing. Listen to my heart. It sounds brave, under these circumstances. Really? – All that, and you keep going? Just going, just the same?

I sit and breathe and stretch open further and further. My heart feels alive; I'm sure it always was, I just forgot, I was frightened and ran away somehow, I abandoned it the same way I feel abandoned. Now I remember it, this basic animal piece of me, the life of me and it reminds me that just this moment is enough to concentrate on and in this moment – I am alive. It seems, as I concentrate closer and closer, that each beat of my heart is telling me something, buying me another moment, at least, to discover something or just to be. Hope. No matter how bad this is, how traumatized and lost I am in the snowstorm of loss and sheer missing and confusion and utter not knowing – hope. *Hope.*

Hope is the name of my fourth cord, the cord of the heart and it is deep green like forests and I measure it out and twine it with the others. I rest for a while, peacefully. I eat. I write in my journal. Then I take a breath and move on, into the work of the fifth strand.

My body. This is the thing that holds it all together – the heart, the voice, what I see and think, how I exist at all to be conscious of the world or of the goddess, a piece of stardust returning, always, to the place we live – body. I put on music and dance. I dance as a hymn of praise to body, my body. I dance each piece of me; fingers, ankles, breasts and belly, thighs and forearms, hips and neck – all of it. I dance until I am sweating and alive in it and I feel acknowledged and held, all of me. When the music changes I start to celebrate, I swing into it, the dips and peaks, this living being of me. I twirl and sweep and leap and lunge and laugh, reckless in my passion for life – this life, mine – until I am exhausted.

This body that holds all my experience, that has been with me ever since I was, this body through which I know the world, meet others, this body that sometimes or maybe every moment embodies the goddess herself, this body that dedicates itself to love and beauty and now back to body again; this body. What if it were the end, the end of this body? How precious would it be to me then, at the end? If these moments, this song, this dance were my last? I am alone and what can I do but keep dancing until the end. I dance, weeping and breathing and sweeping through space, so grateful for life and this body and so in the full beauty of the flesh-blood-bones and molecules of it all. So in the stardust glory that death is acceptable, is a piece of the dance. When the music finishes I drop to the floor. Utter beauty pulsing in tides through and all around me, even death as beauty, the beauty that rounds this earth-body-life of me. *Beauty*.

I lie still for a long time on the floor. When I rise I choose a black cord for the body and measure it out. Its name, still echoing within me from the dance, is *beauty*. It is evening by now. I leave the rest of this work for the next day but I sleep with my cords curled under my pillow, already in a place of transformation, feeling the goddess watching, holding me.

In the morning I begin with the sixth strand, the red womb. I measure out three immensely long strands of red wool and sit down to plait them into a red cord. I let the thoughts come and go as I plait and plait and plait. It takes an hour.

Out of death spins life. My life spun – all our lives spun – out of the wombs of our mothers, their lives from their mothers and so on, back through the ages, infinity almost, a line of mothers stretching back as far as humans, animals, or reproduction stretches back. This red blood is passed to me. Even now, entering menopause and with my mother dead, even now I hold it. I dream of running out of red wool in a workshop, or the fear of running out of it, I didn't bring enough red wool, how could that be? But then there is enough after all, a satisfaction and relief. I dream that I have an unexpected period and when I go to the bathroom everything I touch fills up with blood, the whole roll of toilet paper turns red from my fingers, the bench where I sit, its cushions are soaked with blood, the clothes I brought to change into are cream-colored and I realize they won't do at all; I am about to give a presentation and there is blood everywhere.

I have given birth to just one child, though my mother had two and her mother three, one living and her mother seven living. When I think of the strands of red running through me it is as one of a long line of women, birthed and birthing, of the red threads out of the land of France, of French soil and French women's bodies, though I know the lines are all mixed up in me, with Poland and Italy in there as well, but because the mother line comes from France that is where my imagination sends me.

I remember giving birth and I am grateful unendingly, for having had a child, for who he is and for our relationship. Perhaps this is made more potent by all those years when I longed to have another baby, the one-ness of it has a miracle aspect, that I managed it at all. I always wanted to be a mother. Not just to be a mother but to do the flesh-and-blood, the womb and cervix of it, the birth and breast. I know many women who wanted that and did not have it, others who didn't especially want it but did have it and others still who didn't want it and didn't have it and all the variations in-between. Regardless of all of that we were all born from a woman, all of us with our lives and wishes, choices and circumstances come from that womb place, where we were rocked and held for nine months, when we knew the goddess intimately, held within her.

Bleeding is obvious but the secret times, mid-cycle, the fertile times, they have been my delight. A private delight, although science says we smell fertility; making us more and more attractive like blossoming flowers pushing us out towards the world, towards touch and possibility, held sway in a sense of our own lusciousness. I am stronger, more robust, perhaps more daring in my fertile times and with that an increased sensuality, a strength in it so it is less conditional, more sweeping. I have a sense of brightness in those days. The swell of it, the push and slide of it like waves coming in stronger on those full moon tides, the slip and glide of it so just walking around the world within my own body is a more sensual place than at other times, this promise of potential seems so celebratory, purely of this life.

Every month for a long time, more than half my life, my body has reminded me of this, for a day or two at least. I have been a woman driven by fertility, impelled by it and I have felt those cycles sweep through me, relentless. Has that infused me to the point where I can brew within myself that spell of allure, where I can spin the threads together and send it out when I want? I stand on the brink of fertility, the other brink, that of relinquishing it. Not because I am ready or because I have finished with sexual love or even the yearning for motherhood but because I am fifty-two and my body decides. I hold its mysteries mainly to myself, as I did the mysteries of my blood and my fertility. This womb blessing, the power of it, I feel both how secret, how utterly inner this power is and yet how longing, to be met and celebrated and journeyed with. *Power*.

I reach the end of the red threads, plaited together they are now a cord as long as my other cords. The name of my red cord is *power*. I stretch and move, I wait until I am ready for the last, the seventh cord. To descend into the inner mysteries.

Aphrodite takes me in. Into that sacred place of us, the gate the flower the temple of us, that which declares us, visibly, to be women. I feel grateful that I never struggled with my body, never wanted it to be other than it was and that I have always thought our bodies beautiful, mysterious and sacred. When I feel betrayed or abandoned by a lover I feel a physical shrinking, a recoil as my body cringes in shame, revulsion, anguish; nausea, wanting to purge that from me. *Get out, get out.* So I sit with that, shaking and weeping, asking Aphrodite to make me whole again.

There have been lovers I parted with who honored me, some when it was my choice, some when it was theirs and with them I do not feel this tearing, this repulse when I think of them or someone speaks their name. With those I have a softness in memory, a tenderness and I trust that wherever they are they still hold me in respect and honor and I feel whole in that. So in this newest grief I mourn again, not just for loss though that is always there, someone I gentled towards enough to be lovers, held that space for months or years and now this harshness, scouring shame. Always there is self-blame; have I held sex sacred? Have I really? How then was I choosing a lover who did not hold it sacred, or would not or could not when pressed or pressured by inside or outside forces? Can I now, then, be true to myself? Can I say I am not ashamed to have loved, to have desired, to have welcomed even this one who now denies me?

I want to live as a poem of love and revelry, of delight and passion that's so deep, straight to the goddess that maybe I don't even notice these betrayals or I don't take them on, I dance past them and in the whirl like the stars patterning the universe in becoming and unbecoming they are specks of dust that make and unmake, patterns of change rather than hurt. If I am one breath of the universe I want that breath to be a song, whose resonance touches out, rippling, with softness and depth like a breath of night air filled with promise. I want my skin, outer and inner, to welcome touch and caress whether of ocean waves, of sunlight, a lover, child, the petals of flowers. I want my dedication to Aphrodite to be not just in the secret heart of me but to wear it on the outside, like a sheen of starlight, not exactly wearing it but letting it shine through me from the core and on its way, like starlight, to the outermost edges of the universe, still unfolding.

I stand up and take my clothes off. This vulva part of the human woman of me, from that place I dedicate myself again to Aphrodite, goddess of beauty and love and this is the petals of the flower of me and this is the gateway for the entry into life and here are the halls of the temple and the pearl of me where I touch the center of the universe and blend, am one and formed from them and do not even have to return because I never left. This is me, that is woman, that is pearl that is goddess that is unfolding beauty that is truth that is love is the beating heart of life and soft and strong, serene and deep. I write a poem and in it I name that part of me as *pearl at the center of the universe*. This is the last strand, *pearl*. I choose a delicate pale blue cord for it.

So I have my seven cords of magic to offer Aphrodite. I sit

and plait my girdle from the seven strands and its names are *beloved shining depth hope beauty power pearl* and it is not just for Aphrodite but for myself I chant as I plait the cords together – gold-pink-bright pink-green-black-red-pale blue – singing a spell and it comes out as *beloved pearl shining power depth beauty hope*. It is not just a spell of who I am but of what I am becoming.

Each time I dedicate and rededicate myself to Aphrodite it's another piece. It's a pattern by now, a ritual that allows me to drop deeper and deeper, in through layers, not just of the body but maps of all the times I have taken this path, like a many-layered flower, opening its petals at crown, eye, throat, heart, center, womb, vulva; each cord of this girdle is made of many strands, each time I meet this goddess the depth and breadth of her, the weave of her seems more substantial. My girdle is a seven-stranded plait of colors and tears, of joy and longing and it has shells and bells and beads tied on and a silver locket from my grandmother with a fine braid of hair, some distant woman related to me, it has spells and wishes and each piece of it is a dedication to my self, to love, to beauty, to this goddess who is not separate from me. Aphrodite.

Ereshkigal

Ereshkigal is the Queen of the Underworld in the Sumerian mythos. Dark sister to glorious Inanna, Queen of Heaven and Earth, Ereshkigal's part in Inanna's descent to the Underworld brought death, at least temporarily, to that bright goddess. As Inanna heads blithely into the Underworld to see her sister, Ereshkigal laughs and plans her death. Gate by gate, as Inanna descends, her powers, finery and precious ornaments are stripped away from her and she is constantly reminded *the ways of the Underworld are perfect.* When she reaches Ereshkigal's hall, naked by now, she is killed by a word and look from the Queen of Death and then hangs on a meat hook for three days and nights, until she is rescued. Alone among the dead Ereshkigal cries and moans and screams, engaged in an immense and lonely labor.

Ereshkigal. Say her name in syllables, sound it out with tongue against the roof of the mouth, letting the lips form each shape in turn, like a Japanese word with no emphasis, each piece as deadly as the next; *E-resh-ki-gal. E* spoken *eh* on a low and rusty note, a foretaste, a warning bell; *resh,* a susurrus of whisper in the dark background; *ki* like the knife the cuts the life thread and by now we know there's no turning back; *gal,* the sound of the Underworld, of those gates slamming behind one, clang after clang echoing in unending dropping darkness with no way back. Ereshkigal. What is it like to live in a tomb, a place of the dead, even if a palace, to be living immersed in death?

Surely each one of us can answer that. This service to the dead, by the living; I have done that. I remember driving four hours on a hot summer's Boxing Day with a reluctant partner to the funeral of a friend's only child. There was nothing I could offer but my presence, which was less than nothing in the face of what had happened and yet dozens went and not just for her, who must keep living, but in tribute to a life surrendered.

Seventy of us trekked along a rough track across a creek and through the bush, leading to the hole dug in the ground by his family and friends; his coffin not just carried by men who had cared for and fathered him, but also made by them, physically, from wood and metal in the last days of his dying. My friend Cate said as she sat with her son she could hear them under the house, banging and sawing as they did this work, she said she found it reassuring. That task of hers, to sit by her dying child as his coffin was crafted and listen to the sounds of it; most of us would think that hell.

The mood dropped and dropped through the service for this child, standing in the Australian sun with a backdrop of tall gum trees, the earth clay under our feet, his school class singing for him, people speaking prayers and wishes. When they started to lower the coffin into the ground – not a neat gap in a polite cemetery with marble, mowed lawns and brass plaques but a pit, a hole in the rough clay – I felt a tide, a wave sink through me. Many, most were crying. How to reason with this? How to make space or say this was all right or an end to suffering when surely the suffering, of his parents, had just begun? Then one brave person stepped forward and opened his mouth and began to sing, loudly, *Halle halle halle, lujah*. He sang with conviction and invitation, *halle halle halle* and more and more of us joined in, *halle halle halle* gulping back the tears because this, surely, was a way to redemption, *lujah* a way to have the pulse of the living enter even the halls of the dead, to turn this bleak tide and reforge, with each other, the breath and spirit of life, *hallelujah, hallelujah,* which lasts as long as it lasts and apparently goes on lasting, even in the face of death.

Ereshkigal. I met her once. The patterns of her run through my life. Dark Queen of Mystery.

Once we say *the Underworld* I feel it potent, everywhere, beneath my feet. It is not a precise location, not bordered or limited or confined to any particular place, it is just *below*. This constant presence, hovering, out of sight but not out of mind, waiting for its moment, this seemed to be always with me. As a child I was terrified of it. I felt its jaws were close to me and any moment of inattention on my part could result in obliteration. Fairy tales, especially those of Baba Yaga, Snow Queens or wicked witches, of girls entering impossibly dark places and somehow winning through compelled me. Persephone with her secrets hinted at in that flower, that pomegranate, that story never really let go of my imagination. When I read the story of Inanna and Ereshkigal in my mid-twenties I felt it had been calling me all my life. Here then was the mystery stripped to its essential form. Here were the steps laid out, to enter the world of death and even return. Here was invitation, here was certainty.

I have been in service to death my whole life, we all are. When I was four my mother's father died, after a long illness. I cannot say if it was the day he died or the day after, or the day after that and I cannot ask my mother because now she is dead as well. Before she went out for the day she pulled me aside and spoke to me, I remember it well. She had my whole attention. I think she must have squatted down to my level and looked me in the eye, held me accountable. She said my grandmother was coming to look after my brother and me and that we must be kind to her. I think she said that my grandfather, Paul, had died, though perhaps I did not take that in as fully as the instruction to be kind, this very serious instruction. I was not clear, at that age, of people's relationships to each other, so I did not realize she was telling me her own father, whom she loved deeply, had died.

We were kind, that day, to my grandmother. I remember the sense of it rather than the particulars. My brother must have been not yet three, so it was my responsibility. I think we read books together, that is, she read to us; I think we cuddled her and played outside, by ourselves and let her do whatever she did alone in the house. I remember the largeness of it, an enormity I knew was beyond my reach and yet somehow it impacted right down to a place small enough to contain me; a morning and afternoon in a suburban house with a woman and two children. I remember it feeling completely beyond my grasp and yet my role in it was precise, understandable and punctiliously performed. Maybe the presence of her grandchildren brought my grandmother comfort, or at least distraction; I know we did not talk about death, or about my grandfather and I knew my role was to be performed without commentary, behind the scenes. I was not to explain that we were being deliberately kind, or ask questions, I was just to do it.

Once, in London, I saw an amazing piece of theatre by the Opera Factory that spanned through the Sumerian mythology; perhaps the first half was the story of Inanna and the second half that of Gilgamesh. Three images are burned into my memory from that play and in a way they are all images of death. The first is of Enkidu, the wild man designed by the gods, who lived with the beasts of the field before Gilgamesh found him, tamed him and became his brother, all of which led to Enkidu's death. The theatre company arrayed themselves out across the stage, which was simply the back half of a broad room and they – became animal. They were a herd of gazelles, maybe, with Enkidu among them. It was a perfectly choreographed dance that was not a dance, they conjured up, between them, the grass of the plains, the wind when it shifted, a sense of the herd and the moment, unspelled, of life. An aliveness entered that was not calculated or reserved, that was absolute land and animal, breath and grass and being. This, it was made clear, this was what was stolen from Enkidu when they tamed him, when they civilized him. This wild being-alive-right-now was lost when he became a man like other men, like Gilgamesh; concerned with the past and the future and so given already to Ereshkigal's halls.

Ereshkigal. I remember her. The scene was dark with loud, discordant music and what looked like buckets of red paint thrown about. Ereshkigal lay, high up against the back wall on a series of ledges, on her back, her naked legs splayed open up the wall with her head dangling back off the ledge, screaming. She shone in the dull light with red, I think parts of her body may have been wrapped in plastic wrap, with the wet paint spilled over it. I remember being faintly surprised she was played by a young, slender white woman. She screamed and screamed, not nicely or in an ordered way, with breath and pause between screams; she screamed as if she was giving birth to the world and each piece of it had to be borne through her with all that entailed, all of the bloody dragging and tearing – all of the surrender – out to life and therefore also the turmoil and pain of death. It was unrelenting. I can't recall if anything else at all happened in that scene. I have a vague idea that dark minions scuttled about performing services; but I recall her in the absolute grip of composite creation, the sound we were born from. She was terrifying.

Not the elegant birthing of stars, although perhaps that also, but the bloody, earthy birth of this planet through endless volcanic eras and seismic shifting, plates of continents colliding , electrical storms bathing the surface of the earth searing and igniting, the upthrust of seabed and the collapse of mountain ranges, glaciers and geysers and tsunamis, earthquakes and the forces needed to turn coal to diamond, the ages to petrify rock and fossilize tiny sea beings, to wear boulders to sand, receive the impact of meteorites and the passing dissemination of comets, to heat and ice over, to melt to birth life itself out of this cauldron. Life. Imagine all the lives. Of the algae, of the single-celled. Of bacteria, slime molds, viruses, mosses and insects, seaweed and coral and crustaceans and shellfish and fish. Of plants. Of fungi and bracken, of herb and fruit-growing and flowering, of conifer and nut-bearing, of grass. Of bird. Of animal, lizard, mouse, antelope, tiger, kangaroo, bat, dolphin. Of each human. Imagine giving birth to all that. That's what Ereshkigal conjured for me.

Then the gods. They are given birth to as well, in the stories, from older gods, older ideas, older cultures. Back and back, back to the beginning times and Ereshkigal seemed to me to be birthing that, the beginning. That was why it was so unending, why it went on forever although, as humans, we could only glimpse a little piece of that, maybe the sound of our own mothers giving birth to us or maybe a background music that sounded through our days and nights, birth to death until finally it swallowed us again. No wonder Inanna was overwhelmed. No wonder she was struck dead, with horror or magnificence, to be put on a meat hook until she absorbed the sound of that, seasoned by it, marinated in it. Until she was able to take a piece of it back with her, into the upper, daylight realms and wreak destruction with it there.

The third image is of Gilgamesh with the flower of immortality. He was played by a tall, angular black man. He ran the endless distances required of this role, round and round in big loops on the stage for ten minutes at a time, effortlessly. The flower was pushed on stage. It was encased in a tall box of glass or maybe clear Perspex, six feet high and filled with water. I think they filled it on stage, with a hose. The flower of immortality was down the bottom, something like a water lily. Gilgamesh heaved himself up the side of the box and dropped down into it, his clothes floated up around him as he fought the water to get low enough to pick the flower. It was elegant, timeless, suspended slow motion watching him turn head down and reaching out, reaching for perfection, for godhood, for the dream of never having to die.

Death. I have been in service to it all my life, we all have. My grandmother's funeral, she died in her nineties. We went into the viewing room, before, she lay there quiet, composed. Damon wanted her to be holding flowers so we took a stem of gladioli, from a bouquet someone had sent and he and I arranged her cold stiff hands around it. He was six years old. We did everything, my mother, myself and Damon; made speeches and asked up other speakers. I taught and led the song, Damon lit the candles with tapers and recited poetry. My grandmother let us do it all, in a way she never would have, alive.

The day of my mother's funeral Damon, now twenty-two and I went to the viewing I had insisted on. Now it was my mother who lay in the coffin. She looked small, plain. Living she had a very animated face, now stilled. We stood beside her and recited *The Charge of the Star Goddess*, our voices slipping and word for word catching, eyes gazing at each other, at my mother, hands clinging together, the living. We spoke it to give her into the hands of the goddess, before the ceremony which was non-religious, or not so obviously pagan as to have room for us chanting the words of the goddess, *the dust of whose feet are the hosts of heaven.* And *for behold, I have been with you since the beginning and I am that which is attained at the end of desire.*

Into that coffin, at the end of desire, I had given a red blanket as padding, that was on my brother's bed for many years when he was small. Over that lay a Tibetan blanket, new, in wide stripes of red, dark pink, white that I bought for her to lie on. Also I put in a crocheted lap rug, made by my grandmother, her mother. Her favorite red jumper, in case she got cold. A book I'd read on the plane that – had she lived – she might have read (could it be she'll never read another book again? Who is this woman?) Another book, she was reading, the new Tim Winton only part-way through; her glasses and a small book called *Can't You Sleep, Little Bear?* that I read to my own son, reassuringly, when he was young. I tucked in a copy of the *Dark Goddess*, my book that I don't think she ever read while she was alive. Damon said *that will be useful.*

I made sure she had her watch on, which she always wore; her wedding ring I slipped easily onto the smallest finger of her left hand. A silver bracelet for the other wrist, one that matched the one she gave me. She wore her favorite shirt, black with gold like Cleopatra. She had worn it only days earlier at a party held for her retirement from an organization she was dedicated to for many years. Around her throat and to disguise the marks of autopsy, a linen hand-woven shawl, beautiful, that I gave her last birthday, never worn; I had to take the tag off. Also a necklace with miniature Iceland poppies frozen into time that I had given her. Hope. Hope that she might ever be the mother that I wanted, or I the daughter she might have preferred; I left that in the coffin too.

I wanted to put in the china wombat she had loved, a plaster pig my brother made, I wanted to put in her favorite coffee cup, photographs of her grandchildren; I especially wanted to put those in. Instead I found a soft toy, new never-loved, to journey with her, a psychopomp. Eeyore, from Winnie-the-Pooh, a favorite with us all. Oh when will we stop this endless birthing, the endless bloody tides of it, tides of us, forcing through into – I could have said death instead of life but oh I see they are the same and trade only with each other. I wanted to put coins in. Gold coins. And music. Pens and paper, packets of seeds. I put dark chocolate in, half a block – I ate the other half – maybe I even learnt, somewhere along the way of putting things in my mother's coffin, maybe this is the way to learn to place a piece of me in there, a thread of our connection which was at least this, the red thread of women through the generations, to last us through the ages of forever.

Ereshkigal. Giving birth, screaming as it tears you into pieces; I have done that as I brought a child into the world and I have done that as I let go of a relationship with a man I loved and I have done that to mourn a friend who died. Haven't we all screamed, aloud or inside at the grief and horror in the world, mothers holding their starving babies, fields of young men sacrificed to wars, the ice sheets melting, the Great Barrier Reef dying, the rainforests cleared. Haven't we all felt that? Haven't we had those long silent descents, where voice and motivation are lost to us relentlessly until we are just a shadow, a skeleton moving forward not with any hope of rescue or light but just, if we're lucky, because a small voice inside us whispers *keep moving*. People around us, in the upper world, smiled and talked as if nothing was wrong, they did not even notice we weren't really there. We were lost.

There are years that pass in a fog, that seem unreal even at the time, let alone later if we are lucky enough to have a later, looking back in wonder, awe; how did I survive? How did I get through that, how was I not lost forever? The daze of being responsible for small children, the blur of illness, depression, abuse, neglect, of the wrong job or the wrong family or the wrong choices. Drugs, alcohol, a bad relationship, poverty, mental anguish, grief, injury, chronic pain – the list goes on. The list is long enough that it would be a miracle, unlikely and obviously not even the design, were anyone to escape it. No, we are designed to knock up into it, crash, to collide into that list at some point or many points and go down.

I have dedicated myself to Ereshkigal. She feels chthonic, as old as earth and I don't mean the green-and-pleasant part, but the rocks grinding and churning under the surface, the lava seething and erupting, mountains eroded and sea-beds thrust up into the air and light. Like so many dark goddesses, it isn't really that I chose her but she chose me. She was a seed inside me, nurtured by fear and pain and however hard you turn away, you can't turn away from the darkness inside. She was the raw edge of my emotion, she was what lay underneath the raft I clung to, she gave birth to me and she claimed me as hers long before I wanted to acknowledge her as mine.

I walked towards her once, in ritual, down a long avenue of darkened gates where everything was stripped away from me and I paid no attention to that because I was determined to get there, to confront her. So I was unprepared for the impact of that meeting because I hadn't paid attention to the signs, all along the way; if you walk this path you will lose everything.

Everything. I was careless. I looked at the piece of the script I was interested in, the meeting with Ereshkigal and neglected to note that it actually results in death. Not a timely death, after a full life and involved conversations and cups of tea with one's long-lost sister; actual, immediate, bloody death, unconsenting and abrupt. Without the conversation.

As I approached her in the barely lit dark, naked by then, I was filled with questions and demands, the concerns of the living and she raised her hand calmly, she had done it a thousand thousand times before and she turned her head deliberately, smoothly, in one motion and she opened her mouth and she screamed, short and sharp directly through me and I dropped to the ground, skewered by her. That was my meeting with Ereshkigal. They had to drag me out, across the wooden floor to the doorway of night because I was dead, now. I understood. Well, I understood nothing except this is death, this is how it happens. I still did not understand Ereshkigal, or the purposes of it all or why the living should go through this. But I was changed.

Oh, then to give birth to that part of me, hidden in darkness. To nurture myself through the pains of birth, the stretching and contractions; why on earth are they called contractions when they're expansions? Making room for something to come out, for life to be born into the world. That requires a lot of room, takes a lot of those expansions, to put something new into the world. One has to expand not just one's body, the womb, cervix, vagina – but surely the space in existence, to carve it out and push this new being into a world already full to bursting with events and beings. The space was full, beforehand and now it must be even fuller to accommodate this new one; perhaps this explains the expansion of the universe. I like to think of that, of Ereshkigal down there pushing out the outer limits of unfolding space, birthing something into the nothingness.

That was the first piece of her, dying in ritual by her eye, her word, down there in the Underworld. Dying to be born, changed, reworked into a priestess of Inanna-Ereshkigal; their names married together to be not just one thing but a revealed secret, they are part of each other and even though Inanna is who you notice first, she is the glory and brightness, hers is the name in lights and carved in poetry on the temple walls and sung in the songs on celebration days, hers is the crown and the royal robe and the lapis measuring rod and line and all the rest of it, Ereshkigal is always waiting there at the end of every encounter, she is the end of every sentence, implacable and final. She is the one behind it all, the mastermind, the great mother, that impulse towards life that keeps enfolding and unfolding our planet. Another version of her is Lilith, birthing thousands of demons endlessly; surely a vision of the catapulting assault of life spawning unconsidered and uncontrolled into a pristine world.

Even when we make it pretty and beneficent, the great mother kindly birthing us one after another, she who always cares and always notices and ever stretches out a hand or thought to comfort us, even then. Have you seen a woman giving birth? Have you heard her? Held her hand during a contraction or watched a baby emerge from her body? We might imagine animals are born more gently, or plants, or insects but think of those that eat their own off-spring, or insects torn open by the birth process or the ripping of a seed by pure life expanding within it, the forcing upwards and downwards of stem and root, violence at a cellular level. There's nothing gentle about birth.

I have met Ereshkigal. She rang me up the other night, in a dream. She said I should come and visit her. Really I thought I'd never left but perhaps I've been in the outer chambers for a while, making myself comfortable. I met her in Glastonbury one time, at the Chalice Well, when I was weary and terrified, not of doing the work but of the cost it exacted. Standing on the wrought-iron grid over the top of the well, feeling its dark space echo beneath me I said to her *I want to do this work and I will dedicate myself to it but you cannot take everything from me, each time I do it. Or rather, although you can take everything from me, every time I do it, I choose not to have that happen.* Why would she listen to me, even if I am her priestess? Standing balanced there I drew upon power, not my power but hers, I drew it up from the ground, the water and I felt it fountain through me from the well, straight up from the labyrinthine tunnels under the hills, a dark force and yet water and earth, life-giving water, the earth we are all made of and return to and that was the strength with which I resisted destruction; not final or absolute destruction just the casual everyday destruction that beset me every time I invoked her.

I have been in service to death my whole life; we all have. Each heart-beat beats back the dark, each one counts forward to death, to silence. I am drawn to the cracks, the unhinged edges of creation and possibility, to imagination, mysteries and initiation. I am drawn to the unspoken and not just to observe but to try to speak it, though the words break my voice and its expression is in a language we do not know. When I was eight years old my best friend Kerin died. She was playing outside her house with her brothers and sisters, on a bike on the pavement at the end of a quiet road. A car, too fast, in the wrong place, badly driven, out of control killed her. She was dead. I had loved her because she was the sunniest, happiest and gentlest child I had ever met. She was generous and playful and affectionate, things I desperately needed. New to our school that year, her optimism and warmth thawed my estrangement from my own life, I was entranced by her.

Through years I waited for her death to make sense. It never did. Now I am spending years waiting for the deaths of my mother and Trinda to make sense. I am trying to grow larger, expand, to hold the place for them, for their lives and deaths; giving birth to them, in a way, as I once did for Damon, forcing the world outwards to be big enough to hold them. Screaming with pain as I do so, it isn't easy or soft this expansion, this birthing of the impossible, this making myself broad enough to encompass the dead, this bringing them to life through my own life. Mourning and giving birth, all mixed together. Ereshkigal holds the key to those mysteries. The Dark Goddess always rules birth as well as death.

My relationship with her is just beginning. Maybe I hear her sometimes, moaning and grieving as she struggles to give birth to me, one of her priestesses out here in the world; she rings me up occasionally to tell me I'm overdue for a visit, the next piece of training awaits me. It's not about doing it with grace, nobody says she looks beautiful in sweat and tears but it's about doing it and it is about compassion, the way we receive that pain and acknowledge those births, or deaths; they get muddled down there and are so much the same thing, hard to tell the difference.

Have you stood by and watched, held space for a friend or loved one suffering and not moved to intervene? Perhaps you have been by someone as their life ended; while they struggled to free themselves from a bad relationship, an addiction or to reach the truth of a desperately buried secret? Or you've watched a child, before your eyes, grow into an understanding of how the world is that you would not, even if you could, take from them, as they will need that knowledge to grow into the kind of person you hope they will become. Perhaps you've suffered with them, felt the pangs of childbirth though it wasn't you who was in labor or wept though it wasn't your relationship being torn away. This is the compassion of the Dark Goddess, these are the birthing pains of Ereshkigal and they are real. They don't feel kind; being born isn't kind, its intent is not kind, nor its manner nor much of what will come into that life. It's not kind, but it is great. Enormous, ever-lasting, compassion swells the heart and expands it, reaches out to every suffering being, opens, holds all in a tangible atmosphere of what I want to call love.

Love as it means: that which is life-affirming. Not just being alive, but becoming alive, becoming more and more alive, being born into life. That's what all the screaming's about, down there in the Underworld, being torn apart in order to make more room in the self, in the universe. Being ripped open by the need to be alive. When the last words that someone who's dying speaks to you are *I love you* aren't they offering you their life-blood? A piece of themselves, the last piece they have to give and they give everything, unstinting – not because it will make it easier for you, for me, but because it is the truest, deepest, the strongest thing they can offer. That's what Trinda said to me, the last thing. It is not kindness that gives birth to that baby, brings death, forces through change or growth, but the heartbeat of necessity. Because it is so necessary it is clean, stripped of artifice and I can call it compassion. To hold space for what must be and for the depths and force of life, becoming.

I have been in service to death my whole life, we all are. I am dedicated to Ereshkigal as she remakes the world through each one of us, her screams lingering in our ears as we struggle to stay present, to listen, to echo back our own pain and still, in the face of that, to give birth again and again and to watch others do it, also and still be there, weeping and panting maybe, keening and tearing our hair, down on our knees with the weight and shock of it but eyes open, heart present, breaking. Breaking open like seed pods, like a cervix, like the crust of earth under the force of lava, like heavy clouds into rain.

Ereshkigal, having seen you I can't turn back. I am yours from the same necessity that you exist, in service to this life-cycle, this planet, these birthing, grieving selves of us, these singing panting breathing loving selves who are the pattern life after life, generations on and holding sacred the turn of the seasons, the times of birth and dying, the seeds splitting open, holding sacred women laboring and those who wash the dead and speak with them and holding sacred each transition, birthed in tears and anguish and bringing forth a finer version of that being and holding sacred the birds that flash across my window, red underbelly and blue wings, who nest and raise miniatures of themselves and die and are lost without counting and the trees and rivers and the ferment in the earth, deep down and all that turns and changes, here and out into the stars and even then, in the quiet darkness off the edges which holds the universe expanding.

Ritual – Commit to a Goddess for a Year

Committing to a deity for a year is a powerful way to deepen your understanding and relationship with them. This year may be preparatory to a dedication, you might view it as just this single year or it might be exploratory – you're not sure where it will take you. Committing to anything for a whole year takes us through the cycle of the seasons – we get to explore this through winter, spring, summer and autumn as well as through a year's worth of events, changes and challenges in our lives. We might pair this commitment with a particular branch of study; for example we may commit to Aphrodite while we focus on our sexuality, or to Odin when we intend to study runes.

Usually one would only undertake a commitment for a year if one already felt a great deal of affinity with – and interest in – that deity; other methods, such as walking with or researching, are more appropriate for a goddess we feel curious about or are just beginning to know. But sometimes this is not how it works. A deity can appear in our life and the gravity and power of their presence, how it resonates with everything we have previously done, all that we are seeking and have been unable to find, is so strong and compelling that a commitment of this level may be the only thing we feel will meet it and hold us in it.

I believe a commitment of this kind is binding. That is, if you change your mind during the year it does not undo the commitment. There may be ways to magically extract yourself from this contract, possibly with some sort of cost. Ideally it is best not to have to do this, but instead to be prepared for the consequences of making this commitment. A commitment of this type is going to focus our own attention on this relationship, allow it a priority and offer a willingness towards the remaking of ourselves that always underlies working directly with the divine. However you perceive deity to exist – as discrete, individual beings, as particular shades or facets of a larger force, as projections of the collective unconscious or some other way – it is likely you will feel some return focus from that deity when you undertake any level of commitment ceremony with them. This may not occur during the actual ritual, or it may be subtle – or plainly unmissable – but our belief in this part of the process is an essential ingredient in commitment. It may work purely through our own focus, honing ourselves more and more finely or precisely towards that goddess or it may be returned in some way.

Any commitment ceremony is going to be unique to you and the goddess you have chosen. Creating and undertaking this ritual is a key part – the cornerstone, the opening notes, the first chapter – in your year's commitment.

These are some considerations as you go about the process of designing and performing your ritual of commitment:

- Place. Where will you do this ceremony? Perhaps there is somewhere you associate with this goddess: a temple space, your own altar at home, a forest, beach or park. It may be a place you often go, or rarely; it may be a place you are visiting for the first time. Consider the practical aspects of this place: how you will get there, what you will need to have with you. Is it private and secure enough for what you plan?
- Time. What time of day or night will the ritual take place? You might also like to consider what time of year it will be and what part of the moon cycle, or your own menstrual cycle, it will take place in. Some of these things are easier to arrange than others and usually the time is a blend of arranged and incidental times. I may plan for a full moon ceremony at dusk, when it happens to be spring; or I may choose to do the ceremony at the solstice and the solstice

falls on a gibbous moon. Your goddess may be associated with a season, moon phase or time of day and you might arrange your timing to complement this. Also consider how long your ceremony will last, are you thinking of a three-day vision quest or a ritual that lasts an hour or two?

- What to bring with you. Do you imagine a hundred candles set in a ring inside your temple? Are you planning to camp out? Do you want to have items representing the elements with you, a drum or chimes, Tarot cards, your journal, altar items? Will you need water, food, shelter of some kind?

- Offerings. Most often in a dedication ceremony or any kind of direct communication with a deity we bring an offering. An offering is different than just an item to have on your altar or in your ritual; it is something we give to the goddess – we don't take it back. Sometimes offerings are burnt, buried, hung in trees, sprinkled on the ground or simply left behind when we pack up the rest of our ritual and conclude.

- Several practical points are essential. Never leave a room or other space with an untended, lit flame. Be aware of the environmental impact of what you are planning to leave behind. Never leave non-biodegradable items behind in a natural place and carefully consider the impact of leaving seeds or food or other natural items behind. Leaving a shell on a beach is probably okay, leaving non-native seeds in natural bush is not okay. It may be that the offerings you bring to the ceremony have to be taken away with you, then to be placed on your altar or disposed of in a more appropriate place or way.

- Offerings are not always physical items. Your offering may be an amount of time you offer in service, for example, or an undertaking to perform certain rituals or activities or an amount of money you are donating to a project or cause. With offerings the emphasis is not so much on what we feel like giving as from the other side, what would this deity appreciate and find meaningful?

- Form of ceremony. Perhaps you will follow a classic form of ceremony, particular to the deity you are dedicating to or the tradition they're from, whether Norse, Indian or Roman. Perhaps your ceremony will be quite structured, written out beforehand and performed in a particular order. Or it may be creative, spontaneous and individual; you turn up prepared but open and see where the energies and inspiration take you. Consider what form or forms of ceremony feel most appropriate for your dedication to this particular deity.

- The nature of the commitment. Perhaps your promise will simply be that of dedication for a year, or a year and a day. But perhaps your dedication has a particular focus. For example the goddess Brigid is considered the goddess of healing, smithcraft and poetry. If you are choosing Brigid because of your wish to develop your healing skills, this might be a part of your dedication or promise to her and to yourself.

Ritual – Dedication to a Goddess

If you have decided to dedicate yourself to a goddess this section contains some ideas for how you might do that. Making a formal dedication to a deity is a serious and potentially life-changing decision and is to be taken very seriously. One can work with, love, adore and have a close relationship with a goddess without dedicating oneself to them. As an analogy think of all the people you know and love and ask yourself how many of them you would choose to marry? Dedicating oneself is not necessarily better, or of a higher order, than not dedicating oneself and it is for each of us to work out what we need and wish to do. Some of us might never dedicate ourselves to a deity, others are drawn to dedication, at particular times and in particular ways, with particular deities.

Usually you will have gone through a process, developing a relationship with a deity long before you decide or are called to dedication. Sometimes we may feel already dedicated, without a formal ceremony or perhaps even any conscious act on our part; in that case a ritual marks our willingness in this, our active choice to be in that type of relationship with the goddess. What type of relationship is dedication? It may vary from person to person and goddess to goddess but certainly that is something we should investigate beforehand, perhaps meditating on what it means to us as well as seeking answers about what it may mean in regards to this particular deity. If we are choosing to do this within any sort of social context – a coven, tradition or group – it is important to also understand what dedication means within that setting.

The nature of dedication implies a very special, primary relationship that you will be entering into, or acknowledging, with that deity. It may not be an exclusive relationship – you can dedicate to more than one deity – but it will be a very significant one. As mentioned earlier, usually a dedication is to one deity but it may be to a pantheon – for example, Norse or Greek – or to a pair or trio of linked deities – for example Maiden, Mother, Crone or Isis and Osiris. Sometimes a dedication does not happen individually, but as a group. In that case devote as much time as necessary to discussing where the group's understandings meet and are the same and the points where individuals have different wishes, needs or types of dedication.

Here are some points to consider, prior to dedication:

- What does dedication mean to you? Spend some time, perhaps a full moon cycle (or longer) considering this. You might talk with friends, meditate, attend or create rituals around this goddess and read about the experience of others. Maybe you will also paint or draw, write poetry, undertake vision quests or other forms of exploration.

- What form are you planning for this dedication to take, after the ritual? Are you intending to hold public rituals, to work in a particular field that falls within the domain of this goddess, to devote private prayer or ritual to them, to call yourself her priestess?

- As well as bringing gifts for the goddess you are dedicating to, people often wish to give themselves some gift or visible mark of commitment. This might take the form of a piece of jewelry, a ritual object such as a chalice or athame, a tattoo, a statuette or painting of that goddess or a tree that is planted in her name.

- In what form do you desire the goddess to be present during your ritual? Are you going to create an altar for her? Invoke her? Aspect? Presence? Will you leave it up to her, what form or level of presence she comes through in?

- Do other people play a role in your ceremony? Perhaps you have a coven, a high priestess, or best friend or perhaps you are making your dedication alongside someone else. Perhaps you would simply like a witness, or want a party afterwards, or to have your dedication be a part of another ritual, for example a moon ceremony or a ritual for one of the festivals of the Wheel of the Year.

- Consider the vow or promise you are making to the goddess, in your ceremony. Like a wedding vow I believe these are best written individually – or perhaps you won't write yours at all, it will be spoken spontaneously within ritual, or sung, or danced. What exactly are you promising? What does it mean to you, to undertake this dedication? Is there something you are asking for in return and if so, is your promise conditional upon receiving that? Perhaps you are offering to be of service, to be the hands and eyes and body of the goddess upon the earth and seeking only guidance or a sense of her presence.

- When you are ready to craft a ceremony, read through all the points of the previous exercise, *Commit to a Goddess for a Year*. Consider these elements of your Dedication Ritual: Place, Time, What to bring, Offerings, Form of ceremony, Nature of the commitment. Even if you have previously committed to this same deity for a year, the elements of this ritual may be different, because your knowledge of both yourself and the goddess has developed, your circumstances have changed or because of the different nature of the ceremony.

- However much planning we put into a ritual, the real ritual is the one that happens. It may be that everything will go perfectly to plan and be exactly as you imagined it. Or not. Accepting the way a ritual turns out – who comes, what the weather is, what words come out of our mouth, how the goddess manifests herself – is part of our journey with the ritual and we can choose to experience it, however it is, as the beginning of our dedication to this goddess.

Presencing the Goddess

One way to become familiar with a goddess or god and bring them into ritual or our lives more vividly than walking with them, or purely reading or researching, is what I am going to call *presencing*. Presencing is inviting the deity to be present in our lives. It is similar to invocation, in that we call them in and then different, in that we invite them to stay around. This relationship is assumed to be – and is usually experienced as – an interactive one. We make space in our lives for them, including time to just be together as well as creating actual events, rituals or ceremonies where they – or the relationship between them and us – is the focus. This is like inviting a new friend into our lives, with similarly unpredictable results. We may meet someone immensely interesting, we may find a life-long friend or we may discover a shared interest that leads to shared activities.

A group of people, or one individual from the group, or one person on their own can perform this act of presencing, usually for a specified time period, such as the length of one ritual, a month or a year. Presencing does not require any previous relationship with the deity, although some knowledge and thought preceding it will serve best. Presencing is usually quite particular – we are presencing Charon, out of Greek myth who ferries dead souls across the river to the land of the dead, or the Fairie Queen from Tam Lin's story. It is a process of fine attuning, we know exactly who we want to talk to. Because it is a relatively subtle thing it tends to fade if we don't continue to bring our conscious attention to it.

Presencing certainly can be done purely with intention on energetic or etheric levels, but I prefer to work with altars, with actual objects and with prose. Others choose painting, costume, dance or music. In creating these pieces that are either offered to the deity or created as an expression of their attributes the emphasis is on reflecting the deity in the physical realm. Our relationship to them and their story, and our developing self-knowledge – including layered and revealed knowledge about the connection between ourselves and the deity – occurs through this process, it is not the focus of the process. Thus when I am making a necklace for Freyja I am not thinking about what type of necklace I might like to own or wear, I am thinking about Freyja and the attributes of her necklace. Later I may discover what that means to me and what the connections are between us, through the necklace.

If we are going to presence a myth, for example in a ritual, we may have four different deities from the myth presenced by four different people. Presencing a goddess or other being when we are in a ritual can lend a depth to what we are doing, whether that is leading a trance, playing a part in a sacred drama or bearing witness. Presencing is always context-appropriate – we would be extremely unlikely to presence a Celtic or Tibetan deity during a ritual involving a Greek myth, for instance. We presence a deity to lend a depth and flavor to a ritual that extends from our actual knowledge into a feeling-basis. A little like aspecting, we want to share our awareness with the awareness of the one being presenced; unlike aspecting, our actions and words are not guided by that deity, rather we are simply aware of their presence, within a type of energetic field where we are aware of a response or knowledge not directly our own.

Like other ways of interacting with deity, presencing is ideal when done consciously and deliberately. It can also happen in, for example, sacred drama, dance, prayer or invocation when the power of our own attention and calling is great enough, so that afterwards, or even at the time, we realize we moved into a level of awareness that was more than our own. Presencing is relatively informal and not requiring any special preparation yet for me often results in deep and abiding understandings that shift my relationship to the being and can reveal layers of the story I never previously noticed or considered. It helps create the depth and complexity I prefer to work with, in ritual, where the whole story is cast not simply from a single point of view but from multiple viewpoints.

Once I made a mask for Enkidu, from the Gilgamesh story. He has a rough deal. Created by the gods for their own purposes and cast out among the wild beasts of the plain, he does not even know he is a man. Civilized by a sacred prostitute and brought into awareness of his human condition, he is befriended after a three-day fight with his exact equal, Gilgamesh. He then travels with Gilgamesh performing near-impossible deeds of strength and daring, even when they go against his own nature, such as destroying the forests of Lebanon and their ancient protector. He dies in Gilgamesh's battle against the Bull of Heaven. His whole life, from birth to death, is run by Gilgamesh's story.

I remember what came through my hands; part wild cattle and part plains, camouflaged with stalks of grass resembling a grain field on one side. It was three-dimensional and sat over the top of the head, so the human wearing it was not so much disguised as transfigured. Making and wearing it I learned about Enkidu's wildness, the place where humans emerge from nature not as separate from it but in their deep belonging. It showed me how Enkidu offers Gilgamesh a different, older way to be a king and how Enkidu's death spells an end to that possibility. Wearing that mask in ritual he came to me so gently, so tenderly that I knew his life was a gift and not a burden. The joy of wind and grass on the plains. The infinite pain of love, then the bond of brotherhood. The journey of testing one's strength and discovering morals, values, the offering of one's life and strength upon a battlefield, in service of one's friend. The peace of death.

At the end of this section are several exercises that can assist with and help to focus presencing a deity.

Nephthys

CloudCatcher Reclaiming WitchCamp is birthed like an egg on the ocean of primordial waters. An idea so clear to us, the ones creating it, yet so uncertain to everyone around us. In this tremulous moment we thought and decided to act as if it might be a once-only camp, the first and the last because although we knew we could do it once, it would have to be passed over to community if it were continue. The camp would need participants to love it enough to pay to attend and to bring their friends, as well as organizers to step up and do the work involved in putting it on and nurturing it, year to year.

We chose a story of birth and solidarity that we felt linked us not just into the mythos, but also into the sisterhood of all other Reclaiming WitchCamps, a story that said every child of an idea is different – and equal – and that the whole cannot function without all the parts. Four parts to our story, four children, four gods. Egypt. The great Goddess of Night, of sky, of the Milky Way stretching over us and giving birth, in one birthing, to four beings. Osiris. Set. Isis. Nephthys. Like four sides of a pyramid, holding to the earth and pointing to the sky, four directions anchoring our camp, four pieces of the puzzle of the gods, four different aspects of divinity. Closer than brother and sister, brother and brother, sister and sister – though they are all that, too – closer than lovers, than husband and wife – though they are also that – close as twins, but there are four; a quartet, each bound together from the very first moments of their existence, of the idea of them – and yet, separate.

Osiris. He of the Nile. The river that sustains all life, whose floods yearly bring the rich fertile soil to the fields, feeding, watering the crops. The river-road that leads not just from kingdom to kingdom through the upper, middle and lower realms of Egypt, but even into the Underworld. Bringing life this river also carries death, by its absence in the years it doesn't flood and also as the symbol of the journey of death. The fish, the crocodiles, hippopotamuses – they live in this water of life. Civilization cannot exist without it; cities cannot hold without farmers, storehouses, green and grain and fruit. Everything comes back to this, this rain that runs horizontally along the land instead of falling from the skies; the tears, the blood, the sweat of Egypt. Life is the river.

Isis. She is the throne of the realm known as Egypt. She is its cities and temples, she is the laws and the learning. She it is who teaches all there is to know; how to spin and weave flax, how to write and paint the sacred stories and how to record the crops, the rains, the stored grain. She brings regency, the one who sits with her in the throne is lord of the land, is king, is pharaoh. She is the power on the land, her thoughts and will direct the law. She is order, the way things will be carried out, she is justice. Righteousness, one could say, the right and ordered ways that create a society rich not just in resources, but also in knowledge and power. She holds the east and the sun is born each day within her auspices.

Set. He who belongs to the deserts. The wild, the cannot-be-tamed. That which lives outside the cities, beyond the neat farms and ordered life. The nomadic desert tribes that follow only their own laws. The jackals, snakes, the scorpions. A lineage of desert gods – harsh, patriarchal, absolute and Set claiming his place in that lineage. Laughing in bitterness and strength at the soft cities, the luxury of rivers and fields, how those who live that life grow blind to necessity and miss the subtleties that those who live with nearly nothing, in harsher worlds, hold as close as breath. The desert at night, an immensity of sky. By day, that blaze of heat and the careful, measured cost of survival.

Lastly, always last in their list of names, Nephthys. She of the edges, of the in-between. Of the marshes, the reed-beds, the outlying parts of land that drift to desert. The one who isn't so loud to proclaim anything, own anything, set up boundaries and rules and kingdoms. Her realm shifts all the time, in the winds carrying sand in from the deserts to cover what were once fields, or in the river flooding higher, or lower than previously. Nephthys is not of absolutes but of the deep tiding of patterns, she is always becoming. Part hidden, part revealed, with different parts hidden and revealed at different times she is taken for granted, half ignored but she cannot be ignored, she is crucial; she links everything to everything else.

This story, we thought, would posit that we were a sister, brother, a lover, wife and husband to every other WitchCamp and that every person who came to the camp was an equal, different part of it and our story could not exist without each one of us. So we created a magical gate and went back to Egypt, to invite that story through to cast and hold the container and when we did that we felt the winds blow through. Egypt, so strong in the imagining of Western civilization and occult magic, both; Egypt with its magic and its laws and the great north-south of the Nile and the even greater east-west of sun across the sky, Egyptian myth and magic is the cross at the center of the circle.

Before camp starts we make masks for the deities. There are four of them and three mask-makers. We hold hands, sitting cross-legged around a low table and trance. *How would you like to be portrayed? We ask Set, Osiris, Isis, Nephthys; how will you come through?* We see desert sand and dry grass for Set, the green and brown of growth renewed for Osiris, we get gold inscrutability for Isis and for Nephthys, cool blue and the mystery. We decided to put the masks on sticks, rather than have eye-holes cut for humans to look through, so they can stay themselves and swoop far above human height, remaining partially separate from whoever holds them.

It falls to me to make the Nephthys mask, which I do with great awe and hesitation. Working on her mask, as I draw and cut its shape, choose the colors, I feel her whispering to me, not in words exactly; spells perhaps, shimmering pieces of the in-between realms half felt, half heard. I draw wide eyes white and black on silver, lined with sky blue, with feathers and ribbons trailing down the stick. We make the Isis mask last and match it to Nephthys, in the eyes and the non-human shape of the mask. This was the beginning of my presencing with Nephthys, though I had a history with her, with them all.

Years earlier at an Australian Pagan Summer Gathering run by the Church of All Worlds I had offered a workshop on the myth of these four siblings. About twenty people turned up, including Trinda and a couple who'd just been hand-fasted and still had their right hands bound together. I was fascinated by myths and how they seemed to come alive, once you stepped into them, an opposite to Trinda's more scholarly research. If it's true that these myths are archetypes and we all live with them in our heads all the time, what happens when we bring them into the foreground and – instead of reading them or thinking about them or even rewriting them – we presence them, lending our bodies and voices to discover what comes through?

We were sitting outside, cross-legged on the ground or yoga mats, with a few people in camping chairs. It was a summer afternoon with a breeze and sporadic shade from the gum trees scattered across the site. We discussed the story first, what we remembered, what we thought of it and how and where it resonated with our lives. Siblings, marriage, love, jealousy, betrayal, death, grief and childbirth – there's a lot to choose from and we all had pieces we identified with. The stories of these gods, like those of the Greek gods, echo human concerns and human relationships, even if on a more dramatic scale than in most lives.

I divided the circle into quarters and assigned one of the gods and a quarter of the people to each section. Isis in the east and her sister, Nephthys, across from her in the west; Osiris in the south, our direction in the southern hemisphere for the Underworld and his brother Set across from him, in the north; the quadrant of our summer sun, a blazing heat whose intensity is often unwelcome. In these small groups we travelled further into the myth, examining each character in more depth. I stayed close to the Set quarter, the character I thought most interesting. Who was he, really? Why did he perform such vicious actions, what was going on there?

The group spoke about how wronged he felt, to be neglected in favor of Osiris. Stories of older brothers, more successful friends, rivals in love or work were told. How the most galling thing can be that they don't even notice your striving for attention and offers of friendship and loyalty, how in their generous, out-going even-handedness they never see those desperate to please them, to follow in their footsteps, to be worthy of attention. In Egypt everyone focuses on the Nile, the delta, the civilization of the cities, the wonders of the pyramids and art; they turn their backs on the desert they come from, ignore the wisdom of the sands, their eternity and mystery and obsess instead about flax and grain, flooding and fish. None of that matters in the desert. Hidden waters, shifting sand and following roads laid down in the patterns of the stars are the desert way, listening to the wind, observing the ancient customs and laws within tribes and between tribes.

Those who belong there are relegated to savages, outlaws, the estranged past of this civilized culture that lives for building, for farming, for the priests and pharaohs. They forget where they came from and where, endlessly, everything returns; the harsher laws of minimalist survival, the careful guarding of water, the truce of the oasis. The desert. Sharp-edged and raw-toothed, the measured jars of water, the glistening weight of clusters of dates. In forgetting their past, separating themselves from it with courtyards and temples made of blocks with measured, mathematical perfection and ranks of scribes they forget, also, the

161

old gods, the ones who travelled with them through generations. The new gods can display, order and lecture all they want, from the sideline there are guarded eyes watching every move and awaiting their moment. Set emerges from that background.

The four groups came together, standing in small, tight clumps at the center of the circle and sang to each other. Not in words, but in tone. Each group sang by itself and so we heard Isis in her beauty and power, Osiris' love and generosity, the pacing anger of Set and then Nephthys' cool tones, that weave in and out of themselves. We put all four sounds together and as we stood there, singing to each other, odd resonances began to happen. When Osiris and Set sang together there was the wrestling love of brothers as well as betrayal and shock and an inclination, on Osiris' part, to allow this betrayal, to take this path offered him into death and the mysteries and Set abruptly reminded us of Judas, performing an evil task for which he will be hated through the centuries, but which is, as every other piece, a necessary part of the story.

The song of Isis and Osiris was a great drama, love and grief and separation, reunion and dedication; an opera of emotion, almost staged for an audience filling the temple to hear the epic stories of the gods. Isis and Nephthys sang a pattern of light and dark, holding the sun's path at dawn and dusk, together creating life from death; opposite poles keeping each other stable, focused, balanced. Isis and Set's is a song of opposition – she all sovereignly declaration and outright power, his subtlety, yearning and manipulation which she did not even regard, she sang louder, ignoring him. His song offered all, which was not enough for her, an irritation. Their songs never merged.

Nephthys and Set descended, in their song, into the realm of mystery; all who heard it and sang it recognized it as magic, initiation, a bond to do with contracts forged not in words but older than that; essence and opposite and underground. Here might be the threads of a hidden, occult line of priests and priestesses, bound to the mysteries; here might be the gates that guard and hold the entrance to the secret lore, its key granted only to a few. Their loyalty is not of love but of oath, it binds not flesh but spirit.

Finally Nephthys turned to Osiris. Of all couplings in this group the least obvious, the least marked. As their voices flowered together we heard a woman in love, not in Isis' grand way of announcement and ceremony, but from her self, revealing her truth and trust to one – as we listened we discovered – who would not betray her; who had little to spare between his wife, his kingdom, his rival, but what he gives will be pure and in a way, humble; in the song he offered her love not of a king, but of the heart and we felt, those who listened, that we overheard the murmur of lovers granted a few secret hours.

This was so surprising to everyone listening, and yet felt so right that Trinda rushed off to the car where she had with her, unbelievably, a copy of the *Larousse Encyclopedia of Mythology* and she looked it up and discovered, yes, Nephthys and Osiris were lovers. Surely some of us had read this before and ignored it, but none of us remembered it consciously and we spent the rest of our time discussing how it could be that, in just an hour or two, we could enter so deeply into this realm as to be discovering its secrets in what seemed to us a very primitive way. A circle of people on a summer afternoon at the Pagan Gathering, no special knowledge no hours of trance or meditation, just discussing a story together, bringing it through our voices, lending our bodies and we unveiled all this: a love affair, an occult tradition, a rivalry that contained love and acceptance, and dismissal of a lesser being by she who is esteemed so highly.

At CloudCatcher WitchCamp on the second night we hold a ritual for Set's betrayal of Osiris. We build a cardboard sarcophagus and procession with it down the long driveway to the pond in the night, calling upon the waters of the Nile. The action is all

Osiris-Set-Isis; Nephthys is there, of course, in the shadows, at the edges. We decide, in planning, that Nephthys will lead both the procession and the song of mourning and release, as we reach the water. When we get to choosing roles I am assigned Nephthys and immediately the song is taken away from her, along with leading the procession and given to someone else. I don't think I'm that poor a singer but I observe with interest, already borrowing Nephthys' mask; *so not even that will you grant me. Of the edges and banished to the edges, removed from the ceremony of my brother's funeral.*

As the ritual unfolds I dart with my mask about the fringes of the room, my awareness split between my human body and Nephthys. I watch my husband/lover yearning towards my sister Isis, I see her oblivion in it and her adoration of Osiris; both of whom ignore me entirely and though the human part of me expects to feel slighted, the faint wafts of feeling I get from Nephthys are more of an over-arching love, a loyalty to them regardless, *you do not see me but I see you, and that makes my sight of you even more precious, more loved, to be the only one holding it.* The person presencing Set does bow, formally to me as I hover in the corner and I am glad of it, not to be utterly hidden. But I watch his mounting jealousy, ambition, ruthlessness and I know nothing good can come of that.

I am in a different corner when it comes to the funeral. The mask of Osiris is passed hand-to-hand around the room and each person names what it is they are surrendering to death, before the mask is laid in the sarcophagus and the lid closed. I did not take part in it, I will not be party to his death in that way. I follow the procession, at the back and edges though all the important people are up the front, my sister in grand mourning with all her attendants. High above the humans the Nephthys mask flits and weaves, as much aware of the stars, the mist in the night air, the frogs and insects as this earthly drama.

I push through to nearly the front when they launch the canoe holding the sarcophagus onto the water; I stare at the singer of the song. *That was my job.* I would have done it differently and quietly, with more invitation in it and I feel cold and not exactly discarded; I am disregarded. No-one has noticed what it might be to Nephthys, to lose Osiris, or to have my husband turn killer. Her sister has not called for her. Her husband has not begged for refuge with her. *Perhaps it was only Osiris who saw me, and now he is dead. I will have to hold even more to the in-between spaces, between life and death, so I can be near him, so I can still hear him.* My awareness flares high and wide, like the rays of sunset coloring the whole sky and from up there I can embrace him as he embarks into the mysteries of death and the Underworld.

The next day I am somehow holding the Nephthys mask again, though every other one of the four has switched through two or three people by now. Perhaps no-one else wanted her when we handed out the parts, perhaps no-one really saw her but by now my eyes are fierce with her seeing, I have a whole bodily emotional alignment with her. Another woman, holding Isis, and I are standing at the door as people return from a time outside. We are to bless them as they enter and we agree that we will stand like doorposts, the east and west on each side of the doorway and she will have smoke, a smudge stick, and I will have a bowl of water and that we will not speak at all, but silently greet each person and offer them these blessings of smoke and water. We repeat it several times to each other, we will not speak at all.

After the first two or three people have gone through the doorway she steps forward and speaks to each person approaching, so they turn to look at her. She makes an elaborate smoke ceremony, blocking me out by virtue of where she is standing, so each person turns to face her and has their back to me and is still in the process of turning from her as they enter the room, not seeing me and of course I don't speak, we have agreed not to speak, so I can either fling a few drops of water at their departing backs or do nothing at all. Something begins to ferment in me, a slow burn.

That sister, Isis who must always be the center of everything and take all the attention and do whatever she wants and not even notice, not even hold to our agreement, why is she so important? What am I to do with this? It builds and builds within me and I think of those blithe with power, how they never notice the others who stand by their side, looking to them for sisterhood, for love and friendship, they are so taken up with glamour and self-importance and reflected glory they don't even notice and I begin to understand Set luring Osiris into that coffin, perhaps just to shut him up, sick of that endless song Isis and Osiris sang to each other, to the oblivion of everyone and everything else, feeding each other's glory until even they couldn't see through it anymore.

I cough and the woman holding Isis ignores me, speaks slightly louder to those people approaching and all of them think they are being blessed just by Isis, the wonderful Isis and hardly even notice me standing here and perhaps, if they do, they think I am a servant of the temple, holding a bowl of water, they don't know they are supposed to be receiving a double blessing and only getting half of it and I can't seem to get this part of the ritual back on track so I brood and mutter to myself. *You will see,* I think; *you will see when the time comes, and you can't do without me. You will need me eventually.* I sprinkle my water on the ground, behind those who have passed through. Nephthys flutters about me and her wings stretch out, wider and wider over these workings that neglect her so fiercely. I feel her storing up knowledge and all that neglect – like dark matter, everywhere and unknown – biding her time or getting on with things in a way we do not recognize, cannot see and do not even know to look for.

Oh those in-between spaces. Between being noticed and ignored. Between the love match of Osiris and Isis and the jealous, brooding one, her husband Set, Nephthys is in-between all that. Between having a role at the funeral of her brother and having no role at all, between the blessing at the door, between the importance of Isis, in-between. I was the one who was between Isis and her lover; when he wanted someone to listen, I carved out a secret space, in the in-between. When Isis, pregnant and giving birth needed refuge it was my realms of in-between she came to, the reed beds where I sheltered her, more loyal than you'd expect a neglected sister to be, when the protagonist was my own husband. I was midwife to her son, Osiris reborn, Horus, who inherited qualities from each of us four. I took him through the in-between of being born, emerging from his mother's body into his own mythology.

I linger at the edges, blue and distant; if sunrise is Isis' time, birth of a new day, of reason, logic, law and husbandry of the lands, my time is sunset, when everything blurs again, prelude to night, secrets and darkness. The ushering of cool breezes is mine, the hush of evening as the people return to their houses, huts, tents, but where they turn their backs on the distances opened up by evening, I turn towards them. The sun dies into my embrace, each night. Midwives hold both doors, those of birth and death and I am one who can farewell the dying, who can follow their journey, see into the dimness a little, though most do not even try as their eyes are turned the other way, closed against this, the beckoning of mystery, most do not wish to see.

I am given wings in the jeweled paintings in the tombs, wings to fold the dead within, wings to soar on the heights and spy out all the lands, the comings and goings; not to be committed to one place but inthe breadth and stretch, the vision of it all. I watch history unfold, barely in the script but always there, adding some fourth quality, the flavor it couldn't do without. It wouldn't balance, wouldn't taste the way it should if I were missing yet – mostly – no-one notices that I am there. I step into the roles allowed to me, required by someone else's drama; loyal sister, wife, secret lover…yet these are never my stories. My own story is softer, wider, more pervasive than anyone sees. To Isis the glory of the throne, to Osiris the grandeur of death, to Set the drama of murder and to Nephthys…

The wide-open eyes belong to me. I see, I watch, I observe. The roles I play – if I didn't play them – what then? Who can be husband when there is no wife? What good is one sister, without the other? – not sisters then. And an affair, even with the husband of one's own sister – no-one has an affair on their own, always the parties number two. I begin to see I am the seam stitching them all together. They do not see this, of course. But if I stepped away the stories would unravel. Perhaps I am viewed as a prop, a needed audience, an off-sider, someone who steps in to fill the gap and perhaps I am all those things. But without my care and attention, without my love and dedication this story could not be.

The rest of them do not love as I do. They love with preference, or exclusively, they love their chosen ones and ignore or despise the rest. I – love. To each of them I give this love. To my sister in her time of crisis, but even before that when I watched her admiringly, the throne of Egypt, teacher, ruler, high priestess. Osiris, so noble; the fields and farms, the passage through the Underworld; he shepherded both, in his time, one in life and the other in death. He tried, I believe, to love each one of us, his wife, his brother, his sister. He failed in each of those attempts. His brother turned against him, he left his wife bereft, he… perhaps he did not fail entirely. Then Set, who loved so unevenly; loved me, his wife as duty and companion; loved his sister Isis jealously and intemperately, loved and hated his brother as a rival, enough to kill him.

My love is not like that, weighed and measured, not different for each one of them. My love is like a mother's, flowing out as evenly as the night sky and of us all, I am closest to her who held the four of us together and whispered lore and possibilities into our dreaming selves. She who knew we were really one, each a piece that could be whole only together. One piece of us, me, is the fabric that winds us together, through necessity and blood and love. The other parts are bright and flashy but I alone have the power to hold us together. I am the breath of the nights we were born into and while I remain nothing can tear us apart, not even betrayal and bloody death.

Also, I am secretive. My relationship with each of them is away from the public eye, out of the stories, nearly; it is not a public display like the celebrated love of Isis and Osiris, or the notorious crime of jealous murder. Secretly I have a lover no-one knows about, it is off the side of his noble, reported life and together we hold that space sacred. Everyone knows I am married to Set, but what that marriage is like or what our arrangements are, if we have secret rituals and what they look like, no-one knows except us two. As for Isis – it is known I sheltered her in the reed beds to give birth and be with her infant but no-one knows what stories we shared or how it was for us, lying together night after night with that baby nested between us.

So I am the end-of-day, the fold into night. I am the secrets and that which binds the four of us together, I am the one who sees and the one who loves and the one who is not known. They think, when they step forward to claim the light, take my songs and roles away from me, stand in front of me and speak into a silent ceremony; they think they are taking away my power. But no. They are increasing it with the very acts they thoughtlessly imposed to lessen it. The further back I am, the wider I see, the more I know and the more power I accrue. It is not an active power, true. I am not one to bring dynasties down or demand judgment or re-order the world. It is the power of holding, holding this story as our mother held us in her womb, as I hold the knowledge, all the pieces within my grasp and if I made one move it was to save the baby, who came from all of us. Horus. I choose to save him, give him a place to be born, birth him with my own hands even, shelter him in his infancy against the searching rage of his uncle and in the face of the helplessness of his parents. I use my power for that.

Every night at WitchCamp, when the gods are invoked, people lift their masks from the altars where they lie during the day, and speak with them, or for them, or to them. The invocations to Isis have been bold and showy, glamorous; those to Osiris tinged with reverence, respect; the people who have spoken for Set have tended towards the wild and fierce and those who've held Nephthys' mask have been decorous, gentle. For the final night's ritual my son Damon has been offered an invocation; surprising me, he has chosen Nephthys. Each night the invocations go in birth order as it is reported in the sources; Osiris, Set, Isis, Nephthys. The focus in our rituals has been on Isis, Osiris, Set, Nephthys and one thing stays constant in these lists, Nephthys is always last. Last. The quietest, least dramatic, least noticed; the support role, the side-lined.

Tonight is planned no different, the order of the invocations is written as Osiris, Set, Isis, Nephthys. I have not spoken to Damon about what is happening with Nephthys, what is happening with me as I've held her through this camp, what I've seen or thought or how she's been neglected and somewhat trampled over; I have not really spoken with anyone about it. Part of her condition seems to be the unspoken, the wide eyes and silent mouth, those wings that hold everything and accept everything and a magic that is of the night rather than Isis' daylit style that is established, loud and celebrated.

The first two invocations are spoken, sedately and the woman who is to call Isis steps forward when suddenly Damon grabs the Nephthys mask from her altar and leaps into the circle. He holds the mask out towards the empty space of the center and races with her, around the inside of the circle of people so that the woman who was to call Isis has to step back quickly or be knocked down. The mask swoops and flies, the ribbons and feathers stream and flutter in the wind he makes. He shouts out her name. He is eighteen and pours his energy into this, he calls out that she is of the hidden places and the unknown, she holds the west and mysteries, that she is here and powerful beyond knowing and beyond forgetting and I am startled with everyone else but I look at her mask as she swoops like a bird and I feel her stretching, reveling in this moment of power and recognition.

How to explain this, how to explain any of it? Maybe Damon forgot the order of invocations. Perhaps he chose Nephthys because he had seen me holding her. Maybe she called to him, someone not afraid to tread on a few toes, literally, to shove that pushy Isis out of the way for once, someone who would trumpet her praises and let the world know she existed. So he heard her, followed his intuition or impulse and gave her voice and body, erupting out of the shadows to show herself, righting the balance and claiming her place, just for a moment iridescent with energy, *I am the one you should all be watching. I am of the hidden places and powerful beyond knowing and I am not to be forgotten.*

Damon shouts out her words as he runs, tears two or three times around the circle and he doesn't seem to realize how abrupt it is, how unlike everything else and then he returns her mask to her altar and the woman holding the Isis mask steps forward, warily, waiting for another interruption and speaks her piece, thoughtful and clear but not glittering, not sparkling like stars hard and brilliant and distant as Nephthys did and for once they seem more matched; the days of dedication to Isis balanced by this single reverence of Nephthys in its reach and rawness.

Afterwards I ask Damon, how did he decide to do that? I tell him how for days I have felt Nephthys brooding, the neglect of her and being pushed aside and ignored and he smiles at me. He says it seemed to be what she asked for, what Nephthys wanted. To be seen and heard, to be present. I wish he had more to say about it but the part of me that has been holding her is satisfied, inside. She was there and, on the final night, everyone knew it. Perhaps they carried pieces of her vision and mysteries home with them, as I did.

Freyja

We sat in a small circle, the seven organizers for the second year of CloudCatcher Reclaiming WitchCamp. Our circle included a computer, as one person Skyped into the meeting. Entering a trance we travelled through time to arrive at the beginning of next year's WitchCamp. In the etheric realms – visualizing, sensing, throwing our imaginations forward and out – we gathered together on the familiar slope of lawn at the center of the campsite. The rim of the caldera, the rainforested hills and valleys surrounded us as we asked, what do we meet here? What are the flavors and words and essences of this camp? Then we wrote and spoke and crafted and arrived at an intent, to set the whole camp within. *Here is Animal. Here is Land. We are family of Blood, Bone and Spirit, dancing our surrender into love. Our hearts blaze –*

Every Reclaiming WitchCamp follows a story, usually a myth but sometimes a fairy tale or modern crafting of a story and so, after a break, we discussed stories. So many we listed on that first piece of paper; stories of the beginning of the world, stories of romance, death, transformation; stories from Sumer and Greece and Britain, Russian and Norse stories. One of them was the story of Freyja and the Brisingamen, her magical necklace; several people were very keen for it. We talked about the stories, grouped them, thinned our list down. Freyja was still on it. The more stories we eliminated, the more she stayed on the list.

Freyja was a goddess who chose me. Maybe they always do, maybe it's never really me who reaches out, initiates that delicate conversation between human and divine, or maybe it's always me and I just didn't know it with Freyja; didn't see it coming. At some point I was the only one resisting her and I didn't even know why. I had no knowledge of Norse myths and deities, but I carried an aversion to their war-mongering aspect and how that sometimes shows up in followers of the Norse pantheon, as they present themselves at Pagan gatherings. Really? Was that all? Ignorance and prejudice? I gave way, gracefully I hope; accepting Freyja and her story as our next year's work. I didn't expect to like it; I didn't expect she would take my heart.

Freyja is a goddess of love, magic and war. Her story with the necklace begins when she transitions from the older pantheon of earth-oriented Norse gods, the Vanir, into the newer sky-related pantheon, the Aesir. Like all stories told and retold, there are many versions. Maybe she went as a bride, maybe as a hostage and it could be they are the one thing. There are also different tellings of whom among the Aesir she married. At CloudCatcher we worked with the story where she marries Odin, the All-Father, most famous for the sacrifice of his eye on the world tree, where he gained wisdom and knowledge of the runes.

Freyja wakes in her palace one day and decides to visit the earth, crossing the rainbow bridge to get there. This has many resonances. Since she was from the earth it could be like going back to a childhood home, revisiting her origins, or travelling to the source of her power. Once on earth she discovers the dwarves have made a magical necklace – the Brisingamen – and as soon as she sees it, she will do anything to own it. The price the dwarves ask for the necklace is four nights of love, which she gives. The dwarves themselves are sometimes understood to be the four elements of earth, air, fire and water, or more generally, a race of earth elementals. I look at them in this story and list their qualities: they mine the earth for precious jewels, they labor, they strive to make beautiful objects and gain mastery in magic through those objects, they craft offerings for the divine...and in contrast to the gods, they appear as squat, ugly, earth-bound and mired in the dirt and sweat of labor. I think that describes humans.

Freyja making love with them, whether they were dwarves or humans, is taken as a breach of her divine contract, although apparently not because of sexual jealousy, the way we might be inclined to interpret it. Perhaps because she struck a bargain, her favors were in effect paid for, or because she returned to the earth, or because she claimed an object of such power – there are different understandings. The reason she is discovered in it is because Loki, the trickster god, followed her down the rainbow bridge and spied on her with the dwarves. He rushed back to Odin with the news and between them they decide to trick her out of the necklace. Odin agrees to return it to her only if she promises an endless war...and on earth, we are still trapped in that endless war.

Prior to each CloudCatcher WitchCamp we spend four months in a magical working, one month for each of four different aspects of the story. Right at the beginning of the month with Freyja, my partner left me – abruptly, unexpectedly. My life seemed suddenly to be completely overlapped with Freyja's story. I felt I was drowning in Freyja. I could not even get my head up above the surface long enough to take a look at her; it was all internal, all experience, so overwhelming all I could do was pant through it, that little panting breath you are supposed to use when giving birth, breath that keeps you so focused your mind can't go anywhere else. I was swamped by her. My life was exposed in her story.

I could feel Freyja's pride in being selected, chosen, married into this new echelon of gods, what she would bring them – mirrored by my pride, in my marriage. I had been so proud of it, and the skills and love I brought to it. I caught a glimpse of Freyja standing there, between two groups of gods, the offering, herself the marriage price but removed from her own realm and all she knew. I was living in a city of strangers, away from my friends and community and felt stranded, unable to reach out or ask for help. I felt her frustration, bound into a contract that demanded everything from her – her teaching, magic, love – but that did not begin to recognize her depths, her vibrant connection to the living earth or who she was. I felt her increasing, rising alienation, from everything – what she had left behind and what she had married into until, one day, it all changes.

When Freyja journeys back to the earthly realms she discovers the necklace that is crafted to reveal her own essence. She not only has to *have* the necklace, in some ways she *is* the necklace. Magic, of course, is needed to release it into her keeping; after all she has been split off from part of her self, now revealed to her in the form of the necklace. Her magic is the magic of love and she gives it freely, or as a spell, a price, a binding, a reunion. But when she returns with this emblem of her power, the Brisingamen, a betrayal awaits her. The great Revealer of Truth, the one who strips away the veils of deceit and illusion, also known as the trickster, the untrustworthy or even wicked one, Loki; reveals everything to Odin, Freyja's husband, her student in magic and her lover. Between them, they steal the necklace.

I felt I had lost everything; who I was before my marriage, the promises I had made and even the very essence of my own self was somehow gone. I felt her anger, fear – terror, almost, at the loss of this part of her self – her rage and helplessness. With her I was rocked in waves of shock that greeted me every morning as I woke to my marriage being over, I could only assume that reflected her shock. Just when she claimed her power it was ripped away from her; just when she had learnt who she was and how to wear that, she is denied it again. Freyja will strike any bargain to gain this necklace, regain her self – in the story it is written as if the nights of love with the Dwarves were the price she paid, but I think those nights were her nature and the cost was to recognize and reclaim who she truly is. I take it as a lesson for myself. This is what I need to do.

On the first night at camp I invoked Freyja once the circle was cast. I had forgotten that the first night's casting remains for the length of the entire camp, so this meant I would continue to presence Freyja, in some way, all through camp. Also in that first ritual I took her role, a silent part. I was to be the bridal offering, given from the old gods to the new on the bridge between heaven and earth. I already felt completely mixed up with Freyja. I was bruised in disbelief from my marriage ending; still free-falling through the grief, relief, release. I felt encased in ice, fragile, frozen, hurt beyond measure and bound into not-speaking and not-touching and not-connecting. I thought maybe I wanted never to be in another relationship. That was more believable than that I would abandon myself again. I thought working with Freyja so closely would help me, although that wasn't so much my plan, just what was happening. Perhaps this will remind me of who I am.

In a room bounded by four altars – to Freyja, Odin, the Dwarves and the fourth to Loki – our ritual took place, starting with the marriage of Freyja to Odin. I stood at the beginning of the rainbow bridge, taking a first step from the pantheon of the old gods, those fading in power and towards the new, the sky gods, the ascending powers. I felt my heart beating. Another step. Magic was one of the gifts I brought with me and love the other. They were part of me, I could not leave them behind. Power was what was promised in return. Freyja carries her bloodline with her, the old realms would not be lost in dust as the new powers triumphed. Step by step. I can see him, stepping towards me. I can't tell – was he chosen, did he want this? Did he yearn for me or tremble, venturing out onto this bridge?

Earlier, before the ritual, I stood in my room surrounded by dresses. *White*, I had said to him earlier, *I will wear white.* But when I looked at the white dress, although it did look like a wedding it seemed cold, too harsh for how I had felt Freyja, for the heart of her. I called the two young women who were nearby into the room. *What shall I wear, for Freyja?* I asked. *Put them on,* they said; *show us.* So I dressed in white lace, in gold velvet, in deep rose satin. *Oh, that, the pink,* they said. *Are you sure?* I asked. *It was my wedding dress.* They said *perfect, it will be perfect.* I felt such doubt. Not about the dress but about the turmoil I was in, how can it help to wear that dress again, contract to a marriage, even in a ritual role? Let alone a marriage that goes wrong.

He comes closer, across the bridge. He is dressed in black. He seems solid, powerful, they have chosen a match for me, not a boy I could control or an old man I might bewitch. I must be worth something to them. Further we both step along the bridge, our families arrayed behind us. I can only see my future family now, not where I came from. When we are still paces apart he holds his hands out to me. At the center of the bridge we will meet and seal our alliance and – through us – the alliance of two pantheons. There is no need for him to welcome me, it is decided already. Yet he does. Maybe I smile, or half-smile, I can feel it trembling on my lips. I take a breath and we each take another step, nearly close enough to touch. I meet his eyes and he meets mine, still his hands are held out to me, not imperiously but in a greeting, an offering and I am nearly ready –

Around us it breaks, a shiver, a crack of ice a note struck badly, the air splits, the rainbow trembles as a whisper, a hiss sears about us, reverberating, *something's wrong*. There was nothing wrong, until that second and now our eyes break apart and search and I see – perhaps he wants to be seen – Loki the trickster flitting out of the corner of my eye and that whisper lingering, repeating and gaining volume behind him, something's wrong something's wrong. People are repeating it, *something's wrong, something's wrong* I see it on the faces of those ahead of me, I hear it from behind me *something's wrong* calling out and all around but I have gone too far now, to turn back and he, also...our eyes have broken from each other and his hands dropped before I had reached mine out and something is wrong, now.

I remember wearing that dress for my own wedding, at dawn on a summer morning when storms brewed. We held the ceremony on the verandah – it wasn't actually raining and we would have risked that trek out to the cape, but I couldn't ask the celebrant to do it when at any moment it might start pouring. Other things went wrong before, small things. We had argued, in the lead-up to the wedding, about different things. Perhaps underneath it lay an argument about the meaning of marriage. On the morning of the wedding I got up early, pre-dawn but I miscalculated, there was only one bathroom and it was full of people, all concerned with their own clothing and appearance so I couldn't look in the mirror or arrange my hair and my son Damon was both too young to realize and too old to be asked to help. My friends were not there, we had decided on the tiniest wedding possible; our children and the celebrant.

I walked out on Damon's arm across strewn rose petals. I felt his solid presence and everyone spoke truly beautiful things, poetry and prayers, blessings and speeches from the heart. After the ceremony, when the sun had risen we went down to the rocks, took photos and the storm broke upon us. We rushed back cheerful in torrents of rain for the wedding breakfast. I wept later for how sweet it had been, heart-shaped pancakes and strawberries. All the intent was good but there were cracks. The next day we drove to our honeymoon.

We went to the wrong place, I knew that. He had chosen the place he'd gone for his first honeymoon, with his first wife. I couldn't really understand why he'd choose that. But I didn't say anything, I was scared to upset him. *Something's wrong.* We argue, we can't seem to find a place of softness. I don't understand. I spend hours every day reading, compulsively, book after book with tears sliding down my face while he's shut away in a different room. *Something's wrong.*

I wanted to leave. I thought about just getting in the car and going, but then I'd be leaving him without a car. I thought about walking down the road and hiring a car – then I'd be leaving him with my car, which I didn't want to do. I was married. I'd committed. I went down to the beach and stood in the waves. I felt them break and break and break over me. I went past the breakers, into the swell and was rocked and held by her, the great mother, the ocean. Something's wrong, something's wrong. We patched it together somehow and the relationship lasted another four years. But something went wrong at the very beginning of my marriage, that marriage in the rose pink dress, and I didn't even know what.

On the final night of our WitchCamp with Freyja I go with my friend to the Bower, the space at camp dedicated to acts of love and pleasure. No-one has held me since my relationship broke up and my friend promised that he would do that. But of course there has been no time at all, not even half an hour that we've been able to find and so, when I asked if it would happen at all, he said, *it will have to be tonight.* He is attentive to me in the evening, in spite of being surrounded by his friends and he holds my hand on top of the table as we sit in the midst of supper and conversation and post-ritual exuberance and after a while we stand up and leave still holding hands and though a few people call out after us, no-one follows.

We are both exhausted after long days, countless meetings, groups, classes and rituals but he puts his arm around me as we walk to the room and I feel the solid core of him. He is barely older than my son and for the first several years we knew each other I did not fully trust him. I thought he was sweet, delightful, gifted and amazing but I did not expect, did not look for friendship. Although he showed up. He kept showing up. When things got tough in our tiny community he stayed put, tenacious and loyal and sometimes outraged, but never with me and I admired him in it, especially his refusal to be put aside because of his youth and then, when my relationship broke up so badly, he was there.

I discovered I knew no-one in the city where my partner, son and I had lived for two years, or no-one who could spare an hour or two, except for Damon and his friend who moved in with us, and their friends. I spent a year surrounded by twenty-year-olds talking politics and university courses and student theatre and board games and I was delighted by them, their warmth and clarity, their fierce learning and engagement. This friend of mine was not so different, young as well and he wrote to me, sent messages, every day after my partner left. Not every day for a week, or every day for a month; every day for four months, five. I felt cared for, not in some vague and abstract way but truly, like a friend and not just any friend but a dearly loved and very close friend as I fought my way through coils of what it meant to promise everything and have nothing, of how to free myself from the layers of self-betrayal and silence I had held within and very few people had patience or any interest in that.

But he did. All those messages he sent, they never told me I would be okay, or to get over it or move on, already. They just asked how I was, today. How I felt, what was happening for me. Today. Each day, and it didn't seem to matter what I said, how deep I went or how lost I felt, they kept coming, like sparks of light in the universe, the mystical mending of the world, blessing everything they touch, one after another. So I trust him, not just with words and feelings but with my whole being and when we lie down together, clothed and slightly chilled, he puts both his arms around me and flings one leg across me as well and I let myself be held. He falls asleep and I stay awake, to let it in, being held. Being returned to myself.

I still feel Freyja present and so it's easy for me to claim this as a night of love and I know, by staying with him here and offering and receiving this love I am freed from my marriage. I can declare myself not just left, but leaving, working my way out of its hold on me and of course I think of Freyja and how she was bound by marriage, yet she is the Goddess of Love, mistress of magic, warrior and lover. Now, as morning light filters into the Bower, I feel equal to the task of meeting her, holding her through this camp as I have done; not that I was equal to it at the beginning, when I invoked her, but that these days and this night have brought me equal to it. Holding her has taught me how to hold her and perhaps, now, how to hold the self that I am, again. To remind me that I love, that I risk and break and seek and offer and my magic spins through it all, like the beauty of a necklace that's never been made before and will never be again.

A few months after CloudCatcher WitchCamp I spoke with the woman whose English town I travelled to each year to present a weekend workshop. *We want Freyja's Necklace,* she said, confusing me. *But that's not one of my workshops*, I said. She smiled. *Well, that's what we want.*

I was determined we would have necklaces. We would claim and lose and unmake and remake necklaces. Each woman who came to the workshop brought a beautiful necklace she no longer wanted. I brought one my mother had given me, glass beads strung together, one to the next but each so distinct and colorful – orange, blue, brown, red, green – I could not really imagine wearing it, it had no subtlety, no elegance in my eyes. The beads themselves were beautiful but crammed together, so they struggled with each other. Others brought crystal necklaces, enamel, amber, one woman brought a jet-black necklace of seven long strands, each with hundreds of tiny black, shining beads. I flinched, seeing it, knowing what we would have to do with it.

They gave their necklaces across and we cleansed and blessed them, offered them to Freyja and placed them in a wooden box on the center of our altar. That night we played the scene of the dwarves. I layered all the necklaces between folds of black velvet on a small table and waited, still and quiet beside them, on the floor. We went into the ritual. As Freyja they woke in early morning. As Freyja they tiptoed out and down the rainbow bridge hearing a calling, searching, yearning, following an incomplete thread. One by one they came as Freyja to the cave of the dark corner where I waited. I flung back the top layer of fabric and there, displayed before her, was the necklace she would fall in love with. She could not resist it, she stepped forward to claim it. Freyja. It was taken by her and another came forward. I lifted off the next fold of fabric and there on the black – the necklace she must love and could not resist. She claimed it with her eyes and hands, she took it. Freyja.

Another woman. I throw the fabric over again, the necklace is revealed, she falls in love she reaches out, it is hers, Freyja. Another woman, another necklace, she takes it owns it, it is hers, Freyja and another, the black fabric, the necklace, Freyja and another, another, another; Freyja, Freyja, Freyja. She takes the necklace. It is hers, she is in love with it, it reflects her glory, her beauty her love and she goes off into the ritual with four nights collapsed into one and gives herself over to the elements. A night of love with earth that bore those jewels the necklace is made from, another night with molten fire to cast the golden setting, or silver or copper, a night for air that gives bellows-breath to the fire, and water, the fourth night that cools and she makes love, she forges love between herself and the elements, she dances, she weaves her magic so that, forever, she is bonded to the necklace.

The women go home and sleep with their necklaces. In the morning we play the piece of the story where Freyja's necklace is stolen by Loki. We play it again and again, each woman plays Freyja, waking to find her necklace stolen – the one she fell in love with, last night – each woman in turn plays Loki, stealing the necklace of another Freyja. We watch as he seduces, sneaks, conceals, deceives, pounces, whispers, schemes, conjures that necklace into his fingers. We listen as she cries out in anger, outrage, loss, fear, grief, horror, despair; as she mourns and weeps and as she rants and paces, reasons and pleads. The necklace – this necklace – will not be returned to her.

Instead, we intervene in the story. We call a council with Freyja and Odin. We ask them for peace on earth instead of this endless war they brokered and we offer payment in the form of a necklace; we will remake the necklaces with our own hands and our magic and we offer them one each. Then we sit on the floor and cut apart all of the necklaces. Some have beads streaming everywhere. Some, like my glass beads, clink neatly off into a container, some need each piece to be cut free with the wire cutters. Then we have hundreds of beads, a thousand or more, so we start making necklaces. The tiny black beads are everywhere; on the floor, in our clothes, dozens of them in every necklace we make and still there are infinitely more and more.

We make necklaces. We are the dwarves. We sit and thread and chant and sometimes talk. We make necklaces for Freyja, and for Odin and later we bury those necklaces in the ground, in ceremony. We make necklaces for each of us, we make extra necklaces. As we bead, we re-thread parts of our lives. Women speak of this unmaking and remaking as if they were reordering parts of their lives, breaking down the old to reform it into the new, finding beauty within the brokenness and restringing pieces that didn't go together before into new constructions. After two hours there are still hundreds and hundreds of black beads. I thread endless black beads onto fishing line, onto silver wire, I space out other beads between them, I make long strands of necklace almost entirely of black beads. Finally I make one very long necklace using only the black beads and half a dozen of the glass beads from the necklace my mother gave me. There is six or eight inches between them, each separated by maybe a hundred black beads – and the end result is a thing of such beauty I can hardly breathe, looking at it, or accept that it's mine.

I spaced out my mother's clamorous bright flamboyance with endless tiny shards of shining darkness and it worked. The black beads set off each of those decorative beads to be noticed in a way they never could before, all jammed up together. It is remarkable. Making it I felt the spell of it, that I could co-exist with my mother, have my own terms and make it wearable, this difficult not-pairing of us. I can have, share some of that brightness and loudness of her, interspersed with all of who I am, the dark and deep, the slow and persistent. I only need pieces of what she is and can give the rest away. I see those bright glass jewels strung into many other of these necklaces. The pieces I do keep can be the highlights of who I am, the noticeable parts, the invitations. When I clamp off the end of this necklace I am nearly weeping with it.

Oh I see how loss and brokenness must come first, how one cannot mend and heal without it. I see how one must cut up the accustomed beauty of one's life and how Freyja offers to do that, submits herself to it so we can see; falling in love with the necklace that represents her, the gold and amber of her, the shining beauty mined out of the deep earth and then lets it be taken, stolen, ripped away and from that point, only from that point, allows us to put it back together to let our own beauty shine through. Oh I see it now, I hold it in my hands in this jet-and-glass-bead necklace that will forever speak to me of my mother and my self, strung together in our own way, one offsetting the other but the same, part of the same necklace, that same piece of DNA taken and unbound and bound together a different way, a different aspect of the same shining beauty, I see it now.

Several years later and after my mother has died I go to SpiralHeart WitchCamp, partly because they are working with Freyja. Freyja and her necklace. She draws me there, with her promise of love and magic. Then my friend Trinda dies a few days before I get on a plane and instead of being at the ceremony held for her I am going to be in a WitchCamp on the other side of the world. Getting on that plane and leaving Australia feels like tearing myself out of the fabric of my own life. I am leaving behind my friends and community to travel to a strange place and new people. I am on the rainbow bridge again.

For twenty years Trinda has had my back. She's been the one who thinks I'm marvelous, regardless, the one who always encouraged, never judged, always supported and lent an ear, was interested and available. When my mother died and I was in Paris, I rang Trinda. When something went well for me, it was Trinda I told. When I needed advice, not that she'd give it, I might have asked her. She listened, maybe she'd nod here and there. If I pressed her for opinions she would sometimes offer a delicate question, *well, if it were me, I might ask...* We were friends, and more than that. She was like a mother to me. That bit older, that space for me she always made, I felt special. She told me I was special to her. Partly, I knew I was special because of her.

Over those years we've been in hundreds, literally hundreds, of rituals together. We've written many of them and discussed most of them afterwards, over tea and reference books or coffee and cake, in long winding conversations covering many topics or short, pithy debriefs. We were co-conspirators over the years though she always was the academic one; we used to joke that she knew things and I made them up. Sometimes I would make something up – a ritual, a story, an idea – and then go to her for actual information. Sometimes she would research something and then ask what I thought, not because I knew anything but because I'd make it up.

She's been dying for years and for the last year carefully, precisely, working her Death Project, tying up loose ends, clearing her desk, having important conversations. I know that, I knew that but because my mother had just died I couldn't deal with it very well. Not extensively. I could manage phone conversations about what happened to dead bodies, immediately after death. I could discuss the ritual that might happen, after she died. I could offer to come there, when and as she needed me – I did all those things. But I wasn't there, not actually there and now I won't be anywhere near, I'll be in Pennsylvania with a group of strangers, working with Freyja.

I arrive flooded with grief and jetlag. Trinda – Trinda – every breath, every thought seems to be about her. How can I exist in the world, how can I be who I am, how can I keep imagining myself into the future without her? I will never get over missing her. She is a part of who I am; a part of me is dead. The rawness of my grief meets the immediacies of this story and the way it's being worked here – betrayal, sex magic, loyalty tested, love at the edges of death, love that doesn't stop death, doesn't heal it but holds it. Love regardless.

During the evening rituals, which I'm not responsible for and have no part in other than participant, I'm mainly in a daze, observing things or treading the edges or watching the night sky beyond the trees, but one ritual breaks through to me. It's an excruciating hour-long standing trance, the kind of ritual it's nearly impossible to hold oneself in although it is an important scene, when Freyja sees and falls in love with her necklace. We are outside, it's night, we're in a large circle and at lengthy intervals, following instructions, we turn to face a different direction. East...south...west...north... I amuse myself with vivid trance scenes, interspersed with wondering how I might like to design this ritual. I imagine a dwarf marketplace, a cross between the goblins of George MacDonald's *Princess and the Goblin*, Christina Rossetti's *Goblin Market* and the small Italian town with cobbled streets I was in once at night, close to Christmas with the lights, the bustling, excitement and cold.

At some point in the trance we see the necklace and are asked what price we will pay for it. A lot of people are bored or cross by now, physically uncomfortable with standing so long, impatient for the next part of the ritual, or for it to be over and when eventually it becomes apparent that those running the ritual want us to actually, aloud, name our price they shout out loudly. Five or six ritualists are roaming, leaping about the circle in the guise of the dwarves shouting *Not enough! No, you can't have it! That's not what we want!* and irritating people immensely. They fall into louder shouting, counter-offers, or quiet muttered curses to themselves, some even deciding they don't really want it. I listen for a while, to offers of money and goods and promises – none of which are acceptable prices, according to the dwarves – and I decide to work out the answer. After all, it's in the story, isn't it? All I have to do is go back to the story.

Freyja offers love, in exchange for the necklace. What is that, to her? Well, it's part of her being, part of who she is, she's a goddess of love. So she's offering herself, the price is herself, to claim herself; because I believe the necklace *is* her, fundamentally. So if I offer myself...but that's too vague. She has to – become the qualities of the necklace, in order to have it. That sounds mythic. Be herself fully, in order to own herself. Also, it's not a set bargain, it's a future bargain. What Freyja offers can't be measured or weighed and only comes into being with her future actions. I call out, *I offer to live striving to be worthy of this necklace each day* and am startled to have one of the dwarves stop in front of me and stare into my eyes. *That will be the price, then,* she says, which is immensely satisfying. I solved the riddle. And then it is upon me.

To have the necklace. To live the shining truth of myself. To live all of my love and magic, not conservatively and not waiting for a better day but now and in each moment; to risk love in each heartbeat, to trust myself and all this without Trinda to talk it over with or even tell it to. *I was in a ritual in the woods in Pennsylvania, in this huge stone circle with sixty people under the stars and I was asked...and I understood...and I took the necklace which I already knew was me and I agreed to wear it...* Trinda might add some mythic point I'd been neglecting or never knew about, or she might pull a reference book off the shelf and start leafing through it, all her markers and notes or she might start muttering to herself, cross-referencing and then bring it up days or weeks later or she might ask me, blank-faced, what that means to me, but none of this, none of it can happen because she died and my love did not stop her from dying.

Trinda died and my mother died and still I go on living. Still I can offer love, become the fullness of myself. Freyja shows me how and the presence of Freyja; at CloudCatcher when I was falling apart from my marriage ending, in England re-stringing necklaces and my relationship to my mother, at SpiralHeart in grief for Trinda. Freyja. Who holds the powers of love and magic and whose presence I have brought into my life. If I am to do it, to live worthy of this love and magic of mine I have to say that my marriage ending and Trinda dying does not stop me from loving, from claiming and making and wearing the necklace of myself. I have been taking this journey for years but it is now, under the stars, on the other side of the world from my home, that I really understand what it is, who she is. Presencing Freyja is claiming love, offering love, living love. Veins of gold, drops of amber; the jewels of the earth.

I start to fall in love again.

Exercise – Creating an Altar

Altars are a beautiful way to express devotion, focus our attention on the sacred and begin to create magic. If you are planning to work with a deity, creating an altar can help to make a space for them, in your awareness. As with all altars it may be set up for a specific time or its nature or focus may grow and change over time. Instead of creating a whole new altar you might make room on an existing altar, or maybe the altar you create will be very informal and transient, such as one built on the beach or hanging from a tree in your garden.

Altars can be worked with for many different purposes and easily might accompany dedication, aspecting or researching, as well as presencing a goddess. The distinctions we draw between these things are only guidelines, with no hard-and-fast rules; they allow us to think more clearly about our purpose when we approach a relationship with a deity. I have placed altars in this section as, by their very nature, they presence; they create a space or home for the deity even in our own absence, often in our house. An altar is an invitation for a deity to be present, with or without your immediate attention, once it is set up.

In some ways creating an altar is similar to making an attribute. Both involve physical construction and benefit by some thought, attention or research. I think one of the differences is that we make the attribute *of* a deity (but for ourselves) whereas the altar is actually *for* the deity. There is also the potential of continual – or periodic – change that exists with an altar; it is likely that an altar will be added to, change and develop over time. Perhaps you regularly create altars and need no instruction, or perhaps this will be your first one. There is not really a wrong way to make an altar, so let your instinct and creativity flow. The basic idea of an altar to a deity is that it is a way of communicating, a home place or touchstone for your relationship with them, so each altar will be unique, as that relationship is unique.

How to make an altar for a deity:

- Find a place for your altar. This might be based on practical considerations, aesthetics, or your understanding of who you are working with. For example, I might build an altar in the corner of the living space if I live in a small flat, I might make an altar on a beautiful rock in my garden or I might create Aphrodite's altar on the beach.

- For the initial set-up of the altar bring the items you think you will need – these will be dependent on the goddess the altar is intended for and the location of your altar. For my outside altars I would be sensitive to what materials I was bringing, so although I might leave a crystal on the rock in my garden, I would not leave one on the beach. A picture or photo or precious piece of jewelry I would only leave on an indoor altar. The items you place on your altar may be associated with the goddess; for example grain for Demeter, grapes for Geshtinanna, maybe a stack of books for Athena.

- You might like to set the altar up in sacred space, which may involve grounding, casting a circle and offering a prayer or making an invocation before you begin, or perhaps to you it feels more appropriate to do those things once the altar is set up. At some point invite the deity to her altar, in a way that feels good to you. You may have written a poem, you might chant or sing or make an invocation. You might also like to perform devotional acts such as lighting a candle, meditating or dancing. You may like to journal after you have set up your altar, or take a photo, or just spend some time there. Remember to never leave unattended candles burning.

- The presence of the goddess at, within or around your

altar may be something you feel strongly, occasionally or not very much. You can cultivate this if you wish, as we would cultivate any relationship, with your attention and focus. Or for you simply having the altar may be the main point of it, that when you see it your thoughts are drawn towards the one it was set up for.

- Over the next few days or weeks continue relating to the altar. This might take the form of refreshing flowers kept there, of lighting a candle regularly, meditating, creating ritual next to it or some other form. Transient altars – for example one set up at the beach – are not necessarily less powerful and important for having their whole time of existence concentrated into one event.

Closing your altar:

- Sometimes an altar has been set up for a specific purpose or a specific length of time and other times it just falls into disuse, inattention or changes form into another altar. A formal completion of this space can be an acknowledgement that your focus has shifted for now, as well as an opportunity to thank the goddess for her presence.

Experimenting with altars:

- You might like to try different forms of altars, to find what works for you. Making an outside, transient altar if you have always worked with indoor, formal altars, or experimenting with an altar dedicated to a single deity if you have never done that before can teach youentirely new things.

Process – Making an Attribute of a Deity

Deities usually have a series of emblems, symbols and icons associated with them. Perhaps one particular symbol stands out, Persephone and the pomegranate, for instance, or Christ and the cross or Kali and her necklace of skulls. One way to further enhance our relationship with a divine being and explore deeper meanings of our connection with them is to make an attribute. An attribute is one of these items, usually made in ritual or sacred space. It is then considered sacred or magical, and at the very least, personal to us and them, much as a ring or necklace we've been given is associated with the giver.

It may require some thought to consider how you will create an attribute; the only being who can really make pomegranates is a pomegranate tree. But we could paint a picture of a pomegranate, or shape one from clay, or embroider one onto a sash or wall hanging. We can make a mask for any god or goddess, as we could compose a song or draw a picture or make a costume. But more particular than this is creating the specific symbol that is associated with the god or goddess you are working with. A necklace for Freyja, a raven's wing mask or cloak for the Morrigan, a girdle for Aphrodite.

I love making attributes because in doing so we encounter an older version of the deity, maybe something of the original energy that birthed the deity we currently know. Isis' symbol of a throne, for example, was used in hieroglyphs to mean *Isis*; similarly Inanna's eight-petaled flower stamped into clay was a way of naming her. I imagine that Zeus holding a lightning bolt gives way, back through time, to a lightning bolt. Maybe that actually is Zeus, originally and simply, he is not so much a being with the power of lightning – he literally is lightning, lightning is him. Persephone does not just eat the pomegranate seeds – she actually is pomegranate seeds, which birth and grow into a pomegranate tree, birthing more and more pomegranates, leafing back to life each spring, flowering in summer and fruiting in autumn then to die away each winter, while their seeds germinate deep in the earth.

How to make an attribute of a deity:

- Spend some time reflecting on the symbols or objects associated repeatedly with this deity. Let one call to you. Allow the shapes, colors, feel of the object to ferment in your mind, to intrigue and challenge you.
- If you are not already familiar with the mechanics of how to make the object (for example I had to learn how to make a necklace before I could make one for Freyja), research this.
- Find or buy the materials you will need.
- In sacred space make your attribute. You may cast a circle, meditate and invoke the presence of the deity before beginning. It may take place at a special location; in nature or a place you associate with this deity. It may take place in front of your altar, or in a place you often do ritual. Maybe you will choose to do it at a particular time of the moon, the year or the day, to strengthen its and your connection to the deity; you may choose to work at the new moon, for instance, or at dawn or midnight depending on the qualities of the deity.
- Allow yourself to be in free-flow while making it. You might find yourself in conversation with the deity, revisiting or reworking issues you associate with this object or deity, trancing or falling into a deep meditative space. None of this might happen, or it might occur afterwards. Let yourself be surprised by what emerges in your creative and personal process.
- Once the attribute has been made you might choose to

leave it on your altar, put it away for special or particular rituals or workings, or give it to someone. You may choose to unmake it, immediately or at some later stage, for example leaving an unfired clay object out in the weather. While you are making it, or after you've made it, let its purpose and what to do with it emerge.

Enacting Myth

Enacting a myth is one of my favorite things to do. When we are *enacting myth* we take a story – perhaps Aphrodite being awarded the golden apple by Paris, perhaps the story of Kali and Shiva destroying and saving the world, perhaps the love story between Inanna and Dumuzi – and step within it. Every time I enact a myth, even when it's the same myth repeatedly, I learn new things. I learn about myself as well as about the characters and the myth. Enacting myth is different than presencing, or aspecting a deity because instead of seeking to feel or project the energy of the deity we remain exactly ourselves, while stepping through the actions or storyline of a myth. Bringing our human selves into those places is what brings insight. Once a deity is strongly invoked, aspected or drawn in, they may have no interest in playing out a previously arranged scene. Here it is the human lens we focus on, seeking understanding that way.

To enact a myth we often play a scene out multiple times. Part of the reason myth is so resonant is its paradoxical, multiplicity of meanings and this can best be reached not by a single enactment, by one or two or several people, but by many repeated enactments. Thus if we were to play out a scene with the minotaur in the labyrinth it shows us one set of circumstances and offers one set of understandings; when we repeat it different ones are revealed. So we step further into the mystery; deeper and deeper into the mythos as multiple and co-existent meanings come into play. Partly this is served simply by repetition – trying the same thing again and again results in different nuances, flavors, resonances – but partly it is determined by the people playing those parts, each bringing different understandings and emotions to the actions of the characters and thus revealing another dimension. Goddesses, gods, mythic stories – these are far more complex than a single set of human emotions and actions and thus by repeating the enactment, preferably multiple times, we come closer to revealing the complexity.

There are a few different ways to achieve this multiplicity of viewpoint. One is simply to replay the scene on a number of different occasions. More efficiently, especially if you have many people involved, the scene can be played through multiple times, with each person present having a turn at, for example, enacting Persephone's role picking that flower. When it is done this way everyone gets to see a multitude of Persephones – a curious Persephone, a coy Persephone, a seductive, frightened, determined, daring, enspelled, deliberate Persephone. This shows, more clearly than anything, the complexity and depth of that simple but pivotal action in Persephone's myth; how all those things can be true of Persephone, all at once. This method is ideal for groups up to about twenty in size. A third method, which works for larger groups, if somewhat chaotically, is to allow everyone to have the experience at the same time. For example, multiple Persephones could be let loose into a field of flowers, all at once. There is less witnessing, this way, although still multiple experiences – to gather the information would require a debriefing or sharing and possibly the use of witnesses who are not involved in the enactment.

In the Artemis myth the hunter Actaeon accidently spies upon the goddess bathing in a forest pool, whereupon she turns him into a stag who is chased and killed by his own hounds. The story has a pleasing circularity but has always held a repugnance for me, as if I missed the understanding of its lesson, so I was curious to discover more. Six of us played out their meeting about nine times in quick succession. We created a soundscape as the background for this meeting and did not use words. Taking the emphasis away from spoken language can allow us to tap more deeply into the archetypal and feeling realms, so actions and bodily understanding arise more clearly.

Watching and participating in this repeated play I felt no

difference between a hunter, bound to Artemis, and the hunted, bound to her also. As Artemis I wept when Actaeon turned into a stag, one of her own animals then sacrificed to her. I saw how revealing the mystery – the naked goddess – led to another mystery, shape-changing and how one sparked the other, inevitably. Having seen the goddess one cannot remain the same and must become her creature. To look upon the goddess naked is death to a human; not by choice of the goddess, but inevitably. As Artemis the action flowed through my arm, not my thoughts, this is the next moment that comes, this is what must be. I knew that human life is so tiny bringing it to a close early seems no great thing, a matter of maybe seconds; or even that, at the height of his brightness comes death, darkness and yet it was a pinnacle, to witness that and worth the sacrifice. I watched as Actaeon after Actaeon did not struggle but went gladly, joyfully or in awe to his fate, occasionally surprised or shocked by the change but never contesting it. I felt resonances of the story that had always escaped me before. I discovered he is in service to her in this story in many different ways: as hunter, as witness to her glory, as stag and as sacrifice.

Putting together the pieces of the story after an enactment – in spoken words, drawing, into a ritual or in some other form – is an invaluable part of deepening understanding. At the end of this section are several exercises showing different ways to enact a myth.

Ariadne

Ariadne is a princess of Crete from Greek myth; a goddess, or a maiden, depending on how you read the story. She is the oldest of two daughters born to King Minos and his Queen, Pasiphaë. In the heart of the labyrinth underneath the palace is the minotaur, half man and half bull; Pasiphaë's son and therefore a half-brother to Ariadne and her sister. Perhaps the minotaur is a sacred priest, dedicated to the old ways and although his father is said to be a bull, that could be the form of a god, or a priest, or even the king himself.

The story is told from the perspective of Theseus. He is the hero, bull slayer and bull dancer, royal son of Athens who sweeps forward on the moment of history as Crete falls apart in an earthquake, mythically linked with his penetration of the labyrinth and destruction of the mysteries. It is Ariadne who assists him, showing him the secrets of the labyrinth and holding the end of a ball of thread while he ventures inside, his lifeline back. After murdering the minotaur and in the chaos of the earthquake that breaks the island and the old order apart he takes the sisters with him, later leaving Ariadne on another island, Naxos.

Ariadne's story is set in a time and on an island balanced at the edge of change. She was raised in the old religion, the one of bulls and priestesses and sacred ways. All of that is to finish, to be lost in the earthquake and the coming of kings, the ways of earth replaced by the solar journeys of the hero. Ariadne walks through her story deliberately, the way a labyrinth uncoils within itself, there's only one path. No-one ever suggested she made a mistake when she let Theseus into the secret of the labyrinth, that she didn't know what she was doing, or that she regretted it. She chose; she chose survival. Take this thread, like the thread of my life, I will hold it while you do the unthinkable, create murder and chaos with your brightness, your certainty in this place of darkness, the palace with the labyrinth at its heart.

Whenever I take the first step into a labyrinth I make a commitment. This is the path I shall walk until I reach the center. All the conflicts in me are quietened by this pacing the narrow walkways. There's only one way in, only one place to go and one way out. I have walked labyrinths in England, a beautiful labyrinth constructed of candles at a Green Festival and one laid in stone in Bath; I have walked them in churches in France and San Francisco; a garden labyrinth in Minneapolis; I have walked them marked in paint and chalk, laid out in sticks or stones or ribbons and on the beach marked in sand; I have walked the sandstone labyrinth in Centennial Park in Sydney and the one at the Crystal Castle in Byron Shire. There is a mosaic and brick labyrinth in the Community Gardens near my home in Katoomba.

On New Year's Eve in the first year after my mother died I go there at midnight, to walk the labyrinth. There is a light rain, or heavy mist, the air glitters with dense wetness. I breathe it in. The mosaic is gleaming in reflected light, even though all around is dark. I feel in utter darkness and the brick path itself is dark, it is the mosaic circuits between the paths that gleam; light guiding the darkness. The mysteries. I am utterly alone, only the pattern of the labyrinth, only whatever I carry in me. I think about change. I think about death and its inexplicable, inexcusable slicing through what is known like the fall of a blade, severing. I am severed by it; severed from my understanding of myself, severed from my history and continuity. I know I am the continuity but I feel too insignificant for that, too alone and singular.

I walk the labyrinth in what feels like shock, even though my mother died six months ago. New Year's Eve is also the night I gave birth to my son, twenty-three years before. It's a night that people remember where they were and so I do remember other New Year's Eves; strange parties, resolutions, private celebrations. This unraveling of the path of the labyrinth is like walking backwards through my life, through my mother's life, to birth; hers or mine or Damon's. It's hard to tell the difference, in the dark and the mists. There's an undoing, a becoming, a conscious pulling out of the unknown, of the next piece of the path, the next piece of the story. I feel held by the night, the pause at midnight when I stand in the center, life turning about me. Only me, but my body is tied forever to the stories and bodies of my mother and my son.

Long before in another place four of us enacted Ariadne's story, with her mother Pasiphae, her half-brother the animal-god minotaur and Theseus, her hero. In the mythos all moments are held as alive and present, unfolding right now, this minute and enacting it we stepped into that stream of time. Afterwards memory decides on a story and tells it in a sequence; oh this happened, followed by this and then that. One cannot write down three simultaneous different things unless they are written in columns across the page, or somehow encoded in a labyrinth themselves, twisting about each other like the layered paths. That would conjure the interweaving of it, the rippled manifold conundrum of time, even in the ordinary world let alone the mythic one. Time. As I write of these people, these events they are living, alive; both in the mythic and in this written world of the page...and yet.

Half the people who did this enactment are dead, now. Ross and Trinda have completed the labyrinths of their lives and left the other two of us on the outside, holding the threads of them. Trinda drew the labyrinth for that enactment, white chalk on my concrete floor. The ceiling stretched high above us, unreachable and in the semi-dark, unseeable. We put the entry in the east. Glenn as the minotaur paced in, alone, already bowed with grief or so it seemed. We saw him entering the heart of the mysteries, there to own them but also somehow banished, from light and love and human discourse. Only those who risk transformation would seek him out, he was not to be a part of the daily exchanges of work and family, commerce or love. Who would seek him out?

Trinda, in the role of Pasiphaë, goes to visit him in the darkness. She wants to know, why did we lose the way of the old gods? How are you trapped down here, confined to darkness and alone? The outside shape of him does not matter to her, or perhaps she recognizes the sacred, the body of a man with the head of an animal. How many religions hold that as one of the deep mysteries, where human and animal blend, a man's body wearing the instincts and knowing of the wild? It is ancient, ancient as that time when humans separated themselves from animal. Perhaps they knew what they had lost, civilization breaking them apart from the earth, from deep knowing and connectedness. Their shamans wore cloaks of feathers, bird masks; dancers wore the skull of a horse, dreamers and initiates the skin of an animal; people painted themselves in colored earths with the symbols of their totems, they journeyed for a vision of their spirit animal, they ritually hunted and killed their cousin in animal form.

Pasiphaë goes to say goodbye to the minotaur, she goes to comfort him. Stories are not set in the comfortable continuum of millennia but at their change points, where the land cracks apart and devours all that has been, on the eve of war, at the moment when dynasties shift and change their loyalties and all from then on are born into a new house. She knows this, she is his mother. Every child born is a sacrifice, to the world, to the future. We cannot guarantee their safety or their happiness, we cannot save even one from fate. Certainly not this one, the last of the old, born to be the last, the death of things. Did his mother, truly, mate with the god, with the bull himself? Did she twist magic to create this wonder, this miracle-called-monster, the minotaur in his lair, the priest of the old mysteries, animal and man revealed as one?

She is no longer the young woman who took a god to her bed. She has daughters – Ariadne, Phaedra – who will never be queens after her, of this place, although she has passed them her royal blood and whatever secrets she can. She has a son, hidden away although once he would have been paraded through the streets as the celebration of the highest mysteries. When she paces the labyrinth she understands his death is near – and with his death, the death of a culture, a whole occult knowledge to die in this overturning of earth by sea, of the nature gods by the sky gods – you can see determination in the set of her shoulders, love propelling her forward even though her protection no longer holds. He comes to meet her, the minotaur, paces out of his cell that once was the temple of the innermost mysteries and they stand embracing.

No, it cannot continue, this tentative hold of the old religion struggling to find a place within the new; he will not survive it. He cannot change his face the way those who pick up and put down masks can do, his whole being, bone and flesh, is grafted to the old ways, the god who dances with beasts, as one of them and no less divine for that, rather its most perfect expression. One can hide in a maze, or be hidden only for so long and against only so much determination on the part of the hunters, to scent and find, to commit murder. But in a labyrinth there is no hiding at all. There is one path in and one path out, it is the same path. If there are traps and falls and false turns on the way that may create some delay, but it cannot change the end. Whatever is hidden in the center will be found by those who follow the path.

Like the passage from the womb into the world, there is one way only. As the journey from birth to death it unwinds at its own pace and there may be tripfalls and near misses but in the end, death claims each of us. Pasiphaë knows this because she has given forth offerings to the world, to birth, to death; her daughters, this son. It seems unlikely she can survive the coming changes, her flesh went to make this monster, she nurtured him – revered him and what he stood for – so why should she live longer? It is not just his death she comes to mourn, to acknowledge, to ask forgiveness for, but her own. This is what we see, watching them.

They stand together in the narrow realms of the path and embrace each other, perhaps she is weeping. They speak, heads close together. She is in rage and despair as well as grief, *how can it be that the old ways are ended? – why is the goddess no longer seen or understood? – they will destroy not just this, but everything – all of life must fall before these conquerors.* He answers her with what he has seen in the deep darkness, in the down of things and it is not utter bleakness, but a thread of hope. He speaks of the turning, like the turning of the paths that twist and spin, into the center and then outwards again, ever winding, unwinding, they do not stop. He speaks of how darkness lays down upon the earth and in the minds of men and a long night enters while the world turns. But it does turn and maybe women, close to the birthing of the new, remember and he says that her daughters and their daughters hold the hope, to remember what is birthed from the darkest places.

The old stags lay down their lives – not because they wish to die but as it is the way of the world – and meantime, close by or elsewhere, young stags are racing and leaping, testing themselves against each other and yearning, thrusting into life. The trees that are tallest, oldest can fall – and must fall – not because they are not needed, a host of life lives on them and in them – but because of wind and root rot and lightning and whatever else may fray a tree's life, but they continue to feed their seedlings and the whole forest as they lie dead and rotting, passing back into the earth. Things turn. Great cycles of life unfold and evolve, giving way one unto the next and we, standing on a darkened patch of earth trapped in our own time, cannot call the turning, cannot see it even, but this is the pattern. Things turn.

Pasiphaë, who gave birth to the minotaur learns this from him just as we, aging, have reflected back to us from our children not just what we always knew and sought to teach them, but what we have never imagined, can scarcely glimpse as they outline it to us, because it comes from a world beyond us. But we must trust that they inhabit it. So in this conversation Trinda hears what she says she never understood before; all is not despair. The ending of the great goddess cultures in Europe and Asia was not the end, forever. It was of the turning and the turning does not cease. Even now, walking through this myth, perhaps we contribute to the turning, the returning knowledge of the great goddess, the great mother whose chthonic belly birthed us all and holds all secrets.

As Theseus, Ross enters the labyrinth once Trinda has left. In the myth Theseus is only able to do this because Ariadne has shared the secrets of this Underworld with him. So he walks the paths not from knowledge, learned painfully and piece-by-piece and not from memory, carried there in the arms of his mother, before he could even speak or walk or from ancestral memory, the way his parents and theirs and theirs trod these paths into mystery and initiation, but on Ariadne's thread. It is her knowledge he walks forward on, her ancestral line he seeks to prune, her intuition waiting and listening to the world of dreams and deep archetypal understanding he is following. Perhaps we are initiated even if we don't seek it, walking thus.

He strides, but there is something clipped and rigid in his walk, he is on a mission not in keeping with the mood of this place, which is gentle and dark, enfolding; he carries brightness with him in the sword and the intent he bears, it is a soldier's walk. Soldiers and temples. They come before marching off to war to pray, or to beg for success or just their lives, or ask that if they die their dependents and loved ones will be cared for. Perhaps they offer gold or whatever they have to the gods, hoping for intervention, safety and return. After the killing they return to the temples, take their armor off at the gate and seek absolution. Perhaps they come seeking a different way than war, or healing or perhaps they come in righteous victory, to claim acknowledgement from the gods.

Often, throughout time and history, they come to sack. They

strike the statues from the plinth to shatter on the ground. They come to slash, to desecrate, the hangings and pictures and cushions and also the priestesses, mown down in death and rape and capture; they come to force their victory not just on the town and people but even on the gods. Those who live in the temples, who serve them, what are they to do? Where would they run, that is safer than under the gaze of their gods, in the arms of the goddess? If they run they betray all they lived for. Soldiers plunder the riches of the temple, its gold or jewels or chalices and priceless art and they desecrate as well as destroy. They break the temple open, they damage and scar, they burn temples to the ground.

Theseus walking into the labyrinth at night is just one man, how much damage can he do? Perhaps he can do just one thing, pitch his life against the life of another, the high priest, the god-on-earth, the minotaur. Just that one thing and that at the risk of his own life. Life for life; one to live and one to die. He paces, nervy, inwards. Inwards is a direction he is not familiar with. Outwards has been the direction of his life; to be a prince, a warrior, a hero. To be in the world and perform great deeds, not to reflect, to submit to mystery. He has defeated mystery, forcing circumstances to change to his will, he has rewritten his own history again and again, an actor in a world of action.

The minotaur waits in the center. Ariadne, outside, surely knows this has only one outcome; her lover sent in to kill her brother, her choice cast, her thread unwound and fate chosen. This is the ancient way of kings and gods, to die at the hand of another, who then takes one's place in the long line of gods or kings, indistinguishable, one from the next. But Theseus is an intruder, from a different place and bringing a different time, he will not stay to master the labyrinth, or serve it; he will not become the next bull priest. Unless in this very intimate act of killing he takes on the essence of the other; like making love, as intimate as that, an exchange that is not just physical but energetic, twisting fates together so that ever afterwards he will carry with him something of that magic, the death of the minotaur bound up in him.

The minotaur faces him as he enters the innermost circle of the labyrinth. He holds out his arms as if to greet this other and so is pierced right through, simply and with no fight and collapses on the floor. Theseus spurns the embrace of a brother, a cousin, instead he takes the warrior's way of victory and death. Then he kneels, perhaps to check the monster is dead but from the outside, watching, it looks as if he bows down to the earth. To the greatness of death, at least, if not of his opponent, the wonder born on the earth and hidden in the earth and now buried in the earth; a burial that will be echoed any moment, within hours, by the collapse of the whole temple, the palace by ripping earthquake as the ground itself opens up to shout, to cry aloud, to welcome home the minotaur.

When Theseus leaves the labyrinth he passes by me, standing at the entrance, as Ariadne. He does not speak though it was she who led him to this place, her weight that shifted the story in this direction, her thread that provided the narrative. It is my turn to enter and I do, not exactly reluctantly but coolly, the story has spun out of Ariadne's arc now and her part has narrowed. Narrowed to this, walls of chalk and air, of earth, of block and brick guiding me inwards, seeking to reveal the force of consequences. It is a little time, between one time and the next, this soft treading; between the time of being a girl, a daughter and sister and priestess to being a woman, wife and traitor. Those who betray are always, in turn, betrayed; how could that not be? For a little while, for perhaps the last hour on this island that is her home and birthplace I tread these sacred paths with her, unwinding them. I do not need a thread; she is the thread, her blood and that of her brother is the red thread I follow.

I walk into the labyrinth, enacting the steps of Ariadne. How to explain this, the betrayal of a brother, of a priest maybe and certainly a temple, of a way of life and her whole family? *Survive* whispers inside me. We are born to survive. To take whatever twists and turns we must to come through to the other side. It feels as if the whole of her life lies here, unwound and unwinding beneath my feet, her fate turns on these turns. There is a grander story, yes, the times of the goddess giving way, finally and bloodily to the time of the gods. Earth giving way to sky. The priestesses leaving the temples; in Ariadne's case on the arm of the conquering hero. A war spoil. A bargain, a bag of gold, a rescue. The islands, the outposts coming further and further under the control of centralized rule, the mainstream culture wiping, ruthlessly away, all hidden pockets of resistance, all clinging to the old ways, all powers that are not theirs. But her concern is narrower, narrow like these paths. Love and death as they play out in a single life and the three I enact this myth with are bound to me that way, through love and death.

Ross, who held the part of Theseus, was my lover at the time, is dead now. Glenn who played the minotaur is the father of my child and surely this bond is greater than any except that of child and parent; our DNA twisted together in a living form of the future; that in itself is a labyrinth, the emergence of Damon from those two lineages. Trinda played Pasiphae; Ariadne's mother. She is dead one year and one month, as I write this. Trinda, who mothered me in so many ways, who more than anyone on the planet, living or dead, I've trod these old ways with. That labyrinth of chalk and air was as filled with love and death as Ariadne's Cretan passages. If the labyrinth exists as a form, outside time and manifest in each place as a shimmering aspect or gateway one through to the next, then in every labyrinth and even writing this I am there again.

Ariadne reaches the center of the labyrinth. Perhaps there are torches burning smokily on the wall to show her, or candles still lit on the altar, or she can feel through the dark space, inheritor as she is of her mother's role, the goddess on earth, the goddess-in-the-earth. Never mind that she rejects that role, has chosen another or has let herself be lifted up on the wave of fate sweeping down on this island, still she knows. She knows in her bones and breath, in the touch of her fingertips and the backs of her retinas and in her nostrils and on her tongue and in the quality of stillness. Death is here. Instead of birthing life, she has birthed death. Death of kin. Death of a god, or the priest of a god, in his temple. What punishment awaits that in the mythos of ancient Greece, where punishment is perfectly fitted to the crime? It will not matter to the gods that this crime was in their interests, or prompted and even, almost, carried out by them; they will be happy to punish a human for it and then continue their play on the vast stage of earth.

With Ariadne I pause, hesitate. I feel – not grief exactly, an ancient sadness. The sadness of the earth itself, perhaps; seeping out of the walls, hovering in the air and imbibed with each breath. The sadness of the end times. This death – large, but small compared with the death of a whole culture – is inevitable. How could the minotaur live, if all around him were to fall? With him having fallen, how can anything else now stand? Perhaps this would be the moment, in justice, for the roof to fall in and bury not one but two, sister with brother, maiden priestess with ancient god, servants to the old forces, but the gods have glanced away and the earth does not fall. Perhaps their gaze follows Theseus, glittering bright in his armor and destiny as he ransacks the palace, taking the second daughter for good measure, little Phaedra who has done nothing, the royal blood runs as true in her as in her sister, but without the crime. A purer strand, if one wished to breed from this house.

Ariadne. What is it, to stay true to the thread that unwinds through oneself? The lineage, from mother to daughter, passed through lines of women; lines of priestesses, royalty. A royalty bred not so much to rule as to serve the gods. When your gods are vanquished – murdered, overthrown, stabbed in the place of their own mysteries – when the page is about to turn on the story you've been raised within do you leap, out of that story and onto another page, or stay and die with it? These three siblings, half-siblings, prince and princesses of the Palace of Knossos on Crete, go each a different way. The minotaur, wedded, bone and flesh to the old dies, there is no other choice for him. Ariadne leaps, betraying everyone and helping to bring the end. Phaedra leaps not once but twice; with Ariadne fleeing the doomed island but also a second time, leaving behind her sister. Perhaps these are not choices, but inevitabilities.

If this line is to continue it has three chances and it does not matter which succeeds. Phaedra has two children, sons, with Theseus. The lineage folded gracefully into conquest. It has betrayed and fled, been saved and continued. This is the story. The middle role, Ariadne's, is the role of agency. It turned on her choice. She betrayed and thus condemned her brother to that particular death. Perhaps in recompense she saved, and so replaced herself with her sister as Theseus' wife. I stand as Ariadne in the middle of the labyrinth and think of agency. Of what it takes to be the one making choices, of the prices of that.

Ariadne ended up on another island. The story, surely Theseus' version, is that she was left behind, a woman jettisoned in the conquest of patriarchy. But stepping away from the emotions of the story into the events, we can see that she found a place dedicated to the old ways. She was initiated into Dionysian mysteries, not so far from her origins. I think that was the way she could live with what she'd done. She passed the lineage and the getting of kings to her younger sister, who was not so tainted and perhaps not made so powerful by those events of that other island. Who, after all, calls for the death of the king, the god, but the goddess? She took that part. She stepped into power and I don't know that afterwards she wanted the role of queen to Theseus, subservient and breeding. She walked the twists and turns of fate and yet stepped free.

I go to visit the mosaic labyrinth near my house the day it snows, a year and a half past the New Year's Eve when I walked it in the mist and years after we enacted that story. When I get to the gardens they are bare, white. The trees are mainly apple trees, stripped twig-like structures, artistic and dreaming in winter. I walk the path of snow from the car park, there is one set of footprints ahead of me, but no-one there. All around the labyrinth, in all directions, is a blanket of white, but the labyrinth itself, made of brick and tile, is clear except for a few puddles. It has not been swept clean, there are no piles of snow to the edges; the heat of the brick must have melted the snow. So it stands out, stark and revealed in this winter realm, even more the heart of the mysteries.

At Samhain a few months earlier we walked this labyrinth inwards and did not emerge, making our offerings to the Underworld and choosing to remain there for the weeks darkest in the year. I say *we* but I was not actually there for that ritual. I set it up, I wrote it and then – I was somewhere else. I was in the small house Trinda lived in for so many years, next to the house I don't live in any longer with the concrete floor she drew chalk labyrinths on. A tenant moved out, Damon drove with me, there are a host of reasons but I end up spending Samhain where Trinda lived, in the first Samhain since she died and a thousand kilometers away from the ritual here, in the mosaic labyrinth.

Always at Samhain we walked a labyrinth; drawn by Trinda on the floor. Always we made offerings to the Underworld. The turns of fate twist in on me, there are so many parts of this I have not arranged and yet I find myself inside it, already walking the paths. I sleep the night of Samhain in the place where Trinda slept for so many years, while she lived next door to me. I put my bed where her bed was. I make an altar in the garden for her, an offering, many offerings. A pomegranate, broken open. A candle to burn, for memory. A small silver moon I made, while she was alive. Rose essence and chocolate, rainwater and tears and flowers from the eucalyptus tree in the lawn, its fringed gumflowers brilliant pink. They are too high to reach, you have to wait for the tree or a bird to drop them on the lawn and they were there this morning, when I went to look.

Samhain. We walked in and we didn't walk out. As I walked into Trinda's death, still unemerged from the resounding of my mother's death. I did not walk out. When the Winter Solstice came I was back in the mountains and our ritual included walking out of the labyrinth. I did it, but there was a lot going on and my attention was not fully focused. A month later here I am, standing alone in snow. The footprints led to the labyrinth but no-one is here now. I didn't even wonder that they went only in one direction, towards and not away from the labyrinth; there are other paths out of this garden though now I smile to think of someone entering the labyrinth and not leaving.

When I walk a labyrinth I think of Trinda. I walked so many with her. She mutters at my elbow, sometimes she smiles. I see her serious, intent pacing, head down, I pass her on the circuits. I glimpse her leaving the center just as I am arriving or stepping out, ahead of me off the final step and – elsewhere. So now, when I walk this tender small, local labyrinth in fairytale snow, in joy I feel her approval. I sing as I walk, *out of the dark heart of winter I am walking* and truly it seems I am walking out, of the long winter of these deaths, Trinda's, my mother's; this brief winter of bitter cold and rituals and my relationship slowly failing. Trinda mothered me, as Pasiphaë was mother to Ariadne and I search my mind, what echoes lay there, in that working of the threads between us? Yes, the feminine splitting two ways, one to death and one to life; yes, the learning passed down, guided but also let go of. I walk out of the old life, out of winter, and death, out of Samhain and out of living caught in memories and loss. So Ariadne has taught me.

Inanna

Inanna is the Sumerian goddess of heaven and earth. Her stories were written on clay tablets that have been pieced together to reveal the gathering of her powers, the love poetry between herself and the shepherd Dumuzi and, most famously, her descent into the Underworld. In the descent myth she journeys through seven gates to meet with her sister Ereshkigal, queen of that place; she dies there and is reborn. Inanna is a flamboyant, bold and determined character, she shines out through the centuries. For contemporary women her story reveals a deep mythic pattern about the rediscovery of essential self. Part of the joy of this myth is that it has not been rewritten and reworked countless times through the intervening centuries, as myth cycles from some other cultures have been, so that what we are reading, translated, is what the Sumerians were reading, writing and hearing several thousand years ago.

Inanna has never left me for an instant, in twenty five years. I am dedicated as a priestess of Inanna-Ereshkigal and I've reworked her descent in ritual and stories, trance and workshops dozens of times. Inanna with her seven gates, the meeting with the Dark Goddess. Inanna's story is something I carry on the inside, the depths and colors of it. I have a feeling for it. Like picking out the path of a labyrinth in the dark, I don't need a light to see the way because the map is one I hold inside myself. Every time I follow the map, I learn something new.

My friend Fio says he'll come to Sydney to do an Inanna descent with me and we agree to enact the story together over a few days. Six months ago my marriage broke up and I'm still deep in the realms of the unknown, he's about to move to another country and both of us feel we are floating free; untethered and not quite certain of the future. More than ever before we're feeling like siblings; closer than friends, something bonding us together and inviting us further in, to let our magics weave even more strongly together. Doing this descent together is a way of re-finding ourselves; the metaphor of death and rebirth seems perfect.

I'm living at the seaside, a Sydney suburb wide open to nature. When I walk down the few blocks to the beach half the world is sea and sky, with all its moods. I come here after storms, to swim in the women's rock baths and be washed by waves; there are fish and sea birds, seaweed and crabs and sea urchins. I come at night to the beach for the splash of waves on hard sand, or the glimmer of moonlight on the patterns of swirling water. I walk along the sea front, battling wind and crossing on board walks over pockets of delicate swamp, fresh water trickling down to join the ocean. It is in the east, of course; from the land, everything faces east. I watch moonrises, sunrises; since my marriage ended it seems I watch every sunrise through my east-facing bedroom window, unable to rise and greet it, but the sun comes in anyway; golden, muted, reddish, orange, morning after morning.

On the first night of our enactment of Inanna's descent we walk down to the sea in the dark and out onto the rock ledges. The land is behind us and all the eastern sea ahead. Inanna's star, the planet we call Venus, is associated with the east, morning and evening. Like Inanna it travels through the depths of darkness. We bring offerings of a flower, a song and chocolate, which we lay out on the rocks. We can feel the spray of the sea where we sit. Together we call to Ereshkigal. We tell her we are heading down; to look her in the eye and be devoured by her, to devour. We call to Inanna too, the bright one; we ask to walk in her steps and by her side, to learn with her. Then we call to Ninshubar, Inanna's guardian and wise woman and a wave rolls in and breaks, dramatic and bigger than those before it. I take it as a sign we will be looked after. Later we find out that Ninshubar's name translates to Queen of the East. We hold hands. I feel peace and longing and the darkness coming. It is a ritual of intention, of declaration and we feel met in it, not just by each other but by what we call to.

The next day we drive to the labyrinth. It lies in a Sydney park, not far from my home. I have chosen to begin our descent here since a labyrinth seems to me such an obvious signifier of descent, of journeying through layers. We walk through avenues of trees and bike paths, across a road within the park, past ponds with ducks and reeds. The labyrinth is marked out in white paint, prior to being laid into the ground in stone. It's quite off the main pathways, you wouldn't find it unless you knew it was here or stumbled on it by accident. No-one else is within sight. The labyrinth's entry is in the north, we think it is unusual for a labyrinth in this hemisphere, it's in the hottest, blazing, daylit part of the circle. We see it as a fire gate, with the idea that we have to enter through fire; facing flames and heat to even begin our journey.

Inanna went through seven gates before she reached her sister, sacrificing something precious at each gate and we plan to do that, too. Beginning here. We sit down at the entrance to the labyrinth and write out instructions for each other, just as Inanna gave instructions to Ninshubar before descending; what to do if we don't return. His instructions include visiting his mother to explain what has happened to her only son. Reading them I imagine travelling a thousand kilometers to where she lives and trying to tell her what we did, how I lost him, where he's gone. I hope I won't have to do it, but an Underworld journey always has unknown outcomes. My instructions are practical and immediate; make sure I eat, remind me I am a mother, that I have work to do, that I love life. For safekeeping we tuck each other's instructions into our clothes, for the part of us that will, we think, stay separate and apart from this ritual, the Ninshubar part that acts as guardian.

My intention for this journey is release; to free myself from these knots of the body that I am carrying, to be released. Even though I think that if I really leave that marriage behind – not just in time as the months tick on, but let go of my attachment, my commitment, being held into a relating that doesn't exist now I'll hardly know who I am – I can't wait to begin. It's like a shell I have to crack off, a thin layer of brittleness between me and the world. I am holding myself together on the inside, but I feel buried, hidden. Speaking aloud our intentions space opens up, shimmering; we cast a circle enclosing the labyrinth and our ritual and then we are in the loose, free realm of it, trusting that the story will unfold around us.

Standing before the first step onto the paths of the labyrinth we start to sing a song for Inanna and I pour some of the pomegranate juice we have brought across the entryway. We are in a mix of myths here, the labyrinth for Ariadne, pomegranates for Persephone yet enacting Inanna's story. They all have versions of the Underworld in them. I stamp the ground, like knocking at the first gate and look around me – trees over to the west, a lake to the east, the labyrinth straight in front of me, under my feet and I call out; *I come to visit my sister, and to mourn with her*. Of all Inanna's reasons for visiting the Underworld this is the one that resounds within me; I am in mourning and loss, so disoriented that I hardly know where I am going and down is a good direction. Perhaps it is the only direction.

This step into the labyrinth is our first gate. For each gate Inanna went through one of her powers was taken from her, in the form of one of the sacred and magical objects she wore. In this way she was stripped gradually from her status as the Queen of Heaven and Earth to an ordinary being with no special powers, who could die like everyone else. We have agreed that at each gate we will spend a moment in reflection, to understand what we must let go of in order to continue this descent. Because those things are not just losses, it is the release from them that enables her to travel deeper.

For this first gate it seems to me that, as Inanna relinquished her crown, I must relinquish my own status. I list aloud who I am in the world – author, teacher, mother, community member, facilitator, mentor, ritualist – then I cross over the threshold and walk away from it. Away from those roles and away from the first gate. What do those labels even mean? Surely nothing, just the recognition of a set of actions and if I never undertake those actions again, then I am not that thing. They felt like the frames of photos when I named them, not the photos themselves, just the casing. Without them I am not exactly less, but rather more myself. Even though in a labyrinth there's no freedom at all, I feel free, light; it is easy to walk forward.

I hear Fio behind me, making his own offerings to the first gate, beginning his journey that is in the footsteps of mine, the footsteps of Inanna, but every journey is different, each time and already he feels far distant, would be impossible to reach. I catch glimpses of him as we curve about and then on the long unwinding path we pass and pass each other, or walk in tandem briefly beside each other then to separate and turn and pass again. I cannot lose sight of his presence in this process, he is beside me and with me but also, forever held apart. By age, by gender and history, by the simple fact that I am in one body and he in another.

I am still singing under my breath the song we began when we cast the circle and I feel the motion of it, of the labyrinth; unstoppable, pre-determined. The curves unfold at a measured pace and the turns guide my feet. Time is a blur between the first and second gates. I think of Inanna and how full of purpose she was, how determined I am, to be released from the last six months, the last six years of that relationship. How every step is taking me further away from it, further in time, in distance, in ritual; into the mythic realms. I am leaving all that behind.

Until I come to the entrance to the center of the labyrinth; I stop there. I pour another line of pomegranate juice, which I have carried with me, as an offering and a marker of the second gate. Standing there it seems absurd to think I could hang onto my individuality and my preferences for this or that, already in the Underworld and heading down; so I give them away in less than a thought and cross through the gate. Whoever I am, have been, is changing, in flux right this minute in the labyrinth, never mind in my life, past this marriage. I don't actually know what I want anymore. I am not whoever I've been for the past six years and not the person I was before, either. Fio comes in behind me, beside me and we sit down in the center.

Immediately it feels like we are dropping downwards – through the center of the labyrinth and into the earth, the depths – that everything is giving way beneath us. It is dizzying, almost nauseous and we lie down quickly, both of us, in the dirt in the center of the labyrinth and call out to the third gate as we fall – plummet – and I cry out that I let go of relatedness, relationships. Whatever that was, whatever it did to me, all of them through the years, I release them. I might never have another one. They left me – I fell past them – and we lay in silence. Stilled, at the bottom of something. On an irreversible path; with a long way to go. I felt bereft. As if there's not that much holding me to the world. We lie in silence for a while, then we sit up and eventually we go home, walking straight out of the labyrinth, not along its curving paths. We'll come back later, on the way out to do that, assuming we find the way out. We spend that night between the third and fourth gates, suspended. Caught in the inevitable and I think of our lifelines, winding us ever onwards and I think of Inanna, walking through darkness and I feel the pull in myself, gravitational.

The next evening we plot the rest of our descent. We are planning to go down my long narrow flat, counting the back door as the fourth gate, the doorway between the kitchen and living room as the fifth, the door between the living room and corridor as the sixth and we set up a broom propped across the hallway at the very end, near the front door that's never opened as the seventh gate. We put the broom at waist height with fabric draped over it. Inanna ends up in the Underworld *naked and bowed low* so we undress down to four items of clothing each, one for each remaining gate. Then we retreat outside the back door and close it. We stand in a public walkway to talk, in a strange dissonance of the accepted, ordinary world going on – people parking in the street next to us to visit the gym or pick children up, someone climbing the stairs to the upstairs flat over our heads – while we are shifted, caught into the mythic and seeing things in different layers than anyone else would. It seems bizarre to be standing outside the kitchen talking about the fourth gate and yet more essential than anything else we could possibly be doing. We are a little cold and certainly underdressed for anything except an Underworld ritual.

I dedicate this fourth gate to my heart. Like the fourth chakra that is the heart, it's half way and links the upper body and the divine to the lower half of the body and the earth. Not that Inanna thought in those terms, or maybe she did. Such a mix of things go through my head while we stand there looking at my back door, including *get it over* and a sinking responsibility for him by my side; that I got him into this. When I open the door I usher him in first. Not that I am exactly looking after him, taking him on this journey, but to indicate my care, that I am watching over this other being I am bringing with me. I doubt it would be an adequate defense, if I lose him here and I think again of his letter and his mother.

We enter the kitchen. We haven't turned on any lights and it is dimming here, it looks empty. I think of those long underground paths in the Sumerian Underworld, how much space and air there must be down there, air with nothing in it and although the kitchen is filled with the usual things, food and plates and saucepans, benches, a sink and stove and fridge, it also looks abandoned, like a house no-one has entered for years, somewhere the inhabitants walked out of and never returned to. I think that's partly because the light isn't on and it's so strange to be in a kitchen in the semi-dark but also, and really, because by now we are not fully in this world and where an underground earthen path might feel right to us a kitchen with black-and-white squares on the Lino floor is quite alien. We are in the kitchen but not really relating to it, not paying attention, just passing through.

He takes off his jumper and flings it onto the floor. It's a very small, square room and he throws it down between the fridge and the next doorway. It doesn't belong in a kitchen and adds to the sense of this not being a kitchen any longer, more a station of descent and a place of abandoned things and I, thinking of Inanna's breastplate that she leaves behind at the fourth gate, take off my bra from under my t-shirt. I hesitate, not knowing what to do with it and when Fio indicates his jumper, I throw it on top of that. We giggle, imagining what it will look like if anyone comes in before we finish. A passionate embrace so impatient we abandoned clothes in the kitchen, instead of our actual careful pacing into the realms of death.

It was like a game just then, dim and sneaking into the Underworld through the kitchensand we see the black-and-white squares of the floor, like a chessboard. I think of Alice in Wonderland and her mixed-up worlds, I already thought of her when we fell down through the center of the labyrinth and I think of white squares and black squares, life and death and trap floors and sequences of tiles that should be stepped on in a particular order and then the certain knowledge that none of that matters and the doorway looms like an open mouth, sucking us in and drowning us, an indrawing of breath and we on these tides of dusky air, one item of clothing lighter and me, I left behind my heart at that fourth gate, my emotions and it's a release from heaviness, I don't have to carry that anymore. I am released from softness, from hurt, my pain discarded. I feel light and brittle, snappable.

That fifth gate is so close – only a few steps to the doorway out of the kitchen into the living room. I want to be through it already. Standing looking across at it I decide it is personality, to leave behind my personality and we both stride forward, rapidly. We're in the gate, the doorway in a breath and leaving that gate behind. Then the whole landscape changes, out of the chill kitchen into the empty, shadowy living room. I want to dance. It is darker here and spacious compared with the kitchen; I take off my jeans and he takes off his top. I dance a few steps, through the air, feeling easy, light until I reach the doorway out, into the corridor and I stop then, slammed into the air in front of it. This sixth gate seems foreboding. It leads into even darker spaces; the kitchen was dimming, the living room in shadow and the corridor is dark. I don't want to pass through into the narrowness of the corridor. It looks not just constricting, but sinister.

By now we have gone a little strange; both whispering under our breath, *mind, it has to be mind and thought; concepts, understanding* then he puts one hand on the door jamb and I can't imagine anyone actually going through there, into that corridor, except I have five gates behind me and I know it goes in only one direction. I can't get stuck here, in front of the sixth gate. I run my hands over the wooden doorframe; it is smooth and lets me lean into it. Then – we were in the teeth of it – suddenly, shoulder to shoulder we topple through the doorway almost side-by-side though there isn't really room for that. The corridor is dark and narrow and it doesn't look inviting so much as inevitable. I feel strangely light – oh, this is what it's like without the mind – and take off my underpants, leaving my t-shirt on for warmth until the last moment and he takes off his jeans.

There's a thicker darkness. It is intimate in a strange way, that is, he's by my side, I know he's on a journey the same way I am but it's a different journey and even though we are together in this stripping away and we're getting more and more alike, down towards the bones, I have no spare thought for him, as a separate being, all my attention is consumed by forward steps, down the length of this corridor, past bedroom, bathroom, another bedroom. We're moving further and further away from the light and the outside world but I notice my fear is gone. It was all in the mind and I gave that up. Now it's just space and direction and there's only one direction. We get near the final, seventh gate, its curtain dropping to the floor and I go down on my hands and knees onto the carpet. This is it then; death.

He's down on the floor beside me and I feel the heat of his body, through we're an arm's length apart. We are both muttering, jagged words, *body, flesh, mother, my mother, life, this, body, now* and I'm impatient, I can't wait any longer so I pull the t-shirt over my head and crawl through, under the broom, through the curtain into the dead-end cell at the end of the corridor. Into darkness. It's the end.

I crawl up near the front door and lie down naked on the carpet; I assume he has followed though I can't really tell and I can't bring myself to care or even wonder about it. I lie on my stomach thinking of Ereshkigal, surprised it's not colder. A long time passes while the air seems vast, though I know we are in quite a small space; the hugeness of the Underworld and Ereshkigal in atoms, sprinkled about it like dark matter. Eventually my neck starts to hurt and I roll over onto my side and see him. He's on his side too, with his back to me and I have a sudden vision of thousands of us there, curled up in the Underworld, waiting. Like the dead souls, like fetuses or ideas waiting to be born, like seeds, like potential. Or in hibernation, stasis, the pause between the out and in breaths, just as life is like the length of time between an in-breath and an out-breath. Someone walks past heavily in the corridor in the flat next door, which is really only feet away from us on the other side of the wall. It seems odd but okay; we are dead, after all, with no preferences and no say in anything. Others are still alive, moving around and going about their business. They are in the upper world. But we are down.

Eventually we stand up and go and put some clothes on but we don't talk much, there doesn't seem any point. Everything important has already happened, or has yet to happen or in any case doesn't concern us now. Everything seems strangely easy, to matter less, not to be able to impact me and I observe the world as if from a distant place; though I am right there I am hardly there. Things happen, don't happen, continue to happen and I am held, some part of me, some significant part in a space without parameters, a space of infinite void where I am without preferences, personality, relationships, mind, status, my heart – and really, almost without myself. There's a small, ticking spark of me still down in that corridor, in the Underworld; that seems real and the rest, shadow.

Three nights we stay in the Underworld, like it says in the story. It's quite peaceful, remote. I don't miss those things I left behind. I think of us – our souls, maybe – lying there at the end of the corridor while we – our ghosts – move about the world going places, doing things, interacting with the living. I feel more tired than usual and hungry. As if my reserves of energy are low. It is a time of not-thinking, of release from all that has been cluttering my head, pushing for my attention these past six months, the anxiety, relief mixed with guilt, the distress of failure, of broken promises, the tormenting memories and reworkings and confrontation of an ended relationship. It is a blessing to be claimed by darkness and surrender, to lay everything down, even myself, at the feet of Ereshkigal and just wait. Nothing to solve anymore, nothing to do, nothing to become. Just wait. Let time tick past and trust the story, be held in the lap of the Dark Goddess, be blank and know nothing.

Three days is a brief time to spend in the Underworld, but perhaps it is enough, for now. It is what Inanna has, what the moon does each month. Three days of being held in the Underworld, of being lost before returning, changed. The two of us spend that time apart. He goes to stay with a friend while I have a weekend teaching; I feel clear and calm in it, engaged more with others than with myself. I sleep deeply during the nights and feel focused during the days.

When we come back together, before we reverse our journey to come up we do a ritual-within-a-ritual, to listen to Ereshkigal, the Dark Goddess. Firstly we call to the *kugurra* and the *galatur*, the little creatures made by the god Enki and sent down into the Underworld to rescue Inanna. In the story the act of listening that they undertake is pivotal to Inanna being returned to life. Ereshkigal has been alone in the Underworld and even though she's expressing grief and pain, no-one is listening until the *kugurra* and the *galatur* arrive. We call to them almost in whispers, conjuring them out of the atmosphere, the mythos; calling them to us as if we were making them anew. They are formed from the left-over scraps of life-giving earth, we remake them with our breath. We are sitting cross-legged on my bed, in the room that opens onto the piece of corridor where we laid our bodies down three days ago and died. It could be Ereshkigal's bed, in her underground chamber.

Fio goes first, breathing deeply and speaking as Ereshkigal, all his griefs and uncertainties; the places where the Underworld holds onto him. In the story the *kugurra* and the *galatur* echo Ereshkigal, who moans and groans when Inanna can no longer speak. Each thing he says I echo back to him, in *kugurra* whispers, in *galatur* whispers. I feel their voices sighing through me, sad for the world and all its sorrow, grief and fear. My mission – their mission – is clear in my head; his sighs become mine, his sorrows and hurts are reflected by me. His griefs seem small – human and understandable, brief and simple – and also vast and unending, the pains of living. I feel sad with him and also released with him, at each whisper.

When it's my turn I curl up on the bed. Abandonment is what I feel in my guts, my heart, my story; abandonment and betrayal. I say it again and again, the shock still vibrating through me, rejection and shame, loneliness and how hard it is to reach out and how few, how very few notice if I do or not. Saying it does not undo it, but it does release it. Hearing it said back to me in his voice, each piece, is an acknowledgement that changes something, inside me. One person, at least, has listened and heard. On one thread I am connected again. Once I have said it all I sit up and we offer each other the water of life; dripping and sprinkling it on each other, touching wet fingers to lips and then a piece of dark chocolate as the food of life; an earthy grittiness on the tongue.

We rise and walk back to the corridor where we died, lie down and gather ourselves again. We can return now, put on all our layers again and body, life, is the first one. We crawl back through the threshold of the seventh gate, this blanket folded over a broom wedged across the corridor that has waited here for three days, determining ourselves into life. Into this body that each of us has been given, that we inhabit. Rising we walk down the corridor side by side, pace for pace. At the doorway to the living room we stop and run our hands over the door frame, as if we never imagined to be facing this side of it, heading up. We did never imagine it. It was the sixth gate, that I was so reluctant to enter. I can't quite summon up that feeling now; what was I afraid of?

Through we go. I feel a quickening, a thrill; it's my mind I meet here and I remember I danced through this room. Already we are at the fifth gate, of personality and I promise to be more open, flexible; to allow myself to grow and change. To let my mind expand and not be so fearful, hanging onto things. We walk through it into the kitchen. I pick up my bag and we hesitate a moment before the back door. Heart; feelings, the fourth gate. Then out we go into the world; sunshine and fresh air. I feel my heart but it is not so burdensome. Something has been cleansed from it, released in the ritual and those three days of nothingness, it feels more my own. We close the door behind us – more than halfway out by now, we are on the return.

I drive us back to the park and we walk to the labyrinth, carrying flowers. We enter this time from the south, stepping straight over the rings to the center, where we lie down in the third gate. That was where I left my relationships and, lying on the ground again and trying to think clearly, I can find hardly any to pick up. My son, of course, and Fio who is beside me; a few others and that's it. They are light, perhaps not quite enough. I don't actually remember to pick up the relationship with my ex-partner; I realize that only hours later. I think I left it there, in the dirt of the third gate. We rise and start walking out through the labyrinth.

The second gate is the first step onto the path, out of the center and I step over it without pausing, not aware that I've done it straight away. Then I have to stop a few paces on and integrate it. Oh, preferences, that was what I left behind there. Preferences – to be seen a particular way, to wear this or that label or be defined by certain words. It feels incidental with the strength of the Underworld in me. Though I'm sure they will accumulate again, for now I feel stripped fresh, clean of those fiddly little things. I lead us as we walk the long paths out, singing to Inanna as we go, turning on the paths of her memory. At the entrance, the first gate, I stop and assess. This status-thing, Inanna's crown; I see its usefulness, its beauty. I will wear it again in the world, though I know it's just a token, an emblem. It is of me and from me, an expression of me in the world and I am re-entering the world. I accept it back.

When we are both completely out we turn and place our flowers down at the corners of the entrance. We thank Ninshubar, that part of ourselves that remained outside the descent, waiting and watching able to fetch help when necessary. This journey feels so real, as if we have been on a boat to a foreign land, eaten and slept there and learnt what we could and then returned. We stand at the entrance to the labyrinth, holding hands and gazing into each other's eyes. He calls for love to come into my life; I feel gentle, open and generous and I smile, acquiescing. I turn him back to face the labyrinth and recognize him as holding knowledge of the paths of the Underworld, of Ninshubar; Ereshkigal who is so forgotten; the *galatur* and the *kugara* and this story of Inanna's descent. Now we hold this, together know with Inanna, some of what it is to travel to the Underworld and return.

Process – Enacting a Myth

Enacting myth involves unfolding a piece of the story and physically stepping into it – directly into the mythos, it often feels like. This is most powerful and resonant when done in a group, partly to build and hold the energy and partly because of the number of variations – and therefore the depth and complexity – that can occur with multiple people. Here are three different ways to enact a myth.

Exploring One Moment, Action or Transition in a Myth

This method is great to unpack a single piece of myth – usually a complex motif such as Eve eating the apple, Marduk challenging Tiamat or Theseus heading into the labyrinth. Often I would use a single prop, for example an apple for Eve (you would need multiple apples if working with a group), a spear for Marduk, a ball of thread for Theseus.

- Preferably stand in a circle, with the prop in the center. The circle should be wide enough for the person or people entering it to be able to move freely. If this means there are large gaps between people in the circle, that is fine. Standing is preferable to sitting, when possible, as it enables quick movement both to get out of the way and also into the center.
- After speaking through the intent, instructions and grounding or doing whatever other preparatory work is desired, begin as a group to sound or tone together. Invite this sounding to call in the energy of the mythic character you are working with, to invoke and hold space for them.
- When the sound is steady and confident, the first person enters the circle and interacts with the prop. The group

continues sounding, responding to the actions and mood of the person in the center.

- When the person in the center feels complete – and this is often quite a short time, one to two minutes – they leave the center and someone else enters it. This repeats until everyone has been in the center; sometimes people like to go in twice.

- Discuss all that you saw, heard and felt, while in the center and in the circle. You can begin with a round, where each person can share uninterrupted and then widen the discussion to reflect on the myth and how your understandings have grown, changed or been challenged.

- This method also works with interactions between two, or several characters, with different people stepping in to claim the different parts each time you play the scene through. For example, the division of the world between Zeus, Poseidon and Hades would have three people in the center; the confrontation between Inanna and Dumuzi after she returns from the Underworld would have two people.

Enacting a Significant Interaction Within a Myth

This takes a larger group of people, between ten to twenty is ideal. It is best done using a soundscape, possibly of musical instruments (or just one instrument) for example a drum, harp, harmonium or moyo drum. It employs a method of very light aspecting, where the aspect is drawn not into a person but into an object – a veil, necklace, mask or other prop – and that prop is handed between players as the scene continues. Examples in myth where this might be used are the interaction between Eve and the serpent in the Garden of Eden, the interaction between Freyja and the dying soldier on the battlefield and Ceridwen's chase of Taliesin. Once again, each person present holds – in this case, both – roles.

- Begin with clear instructions, grounding, casting and whatever other preparations you wish to make.
- Ask for a volunteer to begin, by holding the active role, for example the serpent, Freyja, Ceridwen.
- Invoke, and collectively draw the aspect into the object, for example an apple, a necklace, a cauldron.
- All take their places in the scene – for example, everyone but the first person becomes a dying body on the battlefield – the music begins and the first person takes the object and enters the scene.
- The first person chooses one other person to play the scene with, speaking if they wish – if they are the serpent they tempt one Eve, or if Freyja they pick one solider to try to save – and once that interaction is complete, they hand across the object (and thus the active role) to the other person and take that person's place. They use an agreed way to indicate that they have already taken a turn, such as holding a hand over their heart.
- The second person then repeats the scene, now in the active role, with a third person. For example, the person who was the dying soldier now takes the part of Freyja.
- The scene plays through as many times as there are people, with the final person returning to the first person, to complete the circle of interactions.
- To finish, thank the deity or being and release the aspect from the object.
- Discuss what you saw, heard and felt throughout the process. Include discussion on the myth and your understandings of it.

Enacting a Whole Scene Within a Ritual

This could be used for any sized group, even one limited to the number of characters in the myth you are working with. For example you could, with four people, play out the scene from Egyptian mythology where Osiris is murdered at a great feast by his brother Set, with Isis and Nephthys present. Or you could set a scene – for example Tam Lin being rescued from the Faerie Queen by Janet – into a ritual with fifty other people present. To reliably enact a scene from myth the deities or characters are usually not in aspect, they retain full human awareness and control. It is known ahead of time who is playing which character, and the scene is usually only played once. Onlookers may be invited to be part of the story – for example to be part of the Faerie Host, or guests at the feast of Osiris and Isis.

- Put some time into creating the scene and setting, for example creating the crossroads for Janet, or structuring how the feast will work with Osiris and Set. If it is a ritual with a large number of people consider practical elements such as how they will see and hear the scene, where they will be and whether they are purely onlookers or participate in some way.

- This is more likely than the other methods to have words spoken during the enactment. Consider how you will handle this; is there a set script, a storyteller; is it spontaneous or is it held within a certain type of language or form?

- If you are playing out the scene or story on its own, not set within a larger ritual, begin with talking through what will physically happen in the enactment. Ground, cast a circle if you wish and begin. If the scene is within a larger ritual, all that may have already happened, even some time before the scene begins.

- After the scene has occurred and the ritual has finished, you might like to talk through how it went, from a practical perspective as well as any mythological insights you have gained.

Exercise – Finding Your Own Story in a Myth

The story of a goddess – or even a fairytale – will sometimes call to us strongly and we can't really explain why. It may even be a myth we don't especially like or a story that irritates us, yet it nags, catches at the edges of our attention and appears somehow ever unresolved. Its motifs may repeat in our dreams or trance states and emerge, uninvited, into our creative projects; our poetry, gardening, painting or music. We may already be enacting the myth in some way, or living parallel to its themes or storyline.

The following exercise is a way of bringing this material into focus in the context of our own lives. Perhaps this will be a revelation to us, psychologically satisfying or challenging or perhaps it will prove to be a deepening of the mystery. It is a process of discovery as much as one of producing something, yet it also produces something. We create a story – or song or artwork or something else – from the fusion of our own story with a myth, fairytale or goddess story.

A story that has always haunted me – frightened me, really, yet I could not shake free of it – was a Russian tale of a little girl running away from a witch. She threw various – precious – belongings over her shoulder to create barriers between them, a comb, a ribbon and a mirror, which magically transformed to a forest, a river and a mountain. The witch, Baba Yaga, was slowed but never deterred. I can't remember the ending. When I begin to put pieces of my life into that story it makes a horrid kind of sense, including the fact that I can't remember the ending. Obviously the ending is still to come, in some way I'm still being chased by that terrifying witch. But if I was to sit and write it out – I could write my own ending.

The strength of this process lies in the depth of response or connection we have to a story. To pick a random myth or fairytale and write ourselves into it would not be the same. This is about the interplay between our own lives and psyches with the story or mythos; each informing and revealing the other.

This is the method I use to find my own story within a myth or fairytale:

- Choose a mythic story or fairytale with strong resonance for you
- Divide a page into two columns
- List down the first column the characteristics of the main character or the one you are drawn to. If there are two characters you feel a resonance with (for example, Snow White and her stepmother) do this exercise twice, once for each character.
- In the second column comment on each characteristic listed, as it relates to yourself. So your comments might include things such as *I was like this when I was younger, exactly like me, opposite of me, how I wish I was.*
- Divide another page into three columns.
- In the first column chronologically list the events of the story, leaving space between each.
- In the second column list one or more events from your own life that seem related to each event, as if the event was in isolation (not in the context of a story). For example next to the listed item of *the Queen orders Snow White's death* I might have *feeling unsafe as a child, watching my friend at her son's funeral, feeling helpless as a mother.*
- In the third column write down the emotional resonance from the conjunction of these two events, the one from the story and the ones from your own life. For example I might have *the ties of life and death between a mother and child.*

Once these sheets are completed spend some time reading through them. Let the story you wish to write arise from within. We may have begun this project thinking we will write about an incident in our own lives, weaving threads of the goddess story through it, only to discover what we want to write is a first person narrative in the voice of the goddess, made more recognizable by the emotional influences from our own experiences.

I am a writer and would choose to write a story. Maybe that works for you as well, or maybe for you it is a song, a painting, a picture book or craft piece that comes out of this process. This book is filled with different examples of how writing can weave together a myth and parts of one's own life.

Once you have created your story, painting or song you can share it with others, place it on your altar, use it as an entrée into ritual or personal process or just allow it to continue stepping you deeper and deeper into the mythos, both the collective one we all share and your own personal, evolving mythos. This process may inspire you to literally enact the myth or story with others, research it further, or invoke that goddess into your life in some way.

Aspecting the Goddess

Aspecting, sometimes also called drawing down a goddess, is an exciting and dynamic way to work with deity. Strong containers are built into this technique. *Aspecting* is usually done within the context of a ritual, thus there is the container of the ritual itself, its intention and whatever circle has been cast. Others in the ritual will have been instructed on the purpose of the aspecting and guidelines as to how it will take place; for example, which part of the ritual it will occur in and how they may approach or interact with the person aspecting. Ideally very clear guidelines are set into the act of drawing down or invocation of the deity, about the exact nature of the aspecting to take place as well as the length of time it is to continue for, which is usually but not always the length of the ritual. Most importantly there is the discipline, clarity and self-knowledge required from the person or people who are going to aspect.

As with every other act of our lives we cannot separate ourselves from the aspecting. No matter who or what we are aspecting, we are the channel, the container, the filter and everything we receive – and every word or action – comes through us. If we do not recognize and work with this the aspecting becomes muddied. Once we recognize ourselves within the mix we can begin to work more effectively. Understanding our own stories, shadows, desires and emotional triggers means we can more consciously work the thread of aspecting the deity. That thread – and understanding that a deity may be made up of millions of threads – will be different, and differently expressed, from the thread the person standing next to us might receive, were they to be the one aspecting. But ideally it will be recognizable to others that this thread is something extra, other and different than ourselves, even while it is colored or flavored by having been received and passed through us, as the container.

Aspecting is magical. If presencing is holding the hand of the goddess, if enacting myth is stepping into the mythos, aspecting is breathing the air of the gods and being transformed, alchemically, by and with it. Ideally it offers others, not aspecting themselves, some idea of that air, perhaps even a breath or two of it as they watch, listen to or are touched by the person aspecting the deity.

Aspecting, as taught and practiced in the Reclaiming Tradition, is often discussed in terms of percentages. That is, we enter the experience intending to aspect to forty percent or sixty percent. An awareness of this percentage is carried not just by ourselves – who might weaken during the moment and give way to a much greater percentage – but also by someone else, usually designated as a tender for the length of the aspecting (and afterwards). The tender is ideally someone experienced in aspecting themselves, able to follow what is happening with us and talk us down, or through an experience; someone strong enough or who knows us well enough to communicate with us regardless of the deity we are aspecting or how strong that deity's influence on us might be.

Aspecting is different from possession, where a human body is handed to a god or goddess to inhabit, or possess, often for as long as, or in any way that the deity manifests. After possessory rites it is common for the human to have very little or no memory of what has occurred. After aspecting certain things may be blurred, including a sense of time – which may appear to have been either longer or shorter than the actual time – much understanding of the rest of the ritual, and the exact words spoken. Returning after aspecting one can commonly be hungry, tired, emotional, energized, withdrawn. Having a tender helps negotiate this return to one's normal self.

Deities are all different, just as people are all different. So the combination of one person and one goddess has many different ways it can play out. It is not just self-knowledge that will help us in aspecting, but also knowledge of the deity we are intending to aspect. Usually aspecting is prepared for at some length, prior to the ritual. Depending how deep the aspect and how pivotal the ritual piece is, this may be from days to months beforehand. Often the person doing the aspecting is strongly drawn to the deity and the ritual role, but not always. One WitchCamp ritual I had no role in, thinking it would be useful to be on the outside, observing and edge-walking. By the time we decided that Ceridwen should be present in light aspect for a small piece of the ritual, there was no one else left in our planning team who wasn't already doing something at that time.

Ceridwen's part was to address the ritual and speak on abandoning the newly born Taliesin. I had fierce regard for Ceridwen and her power and no particular desire to get that close to her. But I took the role and retreated into writing, revisiting my days of early motherhood, what it was to hold a newborn in my arms. That led me to contemplate those mothers who do give up their babies – to adoption, for example, but also those who are forced to, through war and death. I came into an awareness that we all give up our babies to the future, to their own life paths and the river Ceridwen places Taliesin onto surely demonstrates this. From here I went into aspecting Ceridwen and what she spoke through me, in her tenderness and depth surprised me and revealed previously unseen layers of the story and of mothering, my own mothering.

At the end of this section are two exercises designed to guide you along the path of stepping into aspecting a goddess in ritual.

Eve

Eve called to me out of that first story in the Old Testament in the King James Bible. I didn't know why she was calling or what she was saying. Lilith is usually considered the interesting figure, older and with links back to the pre-Sumerian mythos. She gives birth to demons, marking her as a wise woman, shaman and witch. Yet it is Eve who has the dialogue with the serpent, Eve who picks and eats the apple, Eve whose actions instigate that confrontation with the all-powerful Yahweh and the expulsion of humans from Eden.

Eve. In Ancient Hebrew it means *life*. Eve is the evening; in Jewish lore and also for the Celts days do not begin with a dawn, but at the eve. They are birthed then, entering into darkness and only half way through does each day become bright and blessed by the sun. Eve gives birth, to days and humankind; Eve is our mother. She talked with serpents, ate apples, had sex and gave birth, none of those actions being laid down in the book of rules. Eve broke the rules. It's said, compared with Lilith, Eve was tame, but look at this list – serpent, apple, sex, birth.

When the story of Eve and the Serpent is chosen for CloudCatcher Reclaiming WitchCamp in our third year I think people like the idea of the serpent, though I am listening to Eve. I still couldn't quite hear what she was saying, but it seemed important. This story is on the first pages of a book referred to as our spiritual and cultural heritage in Western traditions. If you only ever read a few pages of the Bible, this is what you would get: Eden and Adam and Eve, the garden and the tree, the serpent and the apple, God and the angel with the flaming sword, curses and exodus. What kind of a cultural inheritance is that? – Unless you want to instill fear and subservience, of course, then it's quite good.

Was Eve bowed by the weight of that or was she just, in the way of a good story, moving as the narrative impelled her to, taking the steps necessary to advance the plot, expose the inconsistencies and the inevitable law of what-must-be? Were she and the serpent in league? Some retellings have Lilith as the serpent, it's a feminist subversion with Adam playing innocent, someone has to be blamed and why should it be him? But by doing that he removes himself from the drama, now it's all about women and snakes and apples; snakes that shed their skins and so have always symbolized rebirth and reincarnation, apples that hold seeds inside themselves, the fruit holding the whole tree, or many whole trees within itself so that it doesn't matter if it was an apple or a fig or a pomegranate or an apricot or a persimmon, they all do that. Hold themselves within themselves. Like snakes, like women giving birth to children, one and many, children out of their bellies, their wombs, who suck from their breasts and grow up, to do it all over again. Birth and rebirth and reincarnation.

At CloudCatcher WitchCamp a beautiful Tree has been constructed out of dead branches, it stands in the middle of the small room where our Path, the morning course of study is held. A dozen of us come here to investigate the way back to Paradise. We tie apples and other fruit onto the branches and we play in the Garden. We read the sentence that says if you eat of the fruit of the Tree of Knowledge *thou shalt be as gods.* We say that line many times, repeating it whispering it singing it out, *thou shalt be as gods, thou shalt be as gods thou shalt be as gods as gods as gods.* We are naked by now, we have been gradually stripping off our clothes day by day until we are used to singing and drumming naked, having discussions naked, processing our emotions naked, writing in our journals naked; when we leave the room at break time it seems a hassle to put on clothes and some people don't, dashing back to their dorms or to the toilets nude. Skin has become a thing of pleasure to wear and other people's nakedness ordinary.

We have wound time back to the Garden of Eden. We wound

the story back too, turning up fully clothed to the gates, guarded by the angel with the flaming sword; we took turns in holding the sword and one by one felt the weariness of that angel – how long has he stood there? Some of us slid by while he turned the other way, others shouted or negotiated or commiserated but he did not seek to stop us, he who had been standing there for maybe four thousand years with his back turned to Paradise and facing only the deserts and exile, though he had done nothing to deserve it but been loyal throughout time.

Inside the garden we stripped down to our underwear, token fig leaves as we stepped further back into the layers of story and confronted the one who told us *thou shalt not* and we shouted and sang and danced and wept our defiance and we said *we shall and we have, look how we live, who we are and we've come to claim our inheritance, this is ours this garden was made for us and here we are* and some said that God welcomed them and others that he was strangely absent and others that he thundered and roared but that did not sway them and they were not bowed down. When we sang and screamed and danced ourselves through all that, then the sound died down and we were one step closer back, to Paradise.

Where was Eve in all this? Waiting. We did not take this journey as Eve, although maybe we acknowledged ourselves as her daughters and sons; we did it in our own right, our modern, Western, personal journeys leading us right back to her, back to that gate locked against us, back to that garden, that tree. To Eve, the mother of people. There's something like birth in this journey, being reborn and claiming original innocence, not sin, claiming we belong to this garden, to Paradise. Paradise, the walled garden. A place of cultivation, where choice has intervened and within those walls we find what is precious, nurtured, where the mind – of humans or of God – has separated out from the wild and built a garden where before was desert, or has built walls to shelter from the wind or contain the warmth. Paradise.

A garden. A place where beauty is cultivated, food, pleasure. A place requiring gardening; it does not happen by itself. Are we offering ourselves as gardeners, then, by our return?

When we approach the tree we are naked; bodies young and old, female and male. We are becoming used to each other so that what is remarkable, now, is not this nakedness, not standing naked in a circle, but the tree in the middle of a room. It is a beautiful construction and in our eyes it leafs, it flowers, it fruits; it beckons to us from the mythic, from Eden, from one of the birthplaces of our culture. We stand in wonder before it. Caught in its branches is a mask on a stick, a half-mask, for the serpent. One of us steps forward, naked and takes that mask, begins to twist it in their hands, twine it through the air, serpent-like with a little hissing and another of us steps forward, naked, we are all naked and the one holding the mask hisses, whispers *thou shalt be as gods* and the rest of us around the edge echo sigh *thou shalt be as gods* and the one of us who walks naked, drawn, curious, awake moves closer to the serpent who twists away to double back and utter again, *thou shalt be as gods.*

Under the gaze of the serpent she/he/they reach up, I reach up, each one of us in turn reaches up to take that offering, that dare, *thou shalt be as gods.* One by one we pick the fruit and yes we bite into it, choice this time, but surely that time, every time, all times it is choice and offered that choice who would refuse? Knowledge. To know – and thus to be as gods. To taste. To ingest. To allow knowledge to infuse one. What do you know? That I am flesh and the fruit is flesh. That the tree offers like to like, the serpent offers what is. Each time this happens the one holding the serpent mask sighs and places it down and the one of us who tasted the fruit twists and picks it up and turns to look at us through the mask and whispers, *thou shalt be as gods.* Then the next one of us, naked, we are all naked, steps forward.

We see the serpent seduce and tempt and dare, slither and strike, hover and weave; we see it as tempter and tempted, we hear it sing and whisper and incant and declaim, again and again those words *thou shalt be as gods, thou shalt be as gods*. Each one of us Eve and not Eve, each one of us in our own bodies, our skin, nothing between us and Paradise, us and the serpent, us and the fruit we step forward, we hear those serpent words of knowledge dripping into our skins more sensual than caresses, as irrefutable as poison and yet the nectar when we bite in and the juice runs into us, down our throats and the serpent, smiling perhaps and laying down the mask for its next incarnation, folds away. The serpent's next incarnation is us, each time, us naked and in the garden and with the taste of the fruit still in our mouths. *Thou shalt be as gods*. Having tasted, we call the next one in, *as gods, as gods*.

That night in ritual with the whole camp we go into the garden. I am aspecting Eve. I have decided I will do it naked and am reassured by the promise of those aspecting the serpent – four of them, who split apart and join together in a sinuous and inhuman manner – that they will be naked as well. I am not young or slender, I am middle aged and although I think nudity is beautiful and important and sacred, to be naked alone in a room of fifty clothed people is an uncomfortable thought. Path is smaller and we are all naked together. For Eve I will do this and trust that when I am Eve, things will seem different, but I give Jarrah, who is my tender, a large shawl and say I do not know that I will want to be naked for the whole ritual. He carries it with him, over his shoulder.

I asked if he would paint my skin, beforehand and we retreated to my room after dinner. I ask for flowers and vines, scattered over my shoulder and cascading down my back and over my breast and stomach on the left side. I have an eye mask to wear, it is green and gold and looks a bit like a garden, a flower, a butterfly. When I take my clothes off we begin singing; a kind of muttered chanting half under our breaths, partly to each other but even more, to Eve. We start with a chant from the camp, but quickly it changes and turns until we are tying words together, hearing them and sending them back and forth between us and I stand there while he paints me with flowers and vines and I feel I am changing.

Something is coming through me, coming into me, like sap or maybe pollen, waking in the sunlight that is the attention of these two people, myself and Jarrah, this young man named for a tree. In this we are both tenders for Eve, though I allow my consciousness to loosen, a little, and float on the painting, on the chanting, on skin and cold air and he keeps his pinned to the moment, to the paintbrush and skin and color and I feel him drawing a circle around me with his concentration and intent and chanting while I stand in the center and deepen, drop, open, awaken and it feels like the threads of Eve are gathered to me through the vining, through the chant and paint and flowering and the spiraling focus of two minds, two bodies in service to this.

I have a satin slip, a dull mauve color. I can slide it off my shoulders so it slithers to the floor. We go down to the ritual and already I feel half-altered, inside a space more real than this night of cold grass and stars, of people gathering and then of drums and the inside space; I go to Eve's altar and stay there like a small homeplace among those gathering. I am human too, but I feel anchored to something larger, something older, to the garden or the roots of the tree maybe. I have said I will go into aspect sixty percent and already, before we have begun I feel I am in forty percent. I listen to all the early grounding, casting and invocations, suspended in a waiting that is just one breath to the next, no impatience or anxiety or anticipation. Just presence. When it is our turn, to invoke Eve and call her into aspect, the thread that Jarrah and I spun earlier holds us together without words and we walk into the center of the circle. I turn to face him and he calls not to me, but through me, to Eve and holding his eyes, only his eyes, I pull first one shoulder strap and then the other over my shoulders so that my slip falls down to the ground and I come another degree of alive.

Jarrah leads me back into the circle but by now I am shimmering, on the inside, although I know I am naked it seems irrelevant. When we are released from this standing in one place I dart, I weave among the people. I am fascinated by them especially the women and I rush up to them and reach out my hands my gaze my longing and they – they reach out to me. To Eve. They weep. Some of them take their tops off to bare their breasts, more than I expected. We laugh together. Something is happening in the ritual and I don't really know what, I don't really care what, all of me is bound here in skin and body and the room is somehow mine, or hers, this is her moment to come through and she does.

There's a stir, a disturbance and a twisting shape comes through the door – the serpent. I look up and see them, four joined into one and I see they are not naked, they wear loincloths and my attention wavers, breaks for a moment. They said they would be naked, too. Shock, enough to break through my daze of Eve and register surprise, distaste. They could have told me, at least. There is a flavor of deceit, I thought we had an agreement but no, they are playing their own game and so I feel divided from them; it speaks to me more clearly than anything else could that the serpent is not on Eve's side, the serpent moves with its own concerns.

The ritual calls for Eve to be intrigued by the serpent, so I play with that but really I am cross and not drawn towards them. I linger at the edges as they split into four and begin their tempting, like spruikers at a fair, tricksters and magicians and ringmasters, calling their wares while brandishing a whip, summoning equal parts temptation and awe. Then – we are allowed out of this room and into the night and I run for the doors. It does cross my mind that it will be cold out there, that I will be cold, but Eve is not interested in that, she is through the door and I do love the freedom of it, listening to that call and just responding. They stream after me, the people, clothed and unclothed and partly clothed and I do not stop to put on my shoes, which is not like me at night in the dark and cold but is exactly Eve. Perhaps she does not even know what shoes are.

Outside as soon as my feet finish with the brick paving and arrive at the grass it is bliss. I am not interested in the people, out here, though inside I liked interacting with them. Here I am more intent on just being. I am a mixture of laughing and crying; I still think I am only sixty percent Eve but the rest of me feels no need to halt or redirect her and I have let go of my hesitations. She wants to lie down and roll on the wet grass, I let her. She wants to be on her hands and knees, digging her fingers through the grass and into the earth, why not? Jarrah is suddenly there, in front of me, I'm sure he has been all along but in this moment he looks fascinating to me, that tug of concern around his eyes, that attention he is giving me. I laugh and smile to show that everything is all right and he lets me smear some of the dark wet earth onto his skin. I have forgotten that he painted those flowers on me, earlier, by now they are a part of me, but perhaps it is a return gift, the soil, the mark of the land.

We seem confined to this small slope of lawn with buildings on three sides. I am not sure why because the dark stretch of downhill, ahead of me is beckoning and when I look up and around and see the sweep of hills, so close, I can easily imagine running up there to be a part of the night in the forest but somehow, when I get near the edges of the space the other people are in, I get turned back. It is not serious enough an impediment for me to want to break it, though the clouded night seems to me ideal for exploration, for discovery, for adventure. Sometimes, in flickers, it crosses my mind that perhaps I was supposed to be doing something in particular, at this part of the ritual but when I search my mind I can't remember anything; perhaps I even ask Jarrah, *do I have to do anything?* and it seems not, it seems Eve can just be here in the garden at night.

I gaze at the sky, away from the close hills backing us; in the east and north and behind and between the clouds I see a glimmer. Of course; it's Easter, which means there is a full moon. It would have risen by now and it's there somewhere, since I am facing east. I feel a tremor go through me, a shiver not of cold but something else. Magic. Power. I can feel the moon there and when I stretch out my arm it feels like threads connect my fingertips to the rays of it, the moon rays blocked by cloud and I start to sing. It's not the quiet muttered singing we did earlier, invoking Eve while painting flowers and vines this is loud, a love song and I'm not afraid and don't bother to be quiet though I don't think anyone else notices particularly, by now all the people are engaged in their own journeys in the garden.

I sing a song to the moon and I feel it vibrating through my body and it's as if I can pull the moon to me, I believe I can, I feel myself doing it. Or, I feel Eve doing it. Because if it were just me I might sit on the slope and wait for it, trusting it will emerge at some stage, or I might sing quietly under my breath, just to keep myself company but I would not sing like this, commandingly and also with longing, enticing, drawing the moon out, which is what Eve does. The clouds are thinning, the shimmer grows and almost I am laughing with the joy of it, the body of the moon I can feel it searching me out I can feel how it belongs with me or I belong with it and I move my hands, my arms, the threads between us impatiently and I watch it reveal itself.

Eve called the moon out. The clouds ribbon apart and there it is and she calls out in triumph and love and I think she calls *the moon, the moon!* and some people turn to look but by now some are headed back inside and anyway no-one knows it was me, it was her who pulled it out from behind those clouds, except Jarrah, he knows, I can feel it in him that knowledge of what he saw and I stand there in the full moon light, Eve stands there and I am so glad for her, that she got this, got to do this and feel her own power, her connection to all this growing of trees and grass and earth in the night and now we let her have this radiance of moonlight called forth.

Jarrah suggests we should go back inside. That is clearly ridiculous, neither Eve nor I have any patience with that idea. Now that we are outside, why wouldn't we stay here forever? I point that out and I hear him negotiating with someone for a bit more time. More people are leaving to return inside but I don't mind if I'm the only one left here; the moon is still out, the moon that I called, how would I leave it now? It came to my call. I can't understand why anyone would choose to go inside but I don't try to understand it.

He waits with me, patiently. At some times through the last half hour he has offered me the shawl he still carries but I don't want it, I'm not cold. In the Eve persona I have forgotten that originally I thought I might not be comfortable being naked for so long. Eve hasn't noticed since she got outside that she wasn't clothed or had any desire to put anything around her. I thought, the forty percent part of me, that Eve would be more interested in these people and at the beginning, inside, she was. But out here the air and grass and earth, the trees and hills and moon have claimed her. She doesn't want to go back.

Eventually nearly everyone else has gone. Jarrah takes my arm and says, *it's time* and he has a different tone in his voice, maybe he's sad. I don't feel sad, more – uncomprehending. To please him, really, I begin to take a few steps towards the building, which is still a little way off. He's talking to me, although I'm not listening, I'm more having a private conversation with the moon. Then my attention is drawn away, I look down at the ground where I'm treading or towards the lighted building and in that flicker, a cloud starts to come back and I stop still. I could call out the moon again, I know I could and it seems such a waste, to leave it, to leave this game, this serenade of the moon and I am beginning to have a more sinister feeling about inside, that I really don't want to go there. That Eve doesn't want to go there.

We do go inside, I let him lead me away from the moon and the grass. Through the doors we are in the ritual again. The ritual. I had more or less forgotten that. I can feel it is drawing to a conclusion and I know Eve is that conclusion. Why else have all these people gathered together to remember me and play with me, even if only for an hour or so, in a garden of our making? There is a basket of apples in the middle of the floor, I know it belongs to me. I walk over to it and stand there quietly, some other part of the ritual is happening with people's attention elsewhere, but I know I will be able to gather them when I have to. This is the piece I had to remember, I had to discover. This is the piece I have been heading towards all this time – not just the time of this ritual, since the invocation of flowers and vines in the cold bedroom – but since I asked to take this role back in the planning, since we chose Eve as a story eight months ago, since Eve called to me out of those pages of the King James Bible. All those whispers I've been half-hearing all this time, now is the time for them to come together, to come into words, to be spoken. Now is the time for her to speak.

I would still say I am forty percent here, that I have not forgotten what has to happen, that I have no hesitation in playing my role in the ritual but something else has occurred, in that time outside. Eve and I have lost our edges. I don't switch back and forwards between aspecting her and thinking my own thoughts, I don't need to shut myself off, even temporarily, to carry her. I am holding both streams at once. I feel her and I know myself and a little of her warmth is lost, in that, knowing what will come, but none of my purpose. I crouch down over the apples, gathering strength, gathering voice. I feel my feet planted on the floor. I am aware of my nakedness but it has long since ceased to feel strange, by now it is just the way I am. I take deeper and deeper breaths, so that when it is time to call out my voice will carry through the room.

Oh it is obvious now, maybe it was always obvious. I felt

it, half-glimpsed it, saw it in the threads of story, asked for it in the image that was made for this camp, Eve and the tree twined together. The tree is grown in Paradise, as Eve is grown in Paradise. It is the Tree of Knowledge, just as a woman's body holds that knowledge, the sexual revelations of body, of fertility, of ecstasy. The tree gives forth flower and fruit as Eve is flower and gives forth fruit, of her womb and these ones gathered here, they are all from that story, from that womb, they are all born from that. I take a deep breath, pick up an apple and hold it up. I stand and speak.

This is what Eve says:

Here is the apple. It is from me, from my body. Perhaps really it is a pomegranate, apricot, persimmon, date or other fruit. It doesn't matter. Fruit, flesh and seeds, this is me. You were born from these apples, from these seeds, from the tree of me. I am the mother of every one of you and only because I tasted and ate the fruit of the Tree of Knowledge was I able to give birth to you. You are born from me, from the fruit, from the tree. I am the tree, this woman's body is the tree, the Tree of Knowledge and the Tree of Life and eating it we know what it is to live and to die, we know who we are. I am not separate from the tree, I am the tree. When you eat of the tree I am offering you life, my life and you also will be part of the tree. The one who offers the fruit is the tree that grew it, I offer the fruit. I am the tree. I am a woman, I am Eve, I am the tree. We are not separate.

Then there are apples being offered from baskets, apples being eaten all around the room and I stand in the center, alone and I feel like weeping. In the midst of people milling one man comes over to me and goes down on his knees to offer obeisance to Eve, to the mother; he saw her. Heard her. It touches me but I know what is coming and so I feel a little sad and cold and as the circle reforms and Jarrah comes up to me in the center I try to tell him *she doesn't want to go* and his eyes look sad as well but there isn't any choice and I feel her desperation, *no, I was made to be in a body, that's what I am, who I am, you can't take it away from me, no – others are fine in disembodied form but I – I am earth and body and flesh and I do not want to go into formlessness and words on a page, I am not an idea, I am body, body* – and then he says the ritual words, thanking and releasing Eve *but I don't want to be released it is not release it is extinguishment, it is nothing, I am not that I am this, let me stay let me stay* and everyone around the circle echoes him, thanking her *I don't want to be thanked, don't want to be gone, not into bodilessness, not gone from the earth and the night and body* and he does something, I don't know what and she is gone.

Torn out of me, away from me and I am left holding her anguish but here I am and I grab at the shawl still over his shoulder, I can't stand to be naked in this circle of people. I feel horrible, awful, sick and shaking and we walk to the edge of the circle and I go through it and beyond, down behind Eve's altar and I huddle there on the floor and weep and weep. The ritual finishes and I see people beginning to leave the room, some look but none come up to me as I huddle on the floor half naked and weeping, except Jarrah.

I see people glance my way then leave the room and I cry harder, how unfair to offer Eve a body for just a few hours when she was all body, that was who she was and then to take it away, she did not want to go. She was desperate, her children doing this to her, dismissing her, sending her out into the long darkness and I ask for my friend and Jarrah brings him and he squats beside me and hugs me and helps me to dress and is calm and sensible and I forgive them, somewhat but I don't forget her. I don't forget Eve, the spirit of the tree, of nourishment and body, of fertility and life that is knowledge. I don't forget her, now that I know what she was always saying to me. She is the tree, the apples are her flesh, they give knowledge of her and to eat them is to choose the life of the body, which is sex and flesh, alive and divine.

Star Goddess

She was huge and dark, her body was the night sky. There were stars through her, spaced apart. It was hard to see her edges because she was so vast and there wasn't much distinction between her and the rest of the sky. But I could see the folds of her, where her arms lay in her lap, her legs crossed, her head bent forward. I could feel her there. She was naked, as the sky or the earth is naked, her flesh was black space with stars and nothing covered it. In my mind I placed myself, a small child, in her arms and she held me while I went to sleep. Enfolded, comforted not just by her arms, but also by her timelessness, the essence of night, the night mother.

Nobody told me about this goddess, I made her up. She came to me. Now I see that her body is the same type as my mother's, so perhaps I was trying to create a sense of my mother's arms. But she was made of – she was – the night sky. I don't know where I got that from. Later I read about sky goddesses and felt shimmers of recognition. In the contemporary Feri and Reclaiming story of the Star Goddess I recognized my own goddess. My mother. Not in the immediate, she-gave-birth-to-me way, but this-is-where-I-come-from, this is the genesis. The Star Goddess and I go back to when I was a frightened child, trying to sleep in the night.

In the Reclaiming Tradition we tell the story of the Star Goddess. We say it is from her body all things are birthed and in my mind she is always that dark, nearly formless form, a woman as huge as the night sky, with stars in her body. The story tells how she was all alone before she reached out into the curvature of dark space and pulled forth an echo, a mirror of herself, the other, her reflection but also the one given birth to, formed from her own body; her sister, daughter her lover Miria. The mirror. In some Australian Aboriginal languages *mirri yannan* means falling star. So this fallen star, borne from and mirror to the Star Goddess, is thrust away or falls away from her, as space is constantly expanding she gets further and further away and starts to change like the planets form from pieces of star and she goes through ages, as our planet and many others have gone through ages and the ages are named *Blue* and *Green* and *Red*. Each one of those is the name of a god that this piece of Star Goddess becomes in sequence; the Blue God, the Green God and finally the Red God.

At the end – and we believe this will happen, at least with our own star, the sun – everything returns to the Star Goddess, completing her; everything emerges from her and everything returns. Expanding through Miria, through Blue and Green, the Red God as her son, her lover, the other is the one who completes the pattern. Maybe he dies in her arms and maybe they dance the dance of lovers and maybe in another universe she will give birth to him again, to them all, to us all and another way to see it is they are aspects of her, seen in a mirror; we are all aspects of her, mirror shards of star from when that star burst into a million, million other stars, great brilliant clouds of galaxies shimmering through eternities in life cycles unimaginable to us. The Star Goddess, her body, is literally what we are made of, here on this planet, scraps of the bodies of fallen stars, the souls of stars and sometimes when we look into each other's eyes or catch glimpses of our beloveds or a stranger in ritual or dance or song or the full force of their passion we see it, that, her, the Star Goddess blazing through them.

The Star Goddess is the mother I was always searching for, the one who would notice me, comfort me and I found pieces of her again and again in the women who encouraged me, who listened to me and noticed me. All my childhood I sought them out; mothers of friends, teachers, neighbors, women who would look at me and see me and sometimes they did, the dark hold of longing in me and sometimes just being in their presence with their bright assumptions was enough or not enough, was something, a taste of what I might want. This story of daughters with mothers is so generic, endless. There are many girls I knew who envied the blithe absence of my mother, how she didn't notice or seemingly require anything from me, while I longed for attention, concern and involvement.

Certainly my mother was not mothered the way she wanted. Her mother, my grandmother, was critical, never pleased. I imagine she was like that while my mother was a child, cold and disapproving. When I was growing up my grandmother did not like my mother's clothes, her work, her weight, the way she cared for or didn't care for her body, her politics, her lifestyle, where she lived and probably who she married. It's amazing she liked me, but she did. Together we liked coloring in, playing games, going for walks, sewing and embroidery and when my grandmother was unexpectedly harsh I burst into tears, so that she was taken aback and had to mend her manner whereas my mother, growing up with it, probably just suffered or defied or ignored it.

My grandmother herself was not mothered the way she wanted. I know less about this, but I do know she grew up the youngest of seven children, with five older brothers and in her childhood lay scenes that now we would not countenance, but at that time perhaps were considered a normal part of growing up with brothers. They cut open and beheaded her dolls. They shut her in dark rooms by herself. They pinned her braids to the top of the door with her feet off the floor, so she swung on the door when they pushed it to and fro. Where was her mother? Her mother was busy, her mother was sick, her mother was worn out and absent.

The third time I went to California WitchCamp we worked with the story of the Star Goddess in the evening rituals throughout the week of camp. I called Miria in, on the first night and thus held her all the way through until the final ritual. Miria, the light sister to my darkness and mirror to the Star Goddess. All of my relationships with women reflect that, the intimacy of friendship, hours spent in conversation, in fascination with the moods and dreams, longings and life of that other one, so like me and yet not me. The entrancement of a woman lover, beloved; her skin, the curves, the softness and the fall of hair, eyes that gaze into a like-mind, touching a body like one's own. Kisses that are softer than soft, that fall into night with their luminescence, their candor their utter, fierce, known quality. I remember those.

I lay on the ground in the dirt redwood earth between rings of people clustered around the fire, my arm outstretched into the center of the circle and called out to her from darkness. The Star Goddess had already been invoked and now is the turn of Miria out of the curving mirror, Miria, beloved, held and released even as I call to her. The attention of a hundred people swings to me, to her, on the ground. Miria falling away and calling back, echoing her beginnings like the outer edges of space still echo the reverberance of that first explosion, still curve around and around even as they get further away, expanding infinitely like waves on a dark sea heading further out, into darkness. Miria holding the threads back to beginning.

Somewhere out there, on the tides of time and space the story of Miria shifts and transforms. The Blue God emerges from her and I held him once, in a mask, a gorgeous dynamic mask my first ever time at California WitchCamp in the Path of Beauty, held him in turn within a small group. When I put that mask on the world burst into life, not just trees and wind and earth, but every shred of it glittering and pulsing with energy and intense, drenched color and I remember that I leapt and growled with joy, really that would not stay down and when I turned to the humans around me they looked pallid and slow, trembling almost with the fear of the blood in their veins and their own heartbeats and I shouted at them, not me but the voice of cells dividing, of ocean, of the beginnings of life and summer sky.

I can see how Blue shifts to the Green, tying the dance of

life from single cells, sky and ocean into structure and holding. At a different WitchCamp, in Australia, we invoked the Green God standing outside in the sunshine holding hands in a large circle. The instructions were spoken from the center, so quietly I couldn't hear them. I didn't know what we were doing and there was a hush, so I didn't ask. I was standing between two women, one I had just met and one I knew, with both of them I felt an intense sweetness and presence so that I didn't mind holding hands for what began to seem like a very long time. We stood there with our eyes closed and I felt the sun falling onto my skin, soaking into it and the slight breezes as they came and went and in the stillness, my feet on the uneven grass-tussocky ground I thought of roots and of staying in one place one's whole life, not like a human staying in one place, but like a tree.

I thought also of the grass under my feet and of the flowers – small, hidden – in the grass and I thought of vines, climbing up and my fingers and hands must have twisted or moved and on each side of me the two women I stood between responded to that touch in the stillness of the afternoon, stroking their fingers over the palms of my hands, around my wrists and arms and on one side we twisted and twined our forearms together and on the other side it was the delicate brush of skin-to-skin with fingers, hand to hand and sometimes barely touching sometimes smoothing and this is a delight and I don't care how long we stand here, whatever we were supposed to be doing surely it can't be better than this, this sensual vining with two of my sisters, and I imagine them as sister trees, sister vines in the sunlight and it's hard to think of anything other than this exact moment.

The Red God comes out of that. If the Star Goddess is the beginning and end of time, Miria the expanding of the universe, the Blue God the seas and the life begun there, the Green God the plants and forests then surely the Red God is this red blood of ours, this distant, unlikely branch of life, randomly specializing into the forms we are most familiar with, cats and zebras and wolves and monkeys and humans. This whole system of evolution that we are so caught up with, imagining ourselves as the pinnacle instead of a small, sideways twig on the tree of life, I can see the Red God defending that. Standing for birth and sex and death. If we destroy our planet, if we save our planet, surely that will be the Red God's doing, that bloody life-and-death edge is the red realm.

For the whole of California WitchCamp we transition through this Star Goddess story and the final night is the completion. It's the Red God's ritual and we have his return to the Star Goddess built into it. Of all the rituals it has been the most difficult to create, to put death and endings into a large-scale ritual that is also ecstatic and transformative and we have changed and rewritten it again and again. The piece I have held onto, all the way through, is the piece of the Star Goddess, who I will be holding, in aspect. Light aspect, enough to be in touch with her but not taken over, not impelled; maybe thirty percent. She shimmers and gleams for me, entrancing but not immediate; I don't know how it will be.

I think of the Star Goddess, alone in infinite time and space through the unfolding of her story and the spinning wheels of change that she gives birth to and it feels like she welcomes us back, stars or humans, with open arms, with the embrace of a lover. I am determined, in this ritual, to welcome this Red God like the lover I've been waiting for always. Beloved. The one so different, now, from her, that she can take him back and be made more, by the knowledge that he brings of what it is to live and die. Red is different from the blue world or the green world, yet also, in this cosmology it carries both of them within it. I think of the sexuality of difference, whether it is difference in mind or body or experience or knowledge, that lure towards union, completion; how it fights with fear of the unknown, the stranger and how it wins, not always, but when it wins it is greeting the lover you have yearned for without even knowing it or watching a child grow into their own self, seeing the spark and the edge that makes each one unique.

This is a camp where people dress for ritual. There are wedding dresses and ball gowns and all sorts of steampunk, faerie, princess, animal, nightclub costumes. There are cloaks and head-dresses, lace and silk, netting and leather and velvet. There is only one way to stand out among all that, dress down. I will wear my plain dull-purple satin slip, in bare feet, with some stars painted on and hope that between the cascading folds of dresses, between the bright colors and extravagance I look different enough to hold something truly non-human, not of this world. I am excited for the Star Goddess, longing for her. She has a minor part in the ritual but is to be there all the way through it and outside on a cold summer night in the Californian redwoods seems the ideal place.

Amazingly there are seven Australians from CloudCatcher WitchCamp here, I choose one of them to be my tender. Although I am thinking I won't need much tending, that this is just a light aspect and I haven't much to do, I won't forget it and I will stay firmly on the ground. When she is invoked everything is fine, I feel the glimmer and prick of her, like pins and needles under my skin and I can dance and move with it, although the ritual suddenly is not that interesting to me. I do move around the circle. I am gleaming and also burning, I don't feel like getting too close to people. I don't know how to actually talk or interact with them. I bring myself mostly out of the Star Goddess, enough to hold hands in a circle and dance a spiral and as we dance I feel her gaining again, when they pull in close together to raise the chant I step back, out of the circle and onto the edge of the ritual.

I see us for a moment as if from high above; a small clearing in a forest with a fire and a tiny, tiny gathering. A hundred or so people. It is as if I span the globe and throughout time and am seeing dozens of these clearings, gatherings, hundreds of them, thousands upon thousands of them. This one is generic and I feel its sweetness for a second but it is not substantially different from all the others and suddenly I am a long, long way away from it in the night and the vastness sweeps at me and I am grappling with the Star Goddess, not to avoid being subsumed but to hang on to her at all. She was interested, for a second or so, attracted and intrigued, she has been but now she's moving on. I don't even consider going with her, then I would be ninety percent, a hundred percent in aspect and not only that, I would be lost on the river of her, not a river of water but the river of the Milky Way spilling stars and black space, dancing in dark matter and any human part of me burnt in less than the first second of the first breath. I can't hold her.

I am human, standing cold at the edge of the ritual. I gather my shawl back to me and reach out again, Star Goddess, or just a memory of Star Goddess, an imagining. I can gather that, but it is slender, maybe five percent; five percent of me, not five percent of her, it is less than the edge of a flicker of a thought of her and even this I don't know if I can hold. People branch off into the darkness on some ritual task and I'm glad, it gives me time to find out what I can do with this wild absence I'm in. I take myself further out, away from the fire and close my eyes. I reach for the Star Goddess, she who birthed this whole universe, this planet, each one of us. I remember how as a child I was fascinated by stars, I wanted to know more and more about them, they seemed to me the beckoners of every mystery, but I feel cold and distant, my feet glued with gravity to the earth. I catch glimmers of her, thoughts of her like trails in the night sky and decide that will have to be enough and I go back to the fire.

I have to concentrate. It's hard, hard to hold her. I feel she's here but no more here than anywhere else, or everywhere else and that one human, me, isn't enough to hold that focus. People are beginning to come back to the circle and I lean back and whisper to my tender *I can't hold her, I can't hold her* and Lorelei holds my shoulders from behind and whispers into my hair some Star Goddessy words, lulling me back towards a light trance so that I feel – not exactly that I am holding her, but that I remember her and in that remembrance there's a softness, the memory creates a pathway out into her vastness.

The ritual progresses with me just linked the tiniest bit to her and comes towards the end, where I stand at the fire and across from me is the Red God. He is the one I have to meet in this ritual, this is why I am here. Not just meet, with the Red God I have to tie them all together, take the Red God back into the Star Goddess and in so doing fold in Miria, the Blue, the Green, all of them. I have in mind two powers meeting in an almost clash that melds to union. I am poised at the brink of it, summoning it and waiting for his ferocity to explode, on the other side of the fire so we can enter the dance of the stars becoming again when he cries out brokenly and nearly runs around to my side of the fire, goes onto the ground on his knees and clutches at my legs, burying his face in my skirt.

The Star Goddess part of me laughs a little, distantly in recognition and I, the human part, am surprised and undone. So the universe folds gently back to itself, returned to the mother; all my longing for a lover was in that vast distance and watching them dance through life, not in the ending. I am the mother of time, it returns not as lover but as beloved child and I think watching the bright sparks of the fire of all those goddesses, lovers and mothers, all our lives and the stories folding in on themselves and repeating in patterns. All the lives, all the stars, all the mirrors of ourselves. Yes I take him back, I take them all back. I speak the words of the ritual, *all of you I take back in my embrace, each one of you I take back. I give life to the universe. All things proceed from me and all things return – I am the beginning and the end. For behold, I have been with you since the beginning and I am that which is attained at the end of desire.* The largeness of it brings her back to me. In that embrace, holding the end which is also the beginning, I feel the Star Goddess again. All things return.

A few weeks later I'm in Paris, sitting at a restaurant table on the footpath. It's later than I wanted to eat, after 8pm but high summer, so still light and warm. For Parisians the evening is just beginning. Gazing abstractedly across the road, to the shops on the other side – and it's not a busy road, I'm in a tourist precinct near Sacré-Cœur and the traffic is mainly people on foot, French and Americans and Germans and English – I have a sudden and extended stabbing sensation, fierce and definite and not like anything I remember. Like someone, a cold hand, grabbed hold of my heart; put their hand excruciatingly through my flesh inside my chest and wrenched, sharply. It's breathtakingly painful, a wrenching moment so still and sharp and critical I have to question everything, a hovering awareness of, *this moment could be the last.*

I try to keep breathing, to breathe normally as the most immediate pain subsides, leaving echoes of instability and fear within me. I realize that no-one knows exactly where I am and no-one in Paris knows who I am. I wonder, what would happen if I had a heart attack here? Now? What if I suddenly died, on this Parisian footpath? How long would it take them to find Damon? Have I even brought my passport to dinner with me? No, of course not. I have my wallet, my driver's license, they could identify me through that. But who would they contact? How would they trace me? I have only just turned fifty, I wonder if this means I should be more careful about how I travel, where I travel. Am I more fragile than I have been imagining all these years?

Gradually the tension in my chest is easing. I wonder about getting up, leaving the restaurant and going back to my room, my quite nice room in the 18th Arrondissement. But I don't feel up to walking, or negotiating the metro and so I stay put for a while longer. My meal is brought to me and I eat it slowly and carefully, not thinking of anything in particular. Still tentative, fragile, rendered uncertain by that visceral shock and how I couldn't compare it to anything. When I get back to my room I turn my phone off and go to sleep. I have a few more days in Paris before going to Chartres and then England where I have work and friends.

I worked out the times later, much later. My mother was still alive when I experienced that sudden, strong and inexplicable pain, for another hour, and her death was sudden. So it was a premonition, or maybe something she felt and not the actual moment of her death. That wrenching – that was her leaving me. I was cut loose into the land of the living and it felt like death, I thought of death in it. I wondered if I would die.

In the morning, maybe because I didn't look at it last night, I turn my computer on and almost instantly Damon messages me, asking can we talk? I don't have time to think how unusual this is. I open Skype and he's calling me and he says straight away in a kind of choked voice that someone called him, he says the name of his boss and I think that is odd, maybe he is having some sort of work crisis and then he keeps talking and I don't understand for a while, it takes me a few seconds to make the jump from the fact that his boss' name is also the name of my brother, who called him this morning to say my mother has died.

Instantly I feel the vastness of time surrounding me, stretching out like a net and I believe it, I am caught in it. I remember that pain last night and it's as if I catch a glimpse of the Star Goddess at the door, just leaving and she is holding a baby in her arms, it is my mother. Birth and death. The Star Goddess holds both gates. I feel more like I am holding the aspect of her now, this instant, than I did back in the ritual. Her body is that which all life comes from, all of our bodies are made from the deaths of stars and I am in the gateway, with her; it's like giving birth to my mother except this is death but it's hard to distinguish, this close up, there doesn't seem to be a difference. I am there, ushering that soul through, in one direction or another and I can't actually tell the difference, or that it makes a difference, or that it matters that she gave birth to me, not the other way round.

I manage to speak through this to my son. It is afternoon there and I ask if he had people to talk to, will someone be there when he goes home? Of all his grandparents he was closest to her and of all people, growing up, she was the one he had the most to do with other than his parents. It's easier and more immediate to think of that than to think of what I might do, who I might talk to or how to get from Paris to Melbourne though of course it's too late really to be of any use. Through all the rest of the day, which I spend mainly on the phone to various people, my father and my mother's cousin in England and Trinda, who is in Australia and the person I really want to talk to, and lots of others including airline people, I still hold a sense of this vastness, this ushering in, or it should be ushering out, but it doesn't feel like that, it feels more like birth.

The Star Goddess is implacably here, all around me and within me and just everywhere, like dark matter is everywhere though somehow undetected and she is like that, her glimmers showing up between everything else. By late afternoon, when I have not yet left the flat or done anything except try to deal with the ramifications – and just the logistics, not any sort of actual ramifications – of my mother dying suddenly and while I am overseas – I go out, to Notre Dame. Because of the time of day, the tourists have ebbed. I know my mother came here, walked here, maybe many times and I have been here also many times, over the years, and Damon and of course millions upon millions of others, threading networks of lives over these paving stones and through these pillars and lighting candles of wishes and prayers and for the dead and I pay for one now and light it, placing it among hundreds though to me it is particular.

The whole world feels alive with ghosts, with trails of paths that people have walked, over years and centuries. I think of the tribe of the Parisis, setting up their camp on this island in the middle of the Seine, and far later the stone masons building the cathedral and of all the pilgrims and tourists and even in among all that it still seems I can pick out one shining thread, my own to follow and loop back upon. I remember arriving from Australia, years ago. It was very early in the morning when Damon and I came up into the streets of Paris from the metro, cold though it was summer and we came here, which was warm and lit and had seats and Damon, who was six, fell asleep sideways on my lap and I sat there awkwardly, holding him, in a place dedicated to mothers, you could say.

In the very center of the cathedral, at the top, top point and they don't advertise this and it's very hard to find it in the books or anywhere at all, except for exactly where it is, there's a painting of a woman dressed in a blue robe with stars all round her. Mary, they say, though if it is Mary you'd think they'd mention it more frequently; and of course it is Mary the goddess, Mary of the moon and stars and there are older names for her as well and when I look up there now – and they don't even light it properly, so it's hard to see in the wrong light and they don't draw attention to the fact that this is a goddess, that this whole thing is a temple to the goddess and Christ is her child – I see her, the Star Goddess who has been called by so many different names at different ages that the names don't matter, the fact of her matters, a woman dancing among the stars, a woman who will take the small, the lost, the grieving and injured, those born and those dying, back into her arms.

All the candles twinkling in lines and lines are like her stars, inside, and I go back to visit the candle I lit, for my mother and I take some photos of it. The news has not really sunk in, or what it will mean, I am still in the vast tides of stars and birth and death, holding space for the bigness of it. Although it is very inconvenient I am in Paris in another way it is perfect, my mother was born of French ancestry. Her father's parents were born here and all four of her mother's grandparents. She came here many times and, as so many people do, loved France. Here I have all this time to think and be whereas, if I were in Australia, I would be caught up in the material and immediate repercussions of death and dealing with lots of people and lists, whereas here I just have phone calls and then all the rest of the time is mine, to drift and muse and hold space for what feels like a birth.

It will never feel like that again. Once I get on a plane, two days later and from then on, I am in the jaws of actual, bodily death of my mother and someone says, it must be like a god dying, to have a parent, that all-powerful presence who literally created your body die and I think yes, a bit like that. Something no myth or story could ever prepare one for, that changes forever who one is and how one lives in the world. Now, somehow, mysteriously, I am both me and her and yet in her absence. But in France I still hold the vastness of it, separate from the layers of emotional undoing that will follow and held within the cloak of the Star Goddess, her mantle, I feel the threads that bind both me and my mother to her and how I am able, it does seem like that, to stand in the doorway and witness or participate in the passing across the threshold of a piece of star, a human life whose entirety, it feels like, birth to death I hold in my hands.

My hands, the hands that she made within her body. My hands, that hold hands with the Star Goddess or that welcome back the living beings into the folds of her skirt, my hands that reach out to the universe creating others to mirror myself, my hands that look like my mother's hands. I remember as a child I always loved her hands. I have a version of her hands. Damon's hands are a male version of her hands. Her hands. That held me when I was small, dressed and bathed me, held my hand when we crossed a road, those hands that cooked for me and wrapped presents and wrote things down for me, her hands that for me were the living hands of the goddess. I think of hands reaching out to grasp a newborn baby, I think of hands preparing a body for burial.

I think of my grandmother, giving birth to my mother; a much-wanted child for the two born earlier had died. Then my mother had a daughter herself, me, and I feel this line of women so sharply, especially while I am in France. In holding this death I am holding also the life of my grandmother, with all its pains and disappointments and we feel like beads on a thread; shining beads of amber or crystal strung one to the next and I can feel them stretching further back, perhaps I can especially feel them because I am in this land where so many of them lived and died, the place where this particular shining thread of starlight, my hereditary female line, is born from the soil and the water and air that's here and I can almost taste it in my blood and the pores of my skin and every breath, my mother's death and the soil of France. I take it in and I fold it back, all of us back, generations of pieces of star and women and French soil, back to the great mother, the Star Goddess.

Process – Preparing to Aspect

Aspecting in a ritual may appear sudden to onlookers, who see an ordinary human, probably someone they know, then immediately after an invocation see an aspect of the goddess. Ideally it is not sudden – the person aspecting and possibly one or more others have usually entered a changed or semi-tranced state earlier, prior to the ritual starting. The invocation is the public and ritual declaration, and perhaps inner confirmation, that this process is now beginning. This will most likely also happen in reverse, when the ritual is closing and the deity is thanked and asked to leave, the person aspecting and those around them will see and sense the change, but it may still take the person who was aspecting some time – minutes or an hour or longer – to return fully to feeling like their normal selves. Dressing in one's own clothes, eating and talking with others can assist.

Prior to the ritual beginning, talk with your tender. This is the person who will probably call in the goddess in the invocation, who will watch out for you during the ritual, as well as being with you immediately afterwards. Usually a tender is someone you know, who is experienced in aspecting and whom you trust. Talk with them about the ritual, the deity, your needs and wishes while aspecting. You might also enter into ritual space together and remain in silence, chant or sing.

Ideally we create a state of calm, grounded centeredness before beginning to aspect. There are other ways to enter into aspecting, such as dancing, drumming or writing, or you may discover yet other ways. Costume, trance and invocation are common elements of aspecting, often they are all used together. Outlined below are considerations regarding these elements of preparation.

Costume

- Choosing a costume for the deity you will be aspecting, preparing that costume and putting it on can be powerful inductions into the readiness to aspect. This costume may include a mask, face-paint, body-paint or make-up, clothes or nudity. The clothes may be your own, borrowed, or constructed for the role.

- Between taking off the clothes you have been wearing and putting on the clothes you intend to aspect in, ideally cleanse yourself in some way. This might be taking a shower, simply washing your face, hands and feet, smudging or censing with incense or some other ritual preparation.

- Allow the time of costuming to be an entry into light trance, or altered awareness, where you begin to take on the mantle of the goddess, robing yourself as her priestess, one willing to receive her and hold her energy during the ritual. By doing this you build in another layer of exiting the aspecting, after the ritual; when you change clothes, remove the mask or paint or shower it will help to reverse the state you have entered into and return you fully to your self.

- If you wish you can say silently, or aloud, *for tonight this will be Hecate's cloak* or *while I am wearing this mask in this ritual I will be able to see with the eyes of the flower maiden.*

Trance

- You may choose to enter a light trance before the formal beginning of the ritual, or prior to the deity you are aspecting being invoked. You can do this while dressing, as detailed above, or after that, in a quiet moment before or as the ritual begins.

- You might enter a light trance state by yourself, or have your tender talk you through it. It should be a state that allows you to freely walk and move about, to retain full awareness of your surroundings and to interact if needed.
- One way to enter into light trance is simply follow the breath inwards, calming and stilling yourself within while allowing your outer senses to expand. You might prefer a different approach, chanting aloud or under your breath, visualizing a doorway, stairs or another entry into a trance state, or some other way.
- Remember, or have your tender remind you when you finish aspecting, that you also need to fully return from this trance.

Invocation

- Usually the invocation to the deity is immediately prior to, or even part of, the *drawing down* or the formal beginning of aspecting. The invocation may be made by the tender, by the person aspecting, by someone else or by everyone present at the ritual together, for example with a song or energy raising.
- The invocation and drawing down can be split into two parts. This may happen if the ritual begins in one place, including an invocation to the deity who will later be aspected in the ritual, while somewhere else the person aspecting prepares, including entering into aspect and later arriving at the ritual as the aspected deity. It may also occur if the invocation is spoken by one person, possibly the person who will aspect, and the drawing down is performed by someone else, possibly the tender.
- The invocation to a deity who will be aspected in ritual is usually both full and specific. Some attention and thought go into the words and nature of this invocation,

especially concerning the qualities and aspect of the deity being invoked. We can easily imagine the different rituals that might ensue if we invoked *Kali, destroyer of all flesh* compared with *Kali, who destroys and rebirths the world* compared with *Kali, Goddess of the Mysteries of Life and Death*. Ideally the deity will be welcomed and recognized as well as specific qualities being called upon. Those watching and listening will have a chance to feel into the nature of this goddess through the invocation.

- The person invoking will ideally be speaking naturally, with emotion and relatedness, loudly enough to be heard both by those at the ritual and with a carrying quality, such as one might imagine addressing the gods. The invocation needs to come from within – from a human heart and voice – and reach out through the worlds to the goddess. Gestures, movements and props might be used to add depth to the invocation. I cannot think of a way that written notes would be helpful.

- During this invocation the person who will be aspecting is often present. They may even be the person invoking. You can allow this invocation to sink deep within you, as well as expand out around you, to begin to welcome in the goddess and feel her particular energy. This process is often described as *drawing down*.

Ritual – Aspecting a Deity

What is aspecting, exactly? What does it look like, or feel like? How do you do it?

Aspecting is a technical term that places some agreed parameters onto *drawing down* a deity. Drawing down is when someone, usually in ritual, invites a deity – which may be a named deity or more broadly *the goddess* or *the full moon* – to enter their body and be present. We indicate that the process will begin and end at set times and that it will be regulated by the human side of the equation. This regulation is a contract, given out as conditions at the beginning of the experience by the person to the deity. It involves letting others, at least the tender, know the details of this. Potentially the contract may need to be reinforced or renegotiated during the experience. During the aspecting experience you may see, hear and feel a variety of things. It can be ecstatic, disappointing, confronting. Afterwards, good self-care is a necessity.

Aspecting is both a gift and a skill. Anyone can learn and practice the skills involved, which include strong abilities to ground, to create and maintain a contract with a deity, to communicate clearly with a tender both before, during and after the aspect, to allow the deity to come through oneself to the degree negotiated as well as the self-knowledge or ability to differentiate the deity from one's own personality, shadow and personal agenda. Some people are particularly drawn towards aspecting and some seem gifted in it. Some may have affinities with particular deities, rather than with aspecting in general, so their willingness or ability to aspect may depend on which deity is being aspected.

Ways to learn and begin aspecting include working in small groups to practice and support each other, working alone or with a partner, taking very small, or non-speaking aspecting roles in ritual or aspecting as a group. A group aspect is where a group of people together aspect one deity, in concert – not all doing their own thing, but all moving and acting as one, many-limbed being. Speaking the invocation in ritual, learning to tend others in aspect and observing and talking with those aspecting or after aspecting are other ways to gain information and sense one's own relationship to it.

Aspecting would be regarded as successful if those present felt, heard or saw the deity *through* the person aspecting. For want of a better term, a luminosity is attached to the human being we know. Their voice may be different, they may move or gesture differently, what they say and do cannot be predicted entirely by our knowledge of them. This luminosity – a shimmering or radiance, as if ripples of energy are emanating through them – will most likely also be experienced by the person aspecting. It may be kinesthetic, felt in the body; aural, heard; visual or any combination of those.

Internally the person aspecting might have an experience where they felt or heard the deity very strongly, not at all, or anywhere on that spectrum. They may have found it easy, difficult or impossible to negotiate with the deity as to the nature of the aspecting. When I am aspecting everything I do and say feels perfectly natural, exactly what I (the human) wants to say and do. Afterwards it seems to me that I have done and said things not outside the range of my personality or wishes, but probably not things I would have done, solely as myself, in that context or at that time.

The deity is being channeled *by* us and *through* us. If this leads us to engage in behavior that afterwards makes us feel uncomfortable, or as if we have been an unwilling partner, either we do not know ourselves as well as we believe we do or our skills in holding the negotiation with the deity need strengthening. Either way, we should probably refrain from aspecting again until we have understood and resolved these issues.

The role of the tender is crucial and not a lesser role than aspecting itself. The tender not only looks after the person before, during and after the aspecting, they are often also in a position to negotiate between the person in aspect and others in the ritual, for example in regards to where that person wishes to move, when they wish to speak (or not speak) and how much interaction and of what type they have with others in the ritual.

Following are some notes regarding the before, during and after pieces of aspecting a deity in ritual. Every time and every experience will be different. The ritual you are aspecting in may be a simple ritual in a small group, where the aspecting is the central or only piece of the ritual, or your aspecting may be a small piece of a much larger ritual, maybe with many people attending. This will also affect your experience.

Prior to Aspecting in Ritual

Create a clear contract with yourself, the deity you are planning to aspect and your tender. The conditions in the contract should be quite specific. They are up to you to set and to enforce. They include, but are not limited to:

- The name of the deity being aspected, and if there are a variety of possibilities inherent in that name, specifics. For example, rather than simply aspecting Persephone, the intention – and therefore the invocation and the aspect – may be called in as, variously and depending: *Persephone, Queen of the Dead* or *Persephone, maiden and kore, Demeter's daughter* or *Persephone returned from the Underworld*.
- The length of time of the aspect, for example *during this ritual,* or *from the time of the invocation until the time of the release*.
- The degree of movement and speech during the aspect, for example *to be able to move freely within the ritual space*

and the freedom to speak with individuals when appropriate or *to remain by the altar and to be able to speak at the closing of the ritual in the space allotted* or *to be able to dance during the dance and enact the planned conversation (or speech or story).*

- The degree of clothing/unclothing, for example *to remain clothed* or *to be as naked or clothed as desired at the time.*

- The degree of touch during the aspect, which is usually also negotiated with those present. For example *to freely touch and be touched by the tender,* or *not to touch or be touched by others* or *to be able to touch others' hands and to hug when that is wished by both.*

- The depth, degree or percentage of the aspect, that is how much control or presence the deity will have and how much the human will retain, within those parameters already listed. If this were sixty percent, then the person would still retain forty percent of their personality, conscious choice and motivation, with the other sixty percent being given over to the deity aspected. If it were twenty percent, the person retains eighty percent. In aspecting we do not give over one hundred percent. Even with the back-up of a tender and a clear contract we still choose to retain some degree of ourselves present – probably a minimum of twenty percent – during all aspecting experiences.

Aspecting in Ritual

Begin with whatever preparation feels best to you, including any of: cleansing, meditating, costuming (see previous section *Preparing to Aspect*). While aspecting in ritual:

- When the deity is invoked, drawn down or invited into you, welcome them into the space you have created within yourself. At this point it is good to remind yourself, and them, of the percentage you are intending to be in aspect, for example, thirty percent or fifty percent. This is a percentage of you, not of the deity.

- Allow yourself to step into the experience of walking in two worlds, holding and expressing the deity while still retaining your understanding of what is happening in the ritual, as well as your own sense of self. This might be quite straightforward to maintain, or might require many adjustments. Make sure to speak to your tender about how you are finding this experience. Speaking with your tender as your human self is also a good way to damp down the deity's presence a little, if you need to do that.
- Where the ritual has allowed for or invited the deity's specific actions or words, you might choose to allow the aspecting to become a little stronger, or to the full percentage you have negotiated. This may feel as if it flows naturally, or as if you have to translate what you feel into spoken language or some other way entirely.
- Allow yourself to be moved or shaped by the deity's presence, within the terms of the contract you have set out. This will mean that you have a sense of their presence, as distinct from your own, and that the others in the ritual can potentially experience the presence of that deity. You can invite specific parts of you – for example your hearing and sight – to be touched by the deity you are aspecting. The differences this creates might be clear to you at the time, or not until afterwards.
- Stay connected with your tender, as a human reference point and also as someone who retains an understanding of the ritual structure and content. If the tender is insisting upon something it is advisable to listen to them and do your best to follow their instructions. Remember that they probably have a more comprehensive grip on what is actually happening than you do, while you are

in aspect.

- When it is time for the aspect to finish, thank the deity you have been working with, no matter what your experience has been. Do your best to assist those working the ritual to complete and finish the aspect, regardless of how that is feeling to you. It might be relief, joy, sadness or any other emotion or combination of emotions. You will be able to process those emotions and your experiences after the ritual is complete.

After Aspecting in Ritual

After aspecting in ritual it is crucial to ground yourself, probably several times. Grounding might include: sitting or lying on the floor or the earth, eating something, talking with your tender or others, showering or washing your face and hands, changing your clothing, taking a walk with your tender or another person and noticing the outside world or anything else that works for you as a grounding practice. Points to consider are:

- Ideally your tender will ask what you need, but you should also ask yourself what you need. Perhaps it is a hug, to eat some protein, to sit outside for a while, to talk or to be silent. Paying attention to your human needs immediately after aspecting will help ensure your whole experience is a positive one.
- You might need to continue thanking the deity you aspected and closing down your end of the aspecting connection several times over the next few hours or days.
- Often someone who has aspected a deity in ritual will be invited to talk about their experience, perhaps shortly after the ritual ends or perhaps the next day or the next time you meet with the others who were present. You may also, or instead, like to write about your experience,

either privately in your journal, or for others who were at the ritual to read.

- At some point, possibly with your tender or someone else who was present at the ritual, analyze what worked well about your aspecting experience, as well as what you have learned and might choose to do differently if you repeated the experience. These may be technical aspects of the ritual or your aspecting, or they might be internal to you, or something else entirely. By unpacking our experiences and seeking to understand them we can begin to work on refining and increasing our skills.

- You may find that your relationship with the deity you aspected has shifted considerably. Find a way to address this that feels appropriate. You might make a thanks offering at your altar or in art, poetry or some other way. You might feel called to learn more about the deity and their story, deepening your relationship with them and continuing to work with them.

Ritual Basics

Grounding

Grounding occurs at the beginning of many rituals and ritual activities. In essence we bring our attention and focus fully present and connect with the earth, partly through a process bringing us into the moment-by-moment lived experience in our bodies and partly by an act of will. Grounding works best when we use the practice over many occasions, so that our ability to ground ourselves, our recognition of what it takes to become and remain grounded and the knowledge of how grounded we might be, at any given time, increases as we continue the practice. It's great to try many different styles of grounding, both by ourselves and with others, to learn what works best for us and to develop our skills at becoming and remaining grounded in many different situations.

Grounding is not a trance and therefore it is ideally done with our eyes open. Some people might prefer to take a moment or two with their eyes closed first, to orient themselves internally before opening their eyes to continue the grounding process aware of their surroundings. Grounding may offer suggestions of things that are not physically present, or cannot be easily sensed, such as the stars overhead or aligning oneself with the idea of a tree whose roots go deep into the earth and whose branches stretch out to the sky. A grounding can focus on the senses: looking around at where you are, feeling the floor or earth beneath you and feeling into your own body, taking a breath or two slowly and maybe opening to senses of taste and smell, listening to whatever can be heard.

Other terms may be used in conjunction with, instead of or overlapping with grounding, such as centering. The concept of centering is to draw one's energy and focus into the center of one's own body. Some people like to place a hand on their stomach, mid-point or heart as they center themselves. Presence and awareness are other terms that may be used. Often a grounding process will be partly spoken aloud, with suggestions about how to ground, although if it is a group experienced in working together they may ground in silence.

Grounding is not just a starting point for magic and ritual, it is an ideal state in which to meet many of life's challenges, including a fractious three-year-old, a commute to work, a delicate inter-personal situation or unstable emotions such as anger, distress and fear. Even in magic and ritual it is not just at the beginning that grounding is encouraged, but also at regular points, or ideally all the way through the ritual or process. When working with a deity grounding is an essential piece that enables us to work fully and effectively. Being grounded allows us to stay connected to our own bodily needs such as food, sleep or rest, toilet breaks and protection from the elements. Being grounded allows us to bring a focus into our interactions with a goddess, to carry our intention throughout the interaction, to remember what happens afterwards and to stick to our own parameters – for example, not to suddenly begin aspecting when we were attempting to presence, or walk with a deity. If we discover we are not much good at these things while working with deity – specifically, attending to our own bodily needs, remaining with our intention, and staying within our own parameters – we might need to cease this work for a while and return to the foundations of magical and ritual work, including developing our grounding practices.

Invocation

Invocation, like grounding, is a basic magical skill that cannot be over-practiced, nor can it be entirely taken for granted. Just as life continues to hand us challenges when we may find it difficult to remain grounded, each invocation is unique in its circumstances. We may become very skilled at invocations, employing our bodies, voice and focus to bring alive varied, evocative and rich invocations – and yet the next time we do it we may be tired, stressed, asked to call in a deity we don't feel familiar with, or be challenged by some other aspect of the ritual. Invocations may be private, done in solo rituals and thus not necessarily spoken aloud, but often an invocation is not just for ourselves but in service of a ritual or event others are attending.

There are various styles of invocation. One style, not my personal favorite, involves reading or reciting a perhaps quite detailed, possibly rhyming piece of verse aloud, calling upon the deity to be present. Another style is to follow a format that exists within a tradition – this may also include verse, but the nature of it is that it is the same, or similar, each time, or according to the ritual or season. For example a Women's Full Moon Circle may call to the Moon Goddess the same way, with similar words each time they meet, regardless of who is invoking. More formal covens or traditions may have very particular formats, words and style for invocations. This style of invocation is potentially very powerful, although much of the power depends on the extent to which the person invoking has internalized the meaning of the words and the depth of their relationship with the practice and the deity. This method of invocation also contains a build-up effect where the repetition, over time, of invocations resonates, each present example carrying echoes with it of past invocations.

The ecstatic style of invocation appears the least formal but, in apparent contradiction to its seeming informality, may require the most preparation. In ecstatic invocation the words, gestures and format are not set and may appear completely spontaneous. In reality they usually rest on a deep knowledge of and familiarity with the deity being invoked. This may have been acquired by any or all of: research, previous ritual or devotional work, soul searching into one's connection with this particular deity, meditation. For this type of invocation the person invoking begins with an opening gesture or phrase towards the goddess or god they are calling to and receives images, concepts or words which they then translate, through their body and voice, into the invocation. They may call out their longing for the presence of the deity, they may speak of or model their qualities, they might offer praises or respect. Usually they allow the invocation to come through not just in the words that are spoken, but also in the tone, cadences and volume of their voice as well as the gestures and actions of their body.

Ideally any invocation makes audible and visible, for a moment, the deity being called to, through a human vessel. The person invoking may feel, for the length of the ritual, that they are holding that awareness or that energy, both in service to the ritual but also in service to the deity. For this reason one does not usually offer or agree to invoke a deity for whom one feels no sympathetic connection or interest. Similarly, careful ritualists do not invoke deities into rituals if there is no place for them there, no reason for them to be called in or they are not, in some way, a part of the ritual about to take place. Invocations can be made by more than one person. People working in pairs or small groups often create very powerful invocations, blending their voices or bodies into an harmonic invocation.

At the end of the ritual or working any beings, energies or deities invoked are, of course, acknowledged. Various terms for this end part are devocation, dismissal or release. All these terms seem problematic and I prefer to stay with honoring, acknowledging and thanking. Devocation, dismissal and release all imply that we can tell a deity what to do, that we have power or authority over them. Similarly I would not use the term summoning. Invocation is more of an invitation; and I feel at the end of a party, for example, one doesn't dismiss the guests, but rather thanks them and offers a leave-taking, perhaps saying how much we enjoyed having them and how we hope to see them again soon. I work within the belief that deity is continuously present and it is really just our own focus we are adjusting when we invoke or leave-take; that is that we, rather than the spirits, gods and goddesses are actually the ones turning up at the beginning of the ritual and leaving at the end.

Entering and Leaving Trance States

An essential skill in working within ritual and certainly when working with deity is the skill to both enter and leave *trance*, more or less independently, although often in rituals we will be guided into both these states. But this does not always happen, or the guiding may on a particular occasion be indistinct, unclear or simply not work for us. Being able to take ourselves in and out of trance, just like being able to ground ourselves, means we are not reliant on others for providing our ritual experience, but can facilitate and potentially enhance our own participation. Trance can be defined as an altered state from our normal waking consciousness, one where we are more attuned to inner, subtle or energetic states. We may think of trance as entering a different plane of reality, of expanding our consciousness, of being in a waking dream, or a deepened state of awareness.

Some people work with a particular style of trance, for example shamanic, hypnotic, guided visualization, sensory or it may be different each time. We may experience trance as mainly visual, primarily kinesthetic or simply a deep state where things are sensed differently than usual. We may hear words that have not been spoken aloud by anyone, trance may sometimes be as rich and convincing as a dream, or watching a film, or more like hearing a story read to us. We may be people who hang on every word spoken during a trance, or people who essentially go off and do their own thing. It's a great practice, when leading a trance, to imagine that everyone is having a different experience and that none of them are the same as our own.

Most trances involve an induction or lead-in, and at the end, an ex-duction, lead-out or return. It is essential to be able to manage our entry and exit from trance ourselves, both in group ritual and when working solo. Books and classes exist that introduce and teach trance states and practicing with a partner or group is always a great idea. Any work with deity involves some level of trance and being able to induce oneself into this state, control it to some degree and leave the trance when we wish or have previously decided to do so is crucial. It is possible to view all of life as a trance and to analyze the different types of trance we enter into during a day – a social media trance, for example, or the trance of a train journey home, the trance of work, the trance of exercise, the trance of sex or conversation. Understanding how we enter and leave these states – and how to do that cleanly and following our intentions and will – may assist us as we learn the skills of more formal, ritual trance.

If we discover that we are quite good at entering into trance states, but often do not leave them very cleanly; feeling muddy, confused or ungrounded after a trance has ended, we should focus on consolidating the basics of entering and leaving trance before doing solo or deep work with deity, such as aspecting or presencing. We may discover that we don't enter or remain in a trance very easily, and thus could work at that, discovering by experiment what it takes to allow us to enter that state and practicing on our own or in a group to increase our ability. Having someone around who knows us quite well can be a good indicator for how effectively we have left a trance state; we may feel all clear, but they can usually tell by one look, or by exchanging a sentence or two with us how deeply we may still be in. Eating is a traditional way to reground, or return from a trance state and other similarly pragmatic ways include walking around, patting our bodies down and saying our own names aloud, or engaging in a conversation about very mundane matters.

Resources

Books that inspired me along the way

Persephone

Life's Daughter/Death's Bride: Inner Transformations through the Goddess Demeter/Persephone, Kathie Carlson. Shambhala Publications, 1997.

The Long Journey Home: Revisioning the Myth of Demeter and Persephone for Our Time, edited by Christine Downing. Shambhala Publications, 1994.

Travelling with Pomegranates: A Mother-Daughter Story, Sue Monk Kidd and Ann Kidd Taylor. Viking Adult, 2009.

Blodeuwedd

The Earth Witch, Louise Lawrence. Berkley Publishing Group, 1986.

The Mabinogion, (numerous translations and versions available). For example, Gwyn Jones and Thomas Jones. Everyman's Library, 1989.

The Owl Service, Alan Garner. Henry Z. Walck, 1967.

Isis and Nephthys

Awakening Osiris: The Egyptian Book of the Dead, translated by Normandi Ellis. Phanes Press, 1988.

House of Eternity: The Tomb of Nefertari, John K. McDonald. Oxford University Press, 1996.

Isis and Osiris: Exploring the Goddess Myth, Jonathan Cott. Doubleday, 1994.

Mary

King Jesus, Robert Graves. Farrar, Straus and Giroux, 1946.

The Magdalen Manuscript: The Alchemies of Horus & The Sex Magic of Isis, Tom Kenyon and Judi Sion. ORB Communications, 2002.

The Wild Girl, Michèle Roberts. Methuen, 1985.

Aphrodite

Aphrodite's Daughters: Women's Sexual Healing and the Journey of the Soul, Jalaja Bonheim. Simon & Schuster, 1997.

The Courage to Heal: A Guide to Women Survivors of Child Sexual Abuse, 20th Anniversary edition, Ellen Bass and Laura Davis. William Morrow, 2008.

Cunt: A Declaration of Independence, Inga Muscio. Seal Press, 1998.

The process of creating an Aphrodite's Girdle is described in *Aphrodite's Magic: Celebrate and Heal Your Sexuality,* Jane Meredith. Moon Books 2010.

Ereshkigal and Inanna

Descent to the Goddess: A Way of Initiation for Women, Sylvia Brinton Perera. Inner City Books, 1989.

Inanna Queen of Heaven and Earth: Her Stories and Hymns from Sumer, Diane Wolkstein and Samuel Noah Kramer. Harper Perennial, 1983.

The Jigsaw Woman, Kim Antieau. Roc Trade, 1996.

The Moon Under Her Feet: The Story of Mari Magdalene in the Service of the Great Mother, Clysta Kinstler. Harper San Francisco, 1991.

The Red Goddess, Peter Grey. Scarlet Imprint, 2007.

The Spell of Rosette, Kim Falconer. Voyager, 2009.

Freyja

Finding God through Sex: Awakening the One of Spirit through the Two of Flesh, David Deida. Sounds True, 2005.

The Fionavar Tapestry (trilogy), Guy Gavriel Kay. Published in one volume HarperCollins, 1995.

The Heroes of Asgard, A. and E. Keary. MacMillan & Co, 1930.

Ariadne

Ariadne: A Novel of Ancient Crete, June Rachuy Brindel. St. Martin's Press, 1980.

The King Must Die, Mary Renault. Longmans, 1958.

Knossos: A Complete Guide to the Palace of Minos, Anna Michailidou. Ekdotike Athenon, 2004.

Eve

God is a Verb: Kabbalah and the Practice of Mystical Judaism, David A. Cooper. Riverhead Books, 1997.

The King James Bible.

Leaving Eden, Ann Chamberlin. Tom Doherty Associates, 1999

The Star Goddess

Gaia and the Theory of the Living Planet, James Lovelock. Updated edition: Gaia Books, 2005.

The Great Cosmic Mother: Rediscovering the Religion of the Earth, Monica Sjöö. Harper One 1987.

NASA's images of space and stars: *https://images.nasa.gov/#/*

Recommended Books on Ritual and Magic

Casting Sacred Space: The Core of All Magickal Work, Ivo Dominguez Jr. Weiser Books, 2012.

Ecstatic Witchcraft: Magick, Philosophy & Trance in the Shamanic Craft, Gede Parma. Llewellyn, 2012.

Elements of Magic, Jane Meredith and Gede Parma (editors). Llewellyn (forthcoming, 2018).

Kissing the Limitless: Deep Magic and the Great Work of Transforming Yourself and the World, T. Thorn Coyle. Weiser Books, 2009.

The Spiral Dance: A Rebirth of the Ancient Religion of the Great Goddess, Starhawk. 20th Anniversary edition, HarperOne, 1999.

Spirit Speak: Knowing and Understanding Spirit Guides, Ancestors, Ghosts, Angels, and the Divine, Ivo Dominguez Jr. New Page Books, 2008.

Reclaiming Tradition WitchCamps

Reclaiming WitchCamps are held around the world. A list of current WitchCamps can be found at: *www.witchcamp.org/* CloudCatcher WitchCamp is at: *www.cloudcatcherwitchcamp.com.au*

About the Author

Jane Meredith is an author and ritualist. She lives in Australia and works internationally. Jane's books include: *Journey to the Dark Goddess, Circle of Eight: Creating Magic for Your Place on Earth* and *Magic of the Iron Pentacle: Reclaiming Sex, Pride, Self, Power & Passion* (co-authored with Gede Parma). Jane offers courses and workshops as distance courses and in person and also teaches within the Reclaiming Tradition. Jane is passionate about earth-based magic, ritual and the invocation of the divine. Some of her favorite things are rivers and trees, white cockatoos, cats and dark chocolate.

Jane's website is: *www.janemeredith.com*
You can sign up for her e-zine or contact her at:
jane@janemeredith.com

Moon Books

PAGANISM & SHAMANISM

What is Paganism? A religion, a spirituality, an alternative belief system, nature worship? You can find support for all these definitions (and many more) in dictionaries, encyclopaedias, and text books of religion, but subscribe to any one and the truth will evade you. Above all Paganism is a creative pursuit, an encounter with reality, an exploration of meaning and an expression of the soul. Druids, Heathens, Wiccans and others, all contribute their insights and literary riches to the Pagan tradition. Moon Books invites you to begin or to deepen your own encounter, right here, right now.

If you have enjoyed this book, why not tell other readers by posting a review on your preferred book site.

Recent bestsellers from Moon Books are:

Journey to the Dark Goddess
How to Return to Your Soul
Jane Meredith
Discover the powerful secrets of the Dark Goddess and
transform your depression, grief and pain into healing
and integration.
Paperback: 978-1-84694-677-6 ebook: 978-1-78099-223-5

Shamanic Reiki
Expanded Ways of Working with Universal Life Force Energy
Llyn Roberts, Robert Levy
Shamanism and Reiki are each powerful ways of healing; together,
their power multiplies. *Shamanic Reiki* introduces techniques to
help healers and Reiki practitioners tap ancient healing wisdom.
Paperback: 978-1-84694-037-8 ebook: 978-1-84694-650-9

Pagan Portals – The Awen Alone
Walking the Path of the Solitary Druid
Joanna van der Hoeven
An introductory guide for the solitary Druid, *The Awen Alone* will
accompany you as you explore, and seek out your own place
within the natural world.
Paperback: 978-1-78279-547-6 ebook: 978-1-78279-546-9

A Kitchen Witch's World of Magical Herbs & Plants
Rachel Patterson
A journey into the magical world of herbs and plants, filled with
magical uses, folklore, history and practical magic. By popular
writer, blogger and kitchen witch, Tansy Firedragon.
Paperback: 978-1-78279-621-3 ebook: 978-1-78279-620-6

Medicine for the Soul
The Complete Book of Shamanic Healing
Ross Heaven
All you will ever need to know about shamanic healing and how to become your own shaman...
Paperback: 978-1-78099-419-2 ebook: 978-1-78099-420-8

Shaman Pathways – The Druid Shaman
Exploring the Celtic Otherworld
Danu Forest
A practical guide to Celtic shamanism with exercises and techniques as well as traditional lore for exploring the Celtic Otherworld.
Paperback: 978-1-78099-615-8 ebook: 978-1-78099-616-5

Traditional Witchcraft for the Woods and Forests
A Witch's Guide to the Woodland with Guided Meditations and Pathworking
Melusine Draco
A Witch's guide to walking alone in the woods, with guided meditations and pathworking.
Paperback: 978-1-84694-803-9 ebook: 978-1-84694-804-6

Wild Earth, Wild Soul
A Manual for an Ecstatic Culture
Bill Pfeiffer
Imagine a nature-based culture so alive and so connected, spreading like wildfire. This book is the first flame...
Paperback: 978-1-78099-187-0 ebook: 978-1-78099-188-7

Naming the Goddess
Trevor Greenfield

Naming the Goddess is written by over eighty adherents and scholars of Goddess and Goddess Spirituality.
Paperback: 978-1-78279-476-9 ebook: 978-1-78279-475-2

Shapeshifting into Higher Consciousness
Heal and Transform Yourself and Our World with Ancient Shamanic and Modern Methods
Llyn Roberts

Ancient and modern methods that you can use every day to transform yourself and make a positive difference in the world.
Paperback: 978-1-84694-843-5 ebook: 978-1-84694-844-2

Readers of ebooks can buy or view any of these bestsellers by clicking on the live link in the title. Most titles are published in paperback and as an ebook. Paperbacks are available in traditional bookshops. Both print and ebook formats are available online.

Find more titles and sign up to our readers' newsletter at
http://www.johnhuntpublishing.com/paganism
Follow us on Facebook at
https://www.facebook.com/MoonBooks
and Twitter at https://twitter.com/MoonBooksJHP